Rave Reviews for
In Harm's Way

"Stanton tensely tells how four days of shark attacks and hypothermia killed hundreds."

—*People* magazine

"Infuriating, mesmerizing and heartbreaking . . . Impossible to put down."

—Rick Atkinson

"Perhaps Stanton's vivid account of the ordeal of the *Indianapolis* will compel the Navy to examine the matter again, since the book seems likely to find many readers and stir strong emotions."

—*The Washington Post*

"*In Harm's Way* is a stunning book. The story of the USS *Indianapolis* is one of the most harrowing tales of World War II—and Doug Stanton takes you through every terrifying moment in a vivid and utterly memorable account."

—Tom Brokaw, author of *The Greatest Generation*

"As hair-raising as *The Perfect Storm*."

—*Newsweek* Special Issue

"Doug Stanton has done this country a service by bringing the incredible yet almost-forgotten story of the USS *Indianapolis* to heartpounding life. Do yourself a favor. Read *In Harm's Way*."

—James Bradley, author of *Flags of Our Fathers*

"Doug Stanton has rendered a public service by providing the first complete account of the tragedy of *Indianapolis*. . . . A grim, poignant story that needed to be told fully and honestly. With painstaking research and an unerring eye for detail, Stanton has set down a riveting, eloquent tale of great power."

—*World War II* magazine

"Stanton reconstructs the tragedy with journalistic bravura, setting forth a vivid cast of characters and revealing the survivors' mind-boggling will to live."

—*Men's Journal*

"The secret to any good history book is for readers to be taught a history lesson without knowing it. *In Harm's Way* does just that."

—*Chicago Tribune*

"The horror here is in the details . . . heart-wrenching."

—*New York Daily News*

"Stanton's *In Harm's Way* is beautifully written. His sharp eye for detail makes the story all the more heartbreaking."

—*The Baltimore Sun*

"A harrowing and fact-filled account of how war, nature and sheer blunder combined to send the crew of the ill-fated warship into a hellish nightmare . . . Stanton weaves a riveting tale that captures the human toll of the disaster as well as the political fallout. Writing in a straightforward and exact journalistic style, Stanton deftly tells the stories of three survivors."

—*Seattle Times/Post Intelligencer*

"A strong, well-made account of one of the most fearful disasters of World War II—tragic not only in its huge loss of life and its fateful destruction of the career of the *Indianapolis*' commander, but for its random and almost meaningless occurrence in the last days of the war."

—Peter Matthiessen, author of *At Play in the Fields of the Lord* and *In the Spirit of Crazy Horse*

"Stanton has written an enthralling, terrifying and moving tale of the sea. Filled with human poignancy as well as revealing historical facts, *In Harm's Way* is a heartfelt tribute to [Captain] McVay and the courageous crew of the *Indianapolis*."

—*Houston Chronicle*

"Vividly re-creates this catastrophic chapter in military history. Weaving together accounts from official records and interviews with survivors, [Stanton] has created a war story that is part *Titanic*, part Stephen King nightmare. Stanton has a sharp eye for the story's awful ironies and telling details."

—*Star-Tribune* (Minneapolis)

"Stanton writes a riveting account of the USS *Indianapolis* . . . and provides a harrowing story of what the survivors withstood."

—*The Christian Science Monitor*

"If *In Harm's Way* is the next step in the path blazed by *Into Thin Air* and *The Perfect Storm*, it's also Stanton's way of paying something back. And by uncovering the meaning behind the suffering of the men of the *Indianapolis*, he also defines a generation."

—*BOOK* magazine

"A wonderfully wrought account of one of the great war-time disasters at sea. The meticulous research puts the reader onto the scene in the South Pacific in a way that is both harrowing and mesmerizing. It is hard to imagine that Stanton's account could have been done any better."

—George Plimpton

"Journalist Stanton has written a compelling, eminently readable account of the *Indianapolis* for the nonspecialist."

—*Library Journal*

"A crisp, well-executed reconstruction of naval warfare's darkest chapter: the sinking and abandonment of the USS *Indianapolis*."

—*Kirkus Reviews*

"Doug Stanton [is] a remarkably gifted storyteller. His gripping narrative of the experiences of the *Indy* is unrelenting. Anyone interested ... [in] World War II history ... should read this book. It is that good."

—Theodore Savas, coauthor of *Nazi Millionaires*

"Superbly crafted, [*In Harm's Way*] ... benefits from sympathetic research on the *Indianapolis* survivors, the horrors of their experiences, and their courage in surviving."

—*Booklist*

"Other writers have told the *Indianapolis* tragedy, but it took Stanton to find the heart of the drama and to tell it with the power and straightforward respect it deserved."

—*Traverse* magazine

"Stanton not only offers a well-researched chronicle of what is widely regarded as the worst naval disaster in U.S. history, but also vividly renders the combatants' hellish ordeal during the sinking, and the ensuing days at sea as well as attempts to cope with the traumatic aftermath. Stanton's omniscient narrative shifts among the individual perspectives of several principal characters, a successful technique that contributes to the book's absorbing, novelistic feel. . . . Illuminating and emotional."

—*Publishers Weekly*

"[A] heart-racing, exhaustively researched book."

—*Milwaukee Journal Sentinel*

"The book's major contribution ... is its water-line account of the horrendous ordeal of the men who survived the explosion."

—*Hartford Courant*

"Chilling."   —*The Atlanta Journal-Constitution*

"A powerfully intimate story of men victimized by the sea and forgotten by their navy. Stanton's book successfully paints a remarkable picture of the unspeakable horror, heroism, and the strength of the human spirit."

—*American History*

"[*In Harm's Way*] fully deserves the acclaim it has received."

—*National Review*

" [A] riveting oral history."

—*The Indianapolis Star*

ALSO BY DOUG STANTON

Horse Soldiers:
The Extraordinary Story of a Band of U.S. Soldiers
Who Rode to Victory in Afghanistan

The Odyssey of Echo Company:
The 1968 Tet Offensive and the Epic Battle
to Survive the Vietnam War

IN HARM'S WAY

IN HARM'S WAY

The Sinking of the
USS INDIANAPOLIS
*and the Extraordinary Story
of Its Survivors*

DOUG STANTON

A HOLT PAPERBACK
Henry Holt and Company
New York

Holt Paperbacks
Henry Holt and Company
Publishers since 1866
120 Broadway
New York, New York 10271
www.henryholt.com

A Holt Paperback® and ⓗ® are registered trademarks of
Macmillan Publishing Group, LLC.

Distributed in Canada by Raincoast Book Distribution Limited

The Library of Congress has cataloged the hardcover edition as follows:

Stanton, Doug.
In harm's way : the sinking of the USS Indianapolis and the extraordinary story
of its Survivors / Doug Stanton.—1st ed.
p. cm.
Includes bibliographic references and index.
ISBN-13: 978-0-8050-7366-9
ISBN-10: 0-8050-7366-3

1. Indianapolis (Cruiser) 2. World War, 1939–1945—Naval operations,
American. 3. Shipwrecks—Pacific Ocean. I. Title.
D774.I5S73 2001
940.54'5973—dc 21   00-068254

ISBN: 9781250853493 (trade paperback)

Our books may be purchased in bulk for promotional, educational, or business
use. Please contact your local bookseller or the Macmillan Corporate and
Premium Sales Department at (800) 221-7945, extension 5442, or by e-mail
at MacmillanSpecialMarkets@macmillan.com.

Originally published in hardcover in 2001 by Henry Holt and Company

First Holt Paperbacks Edition 2003

Revised and Updated Holt Paperbacks Edition 2022

Chapter opener photographs courtesy of the collections of the individual survivors,
with the exception of chapter three (courtesy Bettmann/CORBIS) and the
prologue and epilogue (courtesy Naval History and Heritage Command)

Printed in the United States of America

1   3   5   7   9   10   8   6   4   2

First say to yourself what you would be,
then do what you have to do.

—EPICTETUS

Contents

The Final Crew of The
USS INDIANAPOLIS (CA-35)

* Indicates a survivor

CREW AND OFFICERS

Abbott, George S., S1
Acosta, Charles M., MM3
Adams, Leo H., S1*
Adams, Pat L., S2
Adorante, Dante W, S2
Akines, William R., S2*
Albright, Charles E., Jr., COX
Allard, Vincent J., QM3*
Allen, Paul F., S1
Allmaras, Harold D., F2
Altschuler, Allan H., S2 RDM*
Alvey, Edward W., Jr., AerM2
Amick, Homer I., S2
Andersen, Lawrence J., SK2
Anderson, Erick T., S2*
Anderson, Leonard O., MM3
Anderson, Richard L., F2
Anderson, Sam G., S2
Anderson, Vincent U., BM1
Andrews, William R., S2*
Annis, James D., Jr., CEMA
Anthony, Harold R., PHM3
Antonie, Charles J., F2
Anunti, John M., M2*
Armenta, Lorenzo, SC2
Armistead, John H., S2*
Arnold, Carl Lloyd, AMM3
Ashford, Chester W., WT2
Ashford, John T., Jr., RT3*
Atkinson, J. P., COX
Aull, Joseph Harry, S2
Ault, William F., S2*
Ayotte, Lester J., S2 RDM
Backus, Thomas H., LT (jg)
Baker, Daniel Albert, S2

Baker, Frederick H., S2 RDM
Baker, William M., Jr., EM1
Baldridge, Clovis R., EM3*
Ball, Emmet Edwin, S2
Ballard, Courtney J., SSM3
Barenthin, Leonard W., S1 FC
Barker, Robert C., Jr., RT1
Barksdale, Thomas L., FC3
Barnes, Paul C., F2
Barnes, Willard M., MM1
Barra, Raymond James, CGMA
Barrett, James B., S2
Barry, Charles., LT (jg)
Barto, Lloyd Peter, S1*
Barton, George S., Y3
Bateman, Bernard B., F2 WT*
Batenhorst, Wilfred J., MM3
Batson, Eugene C., S2 RDM
Batten, Robert Edmon, S1 GM
Batts, Edward Daniel, STM1
Beane, James Albert, F2*
Beaty, Donald Lee, S1*
Becker, Myron Melvin, WT2
Beddington, Charles E., S1
Bedsted, Leo A. K., FIMOMM
Beister, Richard J., WT3
Belcher, James R., S1 RM*
Bell, Maurice Glenn, SI*
Bennett, Dean R., HAI
Bennett, Ernest F., B3
Bennett, Toney Wade, ST3
Benning, Harry, S1
Benton, Clarence U., CFCP*
Bernacil, Concepcion P., FC3*
Berry, Joseph, Jr., STMI
Berry, William Henry, ST3
Beukema, Kenneth Jay, S2
Beuschlein, Joseph C., S2

Biddison, Charles L., S1
Billings, Robert B., ENS
Billingsley, Robert F., GM3
Bilz, Robert Eugene, S2
Bishop, Arthur, Jr., S2
Bitonti, Louis P., S1*
Blackwell, Fermon M., SSML3
Blanthorn, Bryan, S1*
Blum, Donald J., ENS*
Boege, Raynard R., S2
Bogan, Jack R., RM1
Bollinger, Richard H., S1
Booth, Sherman C., S1 GM*
Borton, Herbert E., SCB2
Boss, Norbert George, S2
Bott, Wilbur Melvin, S2
Bowles, Eldridge W., SI
Bowman, Charles E., CTC
Boyd, Troy Howard, GM3
Bradley, William H., S2
Brake, John, Jr., S2
Brandt, Russell Lee, F2*
Braun, Neal F., S2
Bray, Harold J., Jr., S2*
Brice, R. V., S2
Bridge, Wayne Aron, S2
Bright, Chester Lee, S2
Briley, Harold V., MAM3
Brooks, Ulysess Ray, CWTA
Brophy, Thomas D'Arcy, Jr., ENS
Brown, Edward A., WT3
Brown, Edward J., S1*
Bruce, Russell W., S2
Brule, Maurice J., S2
Brundige, Robert H., SI GM*
Bruneau, Charles A., GM3
Buckett, Victor R., Y2*
Budish, David, S2
Bullard, John K., S1*
Bunai, Robert P., SM1*
Bunn, Horace G., S2
Burdorf, Wilbert J., COX*
Burkhartsmeier, Anton T., S1
Burkholtz, Frank, Jr., EM3

Burleson, Martin L., S1
Burrs, John W., S1
Burt, William George A., QM3
Burton, Curtis H., S1*
Bushong, John R., GM3
Cadwallader, John J., RT3
Cain, Alfred Brown, RT3
Cairo, William G., BUG1
Call, James Edward, RM3
Cameron, John Watson, GM2
Camp, Garrison, STM2
Campana, Paul, RDM3
Campbell, Hamer E., Jr., GM3*
Campbell, Louis Dean, AOM3*
Campbell, Wayland D., SF3
Candalino, Paul L., LT (jg)
Cantrell, Billy G., F2
Carnell, Lois Wayne, S2
Carpenter, Willard A., SM3
Carr, Harry Leroy, S2
Carroll, Gregory K., S1 FCO
Carroll, Rachel W., COX
Carson, Clifford, FI WT
Carstensen, Richard, S2
Carter, Grover C., S1*
Carter, Lindsey L., S2*
Carter, Lloyd George, COX*
Carver, Grover C., S1*
Cassidy, John Curran, SI*
Castaldo, Patrick P., GM2
Castiaux, Ray V., S2
Casto, William H., S1
Cavil, Robert Ralph, MM2
Cavitt, Clinton C., WT3
Celaya, Adolfo Valdo, F2*
Centazzo, Frank J., SM3*
Chamness, John Desel, S2*
Chandler, Lloyd N., S2
Chart, Joseph, EM3
Christian, Lewis E., Jr., WO
Clark, Eugene, CK3
Clark, Orsen N., S2*
Clements, Harold P., S2
Clinton, George W., S1*

Clinton, Leland J., LT (jg)

Cobb, William Lester, MOMM3

Cole, Walter Henry, CRMA

Coleman, Cedric F., LCDR

Coleman, Robert E., F2*

Collier, Charles R., RM2*

Collins, James, STM1

Colvin, Frankie Lee, SSMT2

Condon, Barna T., RDM1

Connelly, David F., ENS

Conrad, James P., EM3

Conser, Donald L., SC2

Consiglio, Joseph W., FC2

Conway, Thomas M., Rev., LT

Cook, Floyd E., SF3

Cooper, Dale, Jr., F2

Copeland, Willard J., S2

Costner, Homer J., COX*

Countryman, Robert E., S2

Cowen, Donald R., FC3*

Cox, Alford E., GM3

Cox, Loel Dene, S2*

Crabb, Donald C., RM2

Crane, Granville S., Jr., MM2*

Crews, Hugh C., LT (jg)

Crites, Orval D., WT1

Crouch, Edwin M., CAPT. (Passenger)

Crum, Charles J., S2

Cruz, Jose S., CCKA

Curtis, Erwin E., CTCP

Dagenhart, Charles R., Jr., PHM2

Dale, Elwood Richard, F1

Daniel, Harold W., CBMA*

Daniello, Anthony G., Sr SM

Davis, James Clark, RM3

Davis, Kenneth G., F1 EM

Davis, Stanley G., LT (jg)

Davis, Thomas Edward, SM2

Day, Richard R., Jr., S2

Dean, John Thomas, Jr., S2

Debernardi, Louie, BM1*

Defoor, Walton, RDM3

Demars, Edgar Joseph, CBMA

Dement, Dayle P., Sr

Denney, Lloyd, Jr., S2

Dewing, Ralph Otto, FC3*

Dezelske, William B., MM2*

Dimond, John Nelson, S2

Dollins, Paul, RM2

Donald, Lyle Herbert, EM1

Doney, William Junior, F2

Dorman, William B., S1

Dornetto, Frank Paul, WT1

Doss, James Monroe, S2

Doucette, Roland O., S2

Douglas, Gene Dale, F2*

Dove, Bessil Raymond, SKD2

Dowdy, Lowell S., CWO

Drane, James Anthony, GM3

Drayton, William H., EM2*

Driscoll, David L., LT (jg)

Dronet, Joseph E.J., S2*

Drummond, James J., F2

Drury, Richard E., S2

Dryden, William H., MM1*

Dufraine, Delbert E., S1

Dunbar, Jess Lee, F2

Durand, Ralph J., Jr., S2

Dycus, Donald, S2

Eakins, Morris B., F2 WT

Eames, Paul H., Jr., ENS

Eastman, Chester S., S2

Eck, Harold Adam, S2*

Eddinger, John W., S1

Eddy, Richard Leroy, RM3

Edwards, Alwyn C., F2

Edwards, Roland J., BM1

Egolf, Harold Wesley, S2 RDM

Elliott, Harry W., S2

Elliott, Kenneth A., S1

Emery, William F., S1 QM

Emsley, William J., S1

Engelsman, Ralph, S2

Epperson, Ewell, S1

Epperson, George L., S1

Erickson, Theodore M., S2*

Ernst, Robert Carl, F2

Erwin, Louis H., COX*

Ethier, Eugene Edwin, EM3*
Eubanks, James H., S1
Evans, Arthur Jerome, PHM2
Evans, Claudus, GM3*
Everett, Charles N., EM2
Evers, Lawrence Lee, CMMA
Eyet, Donald Archie, S1
Fantasia, Frank A., F2 WT
Farber, Sheldon Lee, S2 RDM
Farley, James W., S1
Farmer, Archie C., COX*
Farris, Eugene F., S1 RM*
Fasthorse, Vincent, S2
Feakes, Fred A., AOM1*
Fedorski, Nicholas W., S1*
Feeney, Paul Ross, S2 RM
Felts, Donald J., BM1*
Ferguson, Albert E., CMMA*
Ferguson, Russel M., RT3
Figgins, Harley Dean, WT2
Firestone, Kenneth F., FC2
Firmin, John Alden H., S2
Fitting, Johnny W., GM1*
Flaten, Harold James, WT2*
Fleischauer, Donald W., S1 Y
Fleshman, Vern L., S2
Flynn, James M., Jr., S1 FCO
Flynn, Joseph A., CDR
Foell, Cecil D., ENS
Fortin, Verlin L., WT3*
Foster, Verne E., F2*
Fox, William H., Jr., F2*
Francois, Norbert E., F1 MM*
Frank, Rudolph A., S2
Franklin, Jack R., RDM3
Freeze, Howard B., LT (jg)
French, Douglas O., FC3
French, Jimmy, Jr., QM3
Fritz, Leonard A., MM3
Frontino, Vincent F., MOMM
Frorath, Donald H., S2
Fuchs, Herman F., CWO
Fuller, Arnold A., F2
Fulton, William C., CRMA

Funkhouser, Robert M., ART2*
Gabrillo, Juan, S2*
Gaither, Forest M., FC2
Galante, Angelo, S2*
Galbraith, Norman S., MM2
Gardner, Roscoe W., F2*
Gardner, Russel T., F2
Gamer, Glenn R., MM2
Gause, Robert P., QM1*
Gause, Rubin C., Jr., ENS
Gemza, Rudolph A., FCO3*
George, Gabriel V., MM3*
Gerngross, Frederick J., Jr., ENS
Gettleman, Robert A., S2 RDM*
Gibson, Buck Warren, GMS*
Gibson, Curtis W., S2
Gibson, Ganola F., MM3
Gilbert, Warner, Jr., S1
Gilcrease, James, S2*
Gill, Paul Edward, WT2
Gilmore, Wilbur A., S2
Gismondi, Michael V., S1
Gladd, Millard, Jr., MM2*
Glaub, Francis A., GM2
Glenn, Jay R., AMM3*
Glovka, Erwin Samuel, S2
Godfrey, Marlo Roy, RM3
Goeckel, Ernest S., LT (jg)
Goff, Thomas Guy, SF3*
Golden, Curry, STM1
Golden, James I., S1
Gonzales, Ray Adam, S2
Gooch, William Leroy, F2*
Good, Robert Kenneth, MM3
Goodwin, Oliver A., CRTA
Gore, Leonard F., S2
Gorecki, Joseph W., SK3
Gottmann, Paul James, S2
Gove, Carroll L., S2
Gray, Willis Leroy, S1*
Greathouse, Bud R., S1
Green, Robert Urban, S2
Green, Tolbert, Jr., S1*
Greene, Samuel G., S1

Greenlee, Charles I., S2*

Greer, Bob Eugene, S2

Gregory, Garland G., F1

Grief, Matthias D., WT3

Gries, Richard C., F2

Griest, Frank David, GM3

Griffin, Jackie Dale, S1

Griffith, Robert Lee, S1*

Griffiths, Leonard S., S2

Griggs, Donald Ray, F1

Grimes, David Elmer, S2

Grimes, James F., S2

Groce, Floyd Vernon, RDM2

Groch, John Thomas, MM3

Guenther, Morgan E., EM3

Guerrero, John Gomez, S1

Guillot, Murphy U., F1 EM

Guye, Ralph Lee, Jr., QM3

Guyon, Harold Lewis, F1 WT

Haberman, Bernard, S2

Haduch, John Martin, S1

Hale, Robert B., LT

Hale, William F., S2

Hall, Pressie, F1

Halloran, Edward G., MM3

Ham, Saul Anthony, S1

Hambo, William P., PHM3

Hammen, Robert, PHOM3

Hamrick, James J., S2

Hancock, William A., GM3

Hankinson, Clarence W., F2

Hansen, Henry, S2

Hanson, Harley C., WO*

Harland, George A., S2

Harp, Charlie Hardin, S1

Harper, Vasco, STM1

Harris, James Davis, F2

Harris, Willard E., F2

Harrison, Cecil M., CWO*

Harrison, Frederick E., S2 QM

Harrison, James M., S1

Hart, Fred, Jr., RT2*

Hartrick, Willis B., MM1

Hatfield, Willie N., S2*

Haurrich, Cloud D., S2

Hauser, Jack Isaac, SK2

Havener, Harlan Carl, F2*

Havins, Otha Alton, Y3*

Hayes, Charles D., LCDR

Hayles, Felix, CK3

Haynes, Lewis L., MC, LCDR*

Haynes, Robert A., LT

Haynes, William A., S1 GM

Heerdt, Raymond E., F2

Heggie, William A., RDM3

Heinz, Richard A., HA1

Heller, John, S2*

Heller, Robert J., Jr., S2

Helscher, Ralph John, S1

Helt, Jack Edward, F2

Henderson, Ralph L., S1

Hendron, James R., Jr., F2

Henry, Earl O., DC, LCDR

Hensch, Erwin F., LT*

Hensley, Clifford, SSMB2

Herbert, Jack Erwin, BM1

Herndon, Duane, S2

Hershberger, Clarence L., S1 FC*

Herstine, James F., ENS

Hickey, Harry Todd, RM3

Hicks, Clarence, S1 SC

Hiebert, Lloyd Henry, GM1

Hill, Clarence Max, CWTP

Hill, Joe Walker, STM1

Hill, Nelson P., Jr., LT

Hill, Richard N., ENS

Hind, Lyle Lewis, S2*

Hines, Lionel Gordon, WT1

Hinken, John Richard, Jr., F2*

Hobbs, Melvin Dow, S1

Hodge, Howard Henry, RM2*

Hodgins, Lester B., S2

Hodshire, John W., S2

Hoerres, George J., S2

Holden, Punciano A., ST1

Hollingsworth, Jimmie L., STM2

Holloway, Andrew J., S2

Holloway, Ralph H., COX

Hoogerwerf, John, Jr., F1MOMM

Hoopes, Gordon H., S2*

Hopper, Prentice W., S1

Hopper, Roy L., AMM1

Horner, Durward R., WO*

Horr, Wesley Alan, F2

Horrigan, John G., F1

Horvath, George J., F1 EM*

Hoskins, William O., Y3*

Houck, Richard E., EM3*

Houston, Robert G., F1

Houston, William H., PHM2

Hov, Donald A., S1 RM

Howison, John D., ENS*

Hubeli, Joseph F., S2*

Huebner, Harry H., S1 CM

Hughes, Lawrence E., F2 WT

Hughes, Robert A., FC3

Hughes, William E., SSML2

Humphrey, Maynard L., S2

Hunter, Arthur R., Jr., QM1

Huntley, Virgil C., CWO

Hupka, Clarence E., BKR1*

Hurley, Woodrow, GM2*

Hurst, Robert H., LT

Hurt, James Edward, S2

Hutchison, Merle B., S2

Igou, Floyd, Jr., RM2

Izor, Walter Eugene, F1

Jackson, Henry, STML

Jacquemot, Joseph A., S2*

Jadloski, George K., S2

Jakubisin, Joseph S., S2*

James, Woody Eugene, COX*

Janney, Johns Hopkins, CDR

Jarvis, James K., AM3*

Jeffers, Wallace M., COX

Jenney, Charles I., LT

Jensen, Chris A., S2

Jensen, Eugene W., S2*

Jewell, Floyd R., SKV1

Johnson, Bernard J., S2

Johnson, Elwood W., S2

Johnson, George Glen, S2

Johnson, Harold B., S1

Johnson, Sidney B., S1

Johnson, Walter M., Jr., S1

Johnson, William A., S1*

Johnston, Earl R., BM2

Johnston, Lewis E., S1 RM

Johnston, Ray F., MM1

Johnston, Scott A., F2

Jones, Clinton Leroy, COX*

Jones, George Edward, S2

Jones, Jim, S2

Jones, Kenneth M., F1MOMM

Jones, Sidney, S1*

Jones, Stanley F., S2

Jordan, Henry, STM2

Jordon, Thomas H., S2

Josey, Clifford O., S2

Jump, David A., ENS

Jurgensmeyer, Alfred J., S2

Jurkiewicz, Raymond S., S1*

Justice, Robert E., S2*

Karpel, Daniel L., BM1

Karter, Leo C., Jr., S2

Kasten, Stanley Otto, HA1

Kawa, Raymond Philip, SK3

Kay, Gust C., S1*

Kazmierski, Walter, S1*

Keeney, Robert A., ENS

Kees, Shalous Eugene, EM2*

Keith, Everette E., EM2

Kelly, Albert R., S2

Kemp, David Poole, Jr., SC3*

Kenly, Oliver Wesley, RDM3*

Kennedy, Andrew J., Jr., S2

Kennedy, Robert A., S1 Y

Kenny, Francis J. P., S2

Kephart, Paul, S1

Kerby, Deo Earl, S1*

Kem, Harry Gilbert, S1

Key, S. T., EM2

Keyes, Edward Hiram, COX*

Kight, Audy Carl, S1

Kilgore, Archie C., F2

Killman, Robert E., GM3

Kinard, Nolan Dave, S1
Kincaid, Joseph E., FC2
King, A. C., S1 Y*
King, Clarence, Jr., STM2
King, James Thomas, S1
King, Richard Eugene, S2
King, Robert Harold, S2
Kinnaman, Robert L., S2
Kinzle, Raymond A., BKR2*
Kirby, Harry, S1
Kirk, James Roy, SC3
Kirkland, Marvin F., S1*
Kirkman, Walter W., SF1
Kiselica, Joseph F., AMM2*
Kittoe, James W., F2*
Klappa, Ralph Donald, S2*
Klaus, Joseph Frank, S1*
Klein, Raymond James, S1
Klein, Theil Joseph, SK3
Knernschield, Andrew N., S1
Knoll, Paul Edward, COX
Knott, Elbern L., S1 C
Knudtson, Raymond A., S1
Knupke, Richard R., MM3
Koch, Edward Chris, EM3*
Koegler, Albert, S1
Koegler, William, SC3
Kolakowski, Ceslaus, SM3
Kollinger, Robert Eugene, S1
Konesny, John Mathew, S1
Koopman, Walter F., F2
Koppang, Raymond I., LT (jg)
Kouski, Fred, GM3
Kovalick, George R., S2
Koziara, George, S2*
Kozik, Raymond., S1
Krawivz, Henry J., MM3
Kreis, Clifford E., S1*
Kron, Herman E., Jr., GM3
Kronenberger, W. M., GM3
Krueger, Dale F., F2*
Krueger, Norman F., S2*
Kruse, Darwin Glen, S2
Krzyzewski, John M., S2

Kuhn, Clair Joseph, S1
Kulovitz, Raymond J., S2
Kurlich, George R., FC3*
Kuryla, Michael N., Jr., COX*
Kusiak, Alfred M., S2
Kwiatkowski, Marion J., S2
Labuda, Arthur AI, QM3
Lafontaine, Paul S., S1
Lakatos, Emil Joseph, MM3
Lake, Muri Christy, S1
Lamb, Robert Clyde, EM3
Lambert, Leonard F., S1
Landon, William W., Jr., FCO2
Lane, Ralph, CMMA*
Lanter, Kenley M., S1 SM*
Lapaglia, Carlos, GM2*
Lapari, Lawrence E., Jr., S2
Lapczynski, Edward W., S1
Larsen, Melvin R., S2
Latigue, Jackson, STM1
Latimer, Billy F., S1 RM
Latzer, Solomon, S2
Laughlin, Fain H., SK3
Laws, George Edward, S1*
Leathers, William B., MM3
Lebaron, Robert W., S2
Lebow, Cleatus A., FCO3*
Leenerman, Arthur L., RDM3*
Leluika, Paul Peter, S2
Lestina, Francis J., S1
Letizia, Vincencio, S2
Letz, Wilbert Joseph, SK1
Levalley, William D., EM2
Leventon, Mervin C., MM2
Levieux, John J., F2
Lewellen, Thomas E., S2
Lewis, James Robert, F2
Lewis, John Robert, GM3
Linden, Charles G., WT2
Lindsay, Norman Lee, SF3
Link, George Charles, S1
Linn, Roy, S1
Linville, Cecil H., SF2
Linville, Harry J., S1

Lippert, Robert G., S1
Lipski, Stanley W., CDR
Little, Frank Edward, MM2
Livermore, Raymond I., S2
Loch, Edwin Peter, S1
Lockwood, Thomas H., S2*
Loeffier, Paul E., Jr., S2 QM
Loftis, James B., Jr., S1*
Loftus, Ralph Dennis, F2
Lohr, Leo William, S1
Lombardi, Ralph, S1
Long, Joseph William, S1
Longwell, Donald J., S1
Lopez, Daniel B., F2*
Lopetz, Sam, S1*
Lorenc, Edward R., S2
Loyd, John F., WT2
Lucas, Robert Andrew, S2*
Lucca, Frank John, F2*
Luhman, Emerson D., MM3
Lundgren, Albert D., S1 FCO
Luttrull, Claud A., COX
Lutz, Charles H., S1
Maas, Melvin Adolph, S1 SF*
Mabee, Kenneth C., F2
Mace, Harold A., S2*
Macfarland, Keith I., LT (jg)
Machado, Clarence J., WT2
Mack, Donald F., BUG1*
Maday, Anthony F., AMM1*
Madigan, Harry F, BM2
Magdics, Steve, Jr., F2
Magray, Duwain F., S2
Makaroff, Chester J., GM3*
Makowski, Robert T., CWTA
Maldonado, Salvador, BKR3*
Malena, Joseph J., Jr., GM2*
Malone, Cecil Edward, S2
Malone, Elvin C., S1
Malone, Michael L., Jr., LT (jg)
Malski, Joseph John, S1*
Maness, Charles F., F2
Mankin, Howard James, GM3
Mann, Clifford E., S1

Mansker, LaVoice, S2
Mantz, Keith Hubert, S1
Marciulaitis, Charles, S1
Markmann, Frederick H., WT1
Marple, Paul T., ENS
Marshall, John Lucas, WT2
Marshall, Robert W., S2
Martin, Albert, S2
Martin, Everett G., S1
Massier, George A., S1
Mastrecola, Michael M., S2
Matheson, Richard R., PHM3
Matrulla, John, S1 FCO*
Mauntel, Paul John, S2
Maxwell, Farrell J., S1*
McBride, Ronald G., S1
McBryde, Frank E., S2
McCall, Donald C., S2*
McClain, Raymond B., BM2*
McClary, Lester Earl, S2
McClure, David Leroy, EM2
McComb, Everett A., F1
McCord, Edward Franklin, Jr., EM3
McCorkle, Ray Ralph, S1
McCormick, Earl W, MOMM2
McCoskey, Paul F., S1 RDM
McCoy, John S., Jr., M2
McCrory, Millard V., Jr., WT2*
McDaniel, Johnny A., S1
McDonald, Franklin G., Jr., F2
McDonner, David P., Jr., F1 EM
McDowell, Robert E., S1 SM
McElroy, Clarence E., S1 GM*
McFall, Walter E., S2*
McFee, Carl Snyder, SC1
McGinnis, Paul W., SM3*
McGinty, John M., S1
McGuiggan, Robert M., S1*
McGuire, Denis, S2
McGuirk, Philip A., LT (jg)
McHenry, Loren C., Jr., S1 RM*
McHone, Ollie, F1
McKee, George E., Jr., S1
McKenna, Michael J., S1

McKenzie, Ernest E., S1*
McKinnon, Francis M., Y3
McKissick, Charles B., LT (jg)*
McKlin, Henry T., S1*
McLain, Patrick J., S2*
McLean, Douglas B., EM3
McNabb, Thomas, Jr., F2
McNickle, Arthur S., F1
McQuitty, Roy Edward, COX
McVay, Charles Butler, III, CAPT*
McVay, Richard C., Y3*
Meade, Sidney H., S1
Mehlbaum, Raymond A., S1 SC
Meier, Harold F., S2
Melichar, Charles H., EM3
Melvin, Carl Lavern, F1 EM
Mencheff, Manual A., S2
Meredith, Charles E., S1*
Mergler, Charles M., RDM2
Mestas, Nestor A., WT2*
Metcalf, David W., GM3
Meyer, Charles T., S2*
Michael, Bertrand F., BKR3
Michael, Elmer Orion, S1
Michno, Arthur R., S2
Mikeska, Willie W., S2
Mikolayek, Joseph, COX*
Milbrodt, Glen L., S2*
Miles, Theodore K., LT
Miller, Artie Ronald, GM2
Miller, George Edwin, F1 MM
Miller, Glenn Evert, S2
Miller, Samuel George, Jr., FC3
Miller, Walter R., S2
Miller, Walter W., B1
Miller, Wilbur H., CMM
Mills, William Harry, EM3
Miner, Herbert Jay, II, RT2*
Minor, Richard Leon, S1
Minor, Robert Warren, S2
Mires, Carl Emeron, S2
Mirich, Wally Mayo, S1
Miskowiec, Theodore F., S1
Mitchell, James E., S2*

Mitchell, James H., Jr., SK1
Mitchell, Kenneth E., S1*
Mitchell, Norval Jerry, Jr., S1*
Mitchell, Paul Boone, FC3
Mitchell, Winston C., S1 FC
Mittler, Peter John, Jr., GM3
Mixon, Malcom Lois, GM2
Mlady, Clarence C., S1*
Modesitt, Gari E., S2*
Modisher, Melvin W., MC, LTQ (jg)*
Moncrief, Mack D., S2
Monks, Robert Bruce, GM3
Montoya, Frank Edward, S1
Moore, Donald George, S2
Moore, Elbert, S2
Moore, Harley E., S1
Moore, Kyle C., LCDR
Moore, Wyatt Patton, BKR1
Moran, Joseph John, RM1*
Morgan, Eugene S., BM2*
Morgan, Glenn Grover, BGM3 *
Morgan, Lewis E., S2
Morgan, Telford F., ENS
Morris, Albert O., S1*
Morse, Kendall H., LT (jg)
Morton, Charles W., S2
Morton, Marion Ellis, SK2
Moseley, Morgan M., SC1*
Moulton, Charles C., S2
Mowrey, Ted Eugene, SK3*
Moynelo, Harold C., Jr., ENS
Mroszak, Francis A., S2
Muldoon, John J., MM1*
Mulvey, William R., BM1*
Murillo, Sammy, S2
Murphy, Allen, S2
Murphy, Paul James, FC3*
Musarra, Joe, S1
Myers, Charles Lee, Jr., S2
Myers, Glen Alan, MM2
Myers, H. B., F1*
Nabers, Neal Adrian, S2
Naspini, Joseph A., F2 WT*
Neal, Charles Keith, S2

Neal, George M., S2
Neale, Harlan B., S2
Nelsen, Edward John, GM1*
Nelson, Frank Howard, S2*
Neu, Hugh Herbert, S2
Neubauer, Richard, S2
Neuman, Jerome C., F1
Neville, Bobby Gene, S2
Newcomer, Lewis W., MM3
Newell, James Thomas, EM1
Newhall, James F., S1 GM*
Nichols, James C., S2*
Nichols, Joseph L., BM2
Nichols, Paul Virgil, MM3
Nielsen, Carl Aage Chor, Jr., F1
Nieto, Baltazar P., GM3
Nightingale, William O., MM1*
Niskanen, John H., F2
Nixon, Daniel M., S2*
Norberg, James A., CBMP*
Norman, Theodore R., GM2
Nowak, George Joseph, F2
Nugent, William G., S2
Nunley, James P., F1
Nunley, Troy Audie, S2*
Nutt, Raymond Albert, S2
Nuttall, Alexander C., S1*
Obledo, Mike Guerra, S1*
O'Brien, Arthur J., S2
O'Callaghan, Del R., WT2
Ochoa, Ernest, FC3
O'Donnell, James E., WT3*
Olderon, Bernhard G., S1
Olijar, John, S1*
O'Neil, Eugene Elbert, S1
Orr, Homer L., HA1
Orr, John Irwin, Jr., LT
Orsburn, Frank H., SSML2*
Ortiz, Orlando R., Y3
Osburn, Charles W., S2
Ott, Theodore Gene, Y1
Outland, Felton J., S1*
Overman, Thurman D., S2*
Owen, Keith Nichols, SC3*

Owens, Robert Sheldon, Jr., QM3
Owensby, Clifford C., F2
Pace, Curtis, S2*
Pacheco, Jose Cruz, S2*
Pagitt, Eldon Ernest, F2
Pait, Robert Edward, BM2
Palmiter, Adelore A., S2*
Pane, Francis W., S2
Parham, Fred, ST2
Park, David E., ENS
Paroubek, Richard A., Y1*
Pasket, Lyle Matthew, S2*
Patterson, Alfred T., S2
Patterson, Kenneth G., S1
Patzer, Herman Lantz, EM1
Paulk, Luther Doyle, S2*
Payne, Edward G., S2*
Payne, George David, S2
Pena, Santos Alday, S1*
Pender, Welburn M., F2
Perez, Basilio, S2*
Perkins, Edward C., F2*
Perry, Robert J., S2
Pessolano, Michael R., LT
Peters, Earl Jack, S2
Peterson, Avery C., S2 FC*
Peterson, Darrel E., S1 FC
Peterson, Frederick A., MAM3
Peterson, Glenn H., S1 RM
Peterson, Ralph R., S2
Petrincic, John Nicholas, Jr., FC3
Peyton, Robert C., STM1
Phillips, Aulton N., Sr., F2
Phillips, Huie H., S2*
Pierce, Clyde Alton, CWTA
Pierce, Robert W., S2
Piperata, Alfred J., MM1
Pitman, Robert Fred, S2
Pittman, Almire, Jr., ST3
Pleiss, Roger David, F2
Podish, Paul, S2*
Podschun, Clifford A., S2*
Pogue, Herman C., S2*
Pohl, Theodore, F2MOMM

Pokryfka, Donald M., S2
Poor, Gerald M., S2*
Poore, Albert F., S2
Potrykus, Frank Paul, F2
Potts, Dale Floyd, S2*
Powell, Howard Wayne, FI
Powers, R. C. Ottis, S2
Poynter, Raymond Lee, S2
Praay, William Theo, S2
Prather, Clarence J., CMMA
Pratt, George Roy, FI EM
Price, James Denny, SI*
Priestle, Ralph A., S2
Prior, Walter Mathew, S2
Puckett, William C., S2
Pupuis, John Andrew, SI BKR
Purcel, Franklin W., S2
Pursel, Forest V., WT2
Pyron, Freddie H., SI
Quealy, William C., Jr., PR2*
Rabb, John Robert, SCI
Ragsdale, Jean Obert, S1
Rahn, Alvin Wilder, SK3
Raines, Clifford Junior, S2
Rains, Rufus Brady, SI
Ramirez, Ricardo, SI*
Ramseyer, Raymond C., RT3
Randolph, Cleo, STMI
Rathbone, Wilson, S2*
Rathman, Frank Junior, S1 FC
Rawdon, John Herbert, EM3*
Realing, Lyle Olan, FC2
Redmayne, Richard B., LT*
Reed, Thomas William, EM3
Reemts, Alvin T., S1
Reese, Jesse Edmund, S2
Reeves, Chester O. B., S1*
Reeves, Robert A., F2
Regalado, Robert H., S1
Relmer, Herbert A., S1 SM*
Reid, Curtis F., S2*
Reid, James Edgar, BM2*
Reid, John, LCDR*
Reid, Tommy Lee, RDM3*

Reilly, James F., Y1
Reinert, Leroy, F1
Remondet, Edward J., Jr., S2
Reynolds, Alford, GM2*
Reynolds, Andrew Eli, S1
Reynolds, Carleton C., F1
Rhea, Clifford, F2
Rhodes, Vernon L., F1 WT
Rhoten, Roy Edward, F2
Rice, Albert, STM1
Rich, Garland Lloyd, S1
Richardson, John R., S2
Richardson, Joseph G., S2
Rider, Francis Alan, RDM3
Riley, Junior Thomas, BM2
Rineay, Francis Henry, Jr., S2*
Roberts, Benjamin E., WT1
Roberts, Charles, S1
Roberts, Norman H., MM1*
Robison, Gerald E., RT3
Robison, John Davis, COX*
Robison, Marzie Joe, S2
Roche, Joseph M., LT
Rockenbach, Earl A., SC2
Roesberry, Jack R., S1
Rogell, Henry Tony, F1
Rogers, Ralph Guy, RDM3*
Rogers, Ross, Jr., ENS*
Roland, Jack A., PHM1
Rollins, Willard E., RM3
Romani, Frank J., HA1
Roof, Charles Walter, S2
Rose, Berson Horace, GM2
Ross, Glen Eugene, F2
Rothman, Aaron, RDM3
Rowden, Joseph Geren, F1
Rozzano, John, Jr., S2
Rudomanski, Eugene W., RT2
Rue, William Goff, MM1
Russell, Robert A., S2
Russell, Virgil M., COX*
Rust, Edwin Leroy, S1
Rutherford, Robert A., RM2
Rydzeski. Frank W., F1

Saathoff, Don W., S2*
Saenz, Jose Antonio, SC3
Sain, Albert F., S1
Salinas, Alfredo A., S1
Samano, Nuraldo, S2
Sampson, Joseph R., S2
Sams, Robert Carrol, STM2
Sanchez, Alejandro V., S2
Sanchez, Fernando S., SC3*
Sand, Cyrus Harvey, BM1
Sanders, Everett R., MOMM1
Sassman, Gordon W., CO
Scanlan, Osceola C., S2*
Scarbrough, Fred R., COX
Schaap, Marion John, Q-M1
Schaefer, Hany W., S2
Schaffer, Edward J., S1
Scharton, Elmer D., S1
Schechterle, Harold J., RDM3*
Scheib, Albert Eddie, F2
Schewe, Alfred Paul, S1
Schlatter, Robert L., AOM3
Schlotter, James R., RDM3
Schmueck, John Alton, CPHMP*
Schnappauf, Harold J., SK3
Schooley, Dillard A., COX1
Schumacher, Arthur J., Jr., CEMA
Scoggins, Millard, SM2
Scott, Burl Down, STM2
Scott, Curtis Marvin, S1
Scott, Hilliard, STM1
Seabert, Clarke W., S2*
Sebastian, Clifford H., RM2
Sedivi, Alfred J., PHOM2
Selbach, Walter H., WT2
Sell, Ernest F., EM2
Sellers, Leonard E., SF3
Selman, Amos, S2
Setchfield, Arthur L., COX*
Sewell, Loris Eldon, S2
Shaffer, Robert P., GM3*
Shand, Kenneth, W., WT2
Sharp, William H., S2*
Shaw, Calvin Patrick, GM2

Shearer, Harold J., S2*
Shelton, William E., Jr., SM2
Shields, Cecil N., SM2
Shipman, Robert Lee, GM3
Shown, Donald H., CFC*
Shows, Audie Boyd, COX*
Sikes, Theodore A., ENS
Silcox, Bumice R., S1
Silva, Phillip Gomes, S1
Simcox, Gordon W., EM3
Simcox, John Allen, F1MM2
Simpson, William E., BM2*
Sims, Clarence, CK2
Sinclair, James Ray, S2*
Singerman, David, SM2
Sipes, John Leland, S1
Siter, Henry Joseph, S2*
Sitzlar, William C., F1
Sladzk, Wayne Lyn, BM1*
Slankard, Jack C., S1*
Smalley, Howard Earl, S1
Smeltzer, Charles H., S2*
Smeraglia, Michael, RM3
Smith, Carl Murphy, SM2
Smith, Charles Andy, S1
Smith, Cozell Lee, Jr., COX*
Smith, Edwin Lee, S2
Smith, Eugene Gordon, BM2
Smith, Frederick C., F2*
Smith, George Robert, S1
Smith, Guy Nephi, FCO2
Smith, Henry August, F1
Smith, Homer Leroy, F2
Smith, James Wesley, S2*
Smith, Kenneth Dean, S2
Smith, Oles Ellis, CM3
Snyder, John N., SF2
Snyder, Richard R., S1 SM
Solomon, William, Jr., S2
Sordia, Ralph, S2
Sospizio, Andre, EM3*
Sparks, Charles Byrd, COX
Speer, Lowell Elvis, RT3
Spencer, Daniel F., S1*

Spencer, James D., LT
Spencer, Roger, S1 RM*
Spencer, Sidney A., WO
Spindle, Orval Audry, S1
Spinelli, John A., SC2*
Spomer, Elmer John, SF2
St. Pierre, Leslie R., MM2
Stadler, Robert H., WT3
Stamm, Florida M., S2*
Stanforth, David E., F2
Stankowski, Archie J., S2
Stanturf, Frederick R., MM2
Steicerwald, Fred, GM2
Stephens, Richard P., S2*
Stevens, George G., WT2*
Stevens, Wayne A., MM2
Stewart, Glenn W., CPCP*
Stewart, Thomas A., UK2
Stickley, Charles B., GM3
Stier, William G., S1 FCO
Stimson, David, ENS
Stone, Dale Eugene, S2
Stone, Homer Benton, Y1
Stout, Kenneth I., LCDR
Strain, Joseph Mason, S2 RDM
Streich, Allen C., RM2
Strickland, George T., S2
Strieter, Robert C., S2
Stripe, William S., S2
Strom, Donald Arthur, S2
Stromko, Joseph A., F2 WT
Stryffeler, Virgil L., F2
Stueckle, Robert L., S2
Sturtevant, Elwyn L., RM2*
Sudano, Angelo A., SSML3
Suhf, Jerome Richards, S2
Sullivan, James P., S2
Sullivan, William D., PTR2
Suter, Frank Edward, S1*
Swanson, Robert H., MM2
Swart, Robert L., LT (jg)
Swindeli, Jerome H., P2
Taggart, Thomas H., S1 RDM
Talley, Dewell E., RM2

Tawater, Charles H., F1*
Teerlink, David S., CWO
Telford, Arno J., RTS
Terry, Robert Wayne, S1
Thelen, Richard P., S2*
Thielscher, Robert T., CRTP
Thomas, Ivan Mervin, S1*
Thompson, David A., EM3*
Thorpe, Everett N., WT3
Thurkettle, William C., S2*
Tidwell, James F., S2
Tisthammer, Bernard E., CGMA
Toce, Nicole, S2
Todd, Harold Crison, GMS
Torretta, John Mario, F1*
Tosh, Bill Hugh, RDM3
Triemer, Ernst A., ENS
Trotter, Arthur C., RM2
Trudeau, Edmond A., LT
True, Roger O., S2
Truitt, Robert E., RM2
Tryon, Frederick B., BUG2
Tull, James Albert, S1 GM
Turner, Charles M., S2*
Turner, William C., MM2
Turner, William H., Jr., ACMMA
Twihle, Harlan M., ENS*
Ulibarri, Antonio D., S2
Ullmann, Paul L., LT (jg)
Umenhoffer, Lyle E., S1*
Underwood, Carey L., S1
Underwood, Ralph E., S1 RDM*
Van Meter, Joseph W., WT3*
Wakefield, James N., S1 QM
Walker, A. W., STM1
Walker, Jack Edwin, RM2
Walker, Verner B., F2*
Wallace, Earl John, RDM3
Wallace, John, RDM3
Walters, Donald H., F1 EM
Warren, William R., RT3
Waters, Jack Lee, CYA
Watson, Winston Harl, F2
Wells, Charles O., S1 RDM*

Wells, Gerald Lloyd, EM3
Wennerholm, Wayne L., COX
Wenzel, Ray G., RT3
Whalen, Stuart D., GM2
Whallon, Louis E., Jr., LT (jg)
White, Earl Clarence, TC1
White, Howard McKean, CWTP
Whiting, George A., F2*
Whitman, Robert T., LT
Wilcox, Lindsey Zeh, WT2*
Wileman, Roy Weldon, PHM3
Willard, Merriman D., PHM2
Williams, Billie Joe, MM2
Williams, Magellan, STM1
Williams, Robert L., WO
Wilson, Frank, F2
Wilson, Thomas B., S1
Wisniewski, Stanley, F2*
Wittmer, Milton R., EM2
Witzig, Robert M., FC3*
Wojciechowski, Maryian J., GM2
Wolfe, Floyd Ralph, GM3
Woods, Leonard T., CWO
Woolston, John, ENS*
Yeaple, Jack Thomas, Y3
Zink, Charles W., EM3*
Zohal, Francis John, S2

THE MARINE DETACHMENT

Brinker, David A., PFC USMC
Brown, Orio N., PFC USMC-O
Bush, John Richard, PVT USMC
Cromling, Charles J., Jr., PLTSGT USMC
Davis, William H., PFC USMC

Dupeck, Albert, Jr., PFC USMC
Greenwald, Jacob, 1ST SCT USMC*
Grimm, Loren E., PFC USMC
Hancock, Thomas A., PFC USMC
Harrell, Edgar A., CPL USMC*
Holland, John F., Jr., PFC USMC
Hubbard, Gordon R., PFC USMC
Hubbard, Leland R., PFC USMC
Hughes, Max M., PFC USMC*
Jacob, Melvin C., PFC USMC*
Kenworthy, Glenn W., CPL USMC
Kirchner, John H., PVT USMC
Larsen, Harlan D., PFC USMC
Lees, Henry W., PFC USMC
Marttila, Howard W., PVT USMC
McCoy, Giles G., PFC USMC*
Messenger, Leonard J., PFC USMC
Munson, Bryan C., PFC USMC
Murphy, Charles T., PFC USMC
Neal, William F., PFC USMC
Parke, Edward L., CAPT USMC
Redd, Robert F., PVT USMC
Reinold, George H., PFC USMC
Rich, Raymond A., PFC USMC*
Riggins, Earl, PVT USMC*
Rose, Francis Edmund, PFC USMC
Spino, Frank J., PFC USMC
Spooner, Miles Lewis, PVT USMC*
Stauffer, Edward H., 1ST LT USMC
Straughn, Howard V., Jr., CPL USMC
Thomsen, Arthur A., PFC USMC
Tracy, Richard I., Jr., SCT USMC
Uffelman, Paul R., PFC USMC*
Wych, Robert A., PFC USM

PROLOGUE

Sailor on a Chain

———

I wish to have no connection with any ship that does not sail fast;
for I intend to go in harm's way.

—COMMODORE JOHN PAUL JONES,
in a letter dated November 16, 1778

WEDNESDAY, NOVEMBER 6, 1968
Winvian Farm, Litchfield, Connecticut

ON a windswept fall day, on a gray morning after the colorful agony of autumn had passed but before the deep, blank snows of winter sealed off the world, Captain Charles Butler McVay III, the former commander of the World War II cruiser USS *Indianapolis*, woke and took stock of his day. He was alone in a drafty bedroom of a colonial house called Winvian Farm, outside Litchfield, Connecticut, adrift in rich horse country. His window looked out at a flagstone terrace built for grand cocktail parties and at a swimming pool; beyond that, he could glimpse the scattered homes of bankers and lawyers whose offices were in New York, 100 miles to the south. The surrounding woods, black and skeletal in the morning light, scratched at a gray sky.

There was much to do. Earlier in the week, the captain had drained the pool for the winter, and this morning he would finish the ritual of closure by putting up snow fences and wrapping the property's hedges with burlap. After lunch, he often played bridge; later in the afternoon, he might putter in his woodshop or go duck hunting on Bantam Lake. The captain was seventy years old, in fine health, with white hair and black eyebrows that framed piercing, but gentle, blue eyes. Always dapper, always self-assured, he dressed in crisply pressed khaki shirt and pants and leather slippers, clothes that had become a uniform for him, a vestige of his life in the wartime navy.

"Vivian!"

His wife's room was across from his own spartan billet, which included just a twin bed and a night table with a Bible that he

3

read every night before turning in at ten. In the room was a desk drawer filled with letters from the families of sailors he'd commanded, bound up in string and rubber bands. The letters troubled the captain; they had always troubled him. Each Christmas even more arrived, and December 25 was fast approaching.

There was no answer from Vivian's room, which wasn't surprising. Vivian was his third wife. Vivacious, beautiful, and tempestuous, she was in the habit of sleeping late. A former fashion model, she sat at the center of the social whirl of Litchfield; by all appearances, she and Charlie—as all his friends called him—made a wonderful pair, a handsome couple. The social events often bored McVay, who could be shy and even recalcitrant, at times preferring the solitude of the duck blind to the patter of a cocktail party.

He made his way down the creaking staircase to the kitchen, where, lately, he'd been spending more and more time talking with the housekeeper, Florence Regosia, a kindhearted young woman who'd worked for him for eight years and who insisted on calling him Admiral. He'd actually been promoted to the rank of rear admiral, his official naval title upon his retirement, what's called a "tombstone promotion." Such promotions, though, are a bit like being named captain of the football team and then sitting out the game. McVay himself usually insisted on Captain; it seemed more honest to him.

After exchanging pleasantries with Florence, he took his black Lab, Chance, for a walk in the woods behind the house. Afterward, he met Al Dudley, his gardener and handyman, and they began work on the shrubs in the front yard, binding them mummy-tight with twine and burlap for the long voyage into winter.

From the yard of Winvian Farm, you can look out at the country road leading north into Litchfield, and south toward the main arteries leading to the sea. There's a stone fence, a bank of apple trees, and beyond that some woods and fields galloping into the distance. Many of the houses in Litchfield were built by nineteenth-century sea captains, and many of them still sport widow's walks. It's a hilly landscape, and the village is sunk in a wooded valley, off a main thoroughfare, as if the wives of these captains had wanted to drag them as far inland as possible, away from the sea, out of danger's way. It's a place people usually come to in peace and prosperity at the end of life; it's a place to come to and forget things. The captain had lived here for nearly seven years.

A barn and machine shed and the cold whisper of the November wind surrounded McVay and his gardener. They worked well together, side by side, McVay chatting, pliers and twine in hand, as if nothing at all was bothering him.

But something was.

After a couple of hours, they broke for lunch, and Al Dudley returned to his own smaller house across the county road. Inside the Winvian farmhouse, Florence was setting out lunch—a sandwich—on the dining room table. Vivian was off somewhere in another room, eating alone. Before sitting down, the captain went upstairs to his bedroom, ostensibly to change into something suitable for an afternoon of playing bridge at the Sanctum, a gentleman's club situated on the trim town green in Litchfield. He closed the door.

Beyond the bedroom windows, the wind was stripping what leaves were left on the trees, and a freezing rain was worming its way under the eaves, looking for a way in.

On the night table sat a holster, and in the holster was a navy-issue .38, a revolver, which the captain picked up.

A knock came at the door.

"Admiral, your lunch is ready." It was Florence.

"I'll be down in a minute."

For all the captain's customary good cheer, Florence had been worried about him. She knew he was having nightmares; he'd told her they were filled with circling sharks. When she'd reminded him, several weeks earlier, that the storm windows also needed installing, he had remarked, "Oh, that won't be necessary."

"Why not?"

"Because," the captain told her, "I won't be here."

Now, Florence returned downstairs, and soon the captain appeared in the doorway, a blank look on his face. He was still dressed in his khaki.

"Admiral," Florence said, "you have to go play cards today."

"Oh, yes," said McVay. "I know."

When Florence asked if he'd like some lunch, he replied, "I'll eat it later."

Florence eyed him, and then she returned to the kitchen.

THE captain pushed open the front door and stepped through a small wooden entryway erected in anticipation of the coming winter snow. He lay down on the stone walk with his head resting on the marble step, his gaunt face tilted up at a gray sky.

Beside him, as he lay alone in the front yard, stood Chance, who watched, head cocked to one side, as the captain brought the cold barrel of the gun to his head.

In McVay's left hand was a set of house keys, and on the key ring, a metal toy sailor, a worn memento from happier times. He'd carried it with him around the world, across several oceans, and into battle. He'd been given the toy sailor as a gift when he was a boy.

Whatever good fortune the captain had enjoyed in his life, it had run out. He pulled the trigger.

A pool of blood sluiced over the step and ran into the matted grass. Reclined as he was, with his head resting upon the step, his hands lying carefully in his lap, his legs stretching easily before him and pointing down the stone walk, Charles Butler McVay looked like a man adrift, cut free—a peaceful voyager now, on a steady sea.

WHEN word of McVay's death began trickling to the outside world, his obituary, carried by major newspapers, described a historic naval career—"Adm. Charles McVay Dies at 70," read the *Washington Post*. Both the *Post* and the *New York Times* noted, however, that his career had been touched by intense controversy and disaster.

Few people in Litchfield understood why he had killed himself; little was known of his life before he moved to the tiny, insular community. By turns private and gregarious, modest yet proud, he was an enigma, a mysteriously stoic man.

What few in his adopted town knew was that Captain McVay was a survivor of the worst naval disaster at sea in U.S. history. This is a dubious distinction, to be sure—one that dogged him throughout his life. He rarely discussed with anyone the nightmarish events of the early morning of July 30, 1945, when his ship, the USS *Indianapolis*, was torpedoed by a Japanese submarine, immediately killing nearly 300 men, and sending as many as 900 others into the black, churning embrace of the vast Philippine Sea, some 350 miles from nearest landfall.

Four days later, when the navy finally learned of the sinking, only 321 of these sailors were still among the living; four of the survivors died shortly after their rescue in military hospitals in the South Pacific. In a story rich with ironies, it turned out that the *Indianapolis* was the first ship the Japanese captain had ever torpedoed and the last major warship sunk during World War II.

In the aftermath of the disaster, two unprecedented events occurred: the navy changed the way it did business at sea, and Captain McVay was charged with negligence in his command and brought to trial. Of the nearly 400 American captains whose ships went down during World War II—indeed, of all the captains in the entire history of the navy—he is the only captain to have been court-martialed whose ship was sunk by an act of war.

In the early 1990s, intelligence reports that might have proved McVay's innocence in the matter were finally declassified. Upon review, however, the navy refused to reconsider its decision. In spite of congressional action passed in October 2000, McVay's court-martial conviction still stands today, and his criminal record lists him as a felon.

Of the original 316 men who survived the ordeal, 124 were still living in 2001 when *In Harm's Way* was originally published, and every two years they met in Indianapolis, the namesake city of their doomed ship, to revisit the sinking and the memory of Captain McVay. These survivors were the gray-haired men in windbreakers and tennis shoes you would see walking in malls in the morning; they were retired ministers, truck drivers, doctors, and wealthy businessmen; they were grandfathers, husbands, uncles, and brothers. And to a man they insisted Captain McVay was not responsible for the calamitous event that utterly changed them. When the nightmare was over—when they were able to stand again and walk away into the rest of their lives—they rarely spoke of what had happened. It took years to unlock the memories of those days and nights.

In many history books, the sinking of the *Indianapolis* isn't mentioned; in some ways, it's as if the ship set sail and has never come home. But to this day, the disaster haunts the Department of the Navy, and it haunted these men. At night, some of them still reach out from sleep to grip a bed they are sure is sinking beneath them.

PART ONE

Sailing to War

CHAPTER ONE

All Aboard

———

Dad, there's a war to be won out there,
and I'm going out to get this thing cleaned up.
I'll be back shortly.

—ED BROWN,
seaman first-class, USS *Indianapolis*

SUNDAY JULY 15, 1945
San Francisco, California

THE ship was still tied up in the harbor at Mare Island, but already the captain felt it was drifting out of his control.

Marching up the gangway of the vessel under his command, the USS *Indianapolis,* Captain Charles McVay was a man perplexed. Reaching the top, he turned toward the stern, saluted the flag, and strode on through the bronze light of the chill California morning, stepping past the electricians, painters, and engineers working on deck. No one watching the forty-six-year-old McVay, dressed smartly in his khaki and crisp campaign hat—its black vinyl bill decorated with gold braid that the enlisted men called "scrambled eggs"—would have guessed the depth of his concern. He hid it well.

He had just come from an early-morning meeting at U.S. naval headquarters in downtown San Francisco. The meeting, with Admiral William R. Purnell and Captain William S. Parsons, had been disappointingly quick and to the point: this morning he was to take his ship from the Mare Island navy yard, thirty miles north of San Francisco, to Hunters Point navy yard, located just outside the city in San Francisco Bay. Once at Hunters Point, McVay was told, the *Indy* would take on board what was described only as a "secret project" before departing for the Pacific.

The meeting was over in less than an hour, and it failed to provide much information on his ship's new assignment.

McVay had a lot on his mind, much of it worrisome. Since May, the *Indy* had been docked at Mare Island, where it had been undergoing extensive repairs that were expected to take at least four months. Then suddenly everything had been accelerated. Three days ago, on July 12, McVay had received mysterious orders from naval command to immediately ready his crew for a secret mission.

Hundreds of telegrams left the ship, calling the crew of 1,195 boys to sea; they had—at the most—just ninety-six hours to execute the command. Some of the veteran crewmen were dispersed across the country, on leave or at temporary training schools.* The majority of the crew had stayed at the marine and naval barracks at Mare Island, killing time by drinking beer, chasing girls, and playing cards. Still others were being called to the ship and to war—for the first time.

They came streaming to Mare Island and to the ship, stepping over tangled nests of air and water hoses, tools, and debris spread on her deck. McVay had watched as the newest crew members came on board, the older veterans cheering them on: "Hey, boys! Look at him," they cried out. "Ain't he pretty? Why, he doesn't even look like he's shaving yet!"

McVay understood how large the war loomed in the minds of these boys, "green hands" and veterans alike, who during these last few days had made love one last time, gotten drunk one last time, written last letters to mothers and fathers, and prepared to settle on board the *Indy,* into the rhythm of getting ready for sea. Rumors had started flying that the ship was headed back to the Philippines, then on to the massive invasion of Japan and its home islands, code

---

* Although 1,195 crew members departed from California, Navy Captain Edwin Crouch boarded the ship at Guam. He was a fellow classmate of Captain McVay's at the U.S. Naval Academy and asked his permission to ride along to the Philippines, according to William Toti, former Special Assistant to the Vice-Chief of Naval Operations. Crouch's presence on board brings the total number who sailed to 1,196 persons. Crouch did not survive the sinking.

names Operation Coronet and Olympic. But this morning, not even Captain McVay had any idea of their final destination.

He'd been told that the earliest the ship would leave San Francisco would be July 16, which was tomorrow. McVay had been given four days to do what seemed impossible. During the past twenty-four hours, he'd been crashing through night fog and heavy seas around the Farallon Islands, thirty miles west of the San Francisco coast, running the *Indy* through abbreviated but punishing sea trials. The crew had practiced radar alerts, radar jamming, and emergency turns. The *Indy* performed well, all things considered.

But how well was good enough? The ship was still fresh from the disaster that had necessitated all the repair work: on March 31, the *Indy* had suffered a nearly fatal kamikaze attack off the island of Okinawa. The incident had left nine men dead, twenty-nine wounded. One of McVay's boys, bugler second-class E. P. Procai, had been laid to rest at sea, accompanied by a twenty-one-gun salute. The remaining eight sailors were interred on one of the tiny islands west of Okinawa, a repair facility for damaged destroyers and a burial ground for the dead.

After the attack at Okinawa, the *Indy* had limped the 6,000 miles back across the Pacific. Two of her propeller shafts, a fuel tank, and her water distillation plant had been badly damaged. Back on land, some of the crew had begun asking for transfers off the ship. "When we get hit again," they were saying, "you'll be able to drive a bus through the hole." The *Indy,* they grumbled, had "turned poor."

They now wondered if she was an unlucky ship.

NOT long after the captain's return, at about 10 a.m., Dr. Lewis Haynes heard the hiss of the *Indy*'s PA system, a sound like air rushing through a hose, which was followed by the shrill piping of the boatswain's pipe. "Now hear this, now hear this!" came the announcement. The doctor listened as McVay's soft voice echoed through the morning air: "Men," he told his crew, "we are headed tomorrow morning to the forward area." This meant they were going back into the war zone.

The boys halted in midstride and in midchore—brooms and water hoses cradled in their arms as they cocked ears to the speakers tacked to the bulkheads, or outer walls, of the ship. They were to depart immediately, the captain announced, for Hunters Point, a supply depot and loading point of final stores for Pacific-bound ships. And then the captain delivered the news that a sailor dreads hearing: all shore liberties for the evening were canceled. McVay signed off, "That is all." The PA line went dead.

A groan went up among some of the boys. They had plans—and these included getting into San Francisco tonight. The city, still a Wild West town, was the last stop for Pacific-bound sailors, who congregated at all-girlie shows at the Streets of Paris on Mason. In the three and a half years since Pearl Harbor, several million soldiers had passed through; in the last four months alone, the army and navy had shipped more than 320,000 troops from the port city.

McVay next gave the order to sail, and minutes later, the *Indy* backed from the pier at Mare Island and cruised past Alcatraz Island into the wide, placid water of San Francisco Bay. Soon, the sun having risen high and the morning's fog burned off, she was snug to the wharf at Hunters Point, standing motionless against her mammoth eight-inch mooring lines sprung from bow and stern.

Dr. Haynes had thought the abrupt change in the ship's plans was odd. The inquisitive physician had been under the impression that preparations were being made to get the ship ready to join Task Force 95 for the invasion of Japan. At the moment, the task force was in the Philippines, and the invasion was scheduled for the end of the year, which was still about four and a half months away.

The war in Europe was over, and the Pacific theater was paused before this final assault on the Japanese homeland. Two months earlier, Germany had surrendered; the D-Day invasion of Normandy on June 6, 1944, had left the U.S. First Army with 6,603 casualties, 1,465 of them fatal. But this paled in comparison to the estimated toll for the invasion of Japan: at least 500,000 American casualties. The boys of the *Indy* talked openly and often with one another about whether they'd survive the battle. On the island of Tinian, which the *Indy* had bombarded and helped secure in 1944, there were reports that Japanese troops were still hiding in the jungle hills, resorting to cannibalism to survive, and that they could hold out another five years against an invading force. The end of the war seemed near to some, Haynes knew, yet to many it still felt like a dream.

This morning, he wondered how a ship like the USS *Indianapolis* was going to shorten the war. And he thought of home.

During the *Indy*'s furlough, Haynes had been lucky enough to return to Connecticut for several weeks, where he played in the surf with his wife and two young sons and felt the pure joy of not being at war wash over him. At thirty-three, he was one of the oldest, most well-seasoned sailors aboard the ship. In 1941, on the destroyer *Reuben James,* he'd ridden out a North Atlantic hurricane that no one aboard thought they'd survive. He also held an informal record for continuous duty at sea. Before being assigned to the *Indy,* he'd logged thirty-nine months without a leave while aboard destroyers and the battleship USS *New Mexico.* He never complained to his superior officers about his unusually long stint—except once, which was the same day he was awarded leave. His thinking was: he had an important job to do. And that was saving boys' lives.

He almost hadn't made it home to Connecticut last month. Scraping by on his meager lieutenant commander's pay, Haynes had decided he couldn't afford the train fare. He hadn't seen his wife or sons in six months, but he was broke. Then one afternoon as he was sitting at the tiny desk in his berth reading a Zane Grey novel borrowed from the ship's library, Father Conway, a priest from Waterbury, Connecticut, scratched at the black curtain that served as Haynes's door.

Haynes and the ship's dignified priest were friends, and sometimes they went on liberty together. Conway asked Haynes when he was going home. "Well, Tom," Haynes replied, "I have this problem. I can't afford it." Conway left, and Haynes returned to his novel. The next day, the priest tossed a handful of bills on the doctor's desk. "There now," he said, smiling, "you *are* going home!" Haynes could have wept over the kindness.

He had been back on the ship two weeks now, working temporary duty in the naval yard's medical dispensary. Besides the usual cases of tonsillectomies and circumcisions—many of the boys, apparently, hadn't been able to afford, or had never considered, getting a circumcision before joining the navy, and Haynes performed so many for the *Indy*'s crew that they'd renamed her the "clipper ship"—there were more disturbing, war-induced maladies. One crew member was admitted to the hospital with a case of tuberculosis. Another walked in with a harder-to-treat diagnosis of "nightmares." Haynes, like Conway, understood how hard it was for some of these boys to come back to the ship. He had heard them refer to the *Indy*'s hurried departure from San Francisco as a major piece of "grab ass." How were they supposed to say good-bye so quickly to a place that had become their home away from home?

AFTER the *Indianapolis* had sailed into San Francisco for repairs in May, many of the crew had telegrammed girlfriends, wives, and family members, who flocked to the city and rented apartments, found jobs, and set up housekeeping. New lives had quickly taken root on land. Some boys got married. Women got pregnant. Brothers were reunited.

The boys of the *Indy* fell in love with San Francisco, where in diners and soda shops Benny Goodman was on the radio; beer cost fifteen cents a bottle; Luckies were a dime a pack. In July, the Fillmore was showing Bob Hope's flick *Give Me a Sailor*, and the Paramount was playing *The Call of the Wild,* starring Clark Gable. If the boys were feeling flush, they'd drink at the Top of the Mark hotel overlooking San Francisco Bay; if they were broke, they would stumble into Slapsy Maxie's and drink on a tab the patriotic bartender was in no hurry to collect on. Their average age was nineteen, and for many this was their first time on their own.

During the summer, there had been no end to the ways the boys could get into trouble. (*The Bluejackets' Manual,* a sailor's handbook of proper conduct, had warned of all sorts of dangers: "Bad women can ruin your bodily health," admonished one chapter. "Bad women especially are the cause of much grief. Sexual intercourse is positively not necessary for healthy and proper manly development." And this bit of advice to the downhearted: "You will be homesick for a while. We all were. You are starting a new life. Grin and bear it as we all did. No man ever succeeded by hanging on to his mother's apron strings all his life.") One sailor was arrested for "attempting to urinate in public view," and another was cited for "possession of a knife while on liberty." The knife-wielding sailor lost the privilege of five future liberties, and the urinator was fined and sentenced to twenty days' confinement in the ship's brig, an airless cell deep in the *Indy*'s stern. He was fed bread and water.

Captain McVay was billeted, along with his newlywed wife of one year, Louise, in a comfortable but spare officers' community of apartments named Coral Sea Village located within the confines of the Mare Island navy yard. With time on his hands while the *Indy* was undergoing repairs, McVay, like his young crew, also found ways to enjoy himself. Shortly before receiving his surprise orders, he'd taken a brief, impromptu fishing trip to a steelhead trout river north of San Francisco.

The more serious business of preparing the ship for departure was a round-the-clock affair, however. Thousands of rounds of ammo were loaded and dropped by elevator into the ship's magazine near the bow. Over 60,000 gallons of fuel oil were pumped into her tanks, and she took on 3,500 gallons of aviation fuel for the ship's reconnaissance plane. Food for the crew came aboard and was measured by the ton. One of the urns in the ship's galley could brew 40 gallons of the precious, eye-opening coffee in a single batch. A typical list of stores consumed each week included 300 pounds of bread, 295 pounds of squash, 26 pounds of avocados, 672 pounds of apples, 1,155 pounds of oranges, 670 pounds of grapefruit, 305 pounds of celery, 476 pounds of tomatoes, 845 pounds of cabbage, 300 pounds of turnips, 70 pounds of fresh fish, 423 pounds of carrots, 341 pounds of cauliflower, and 665 pounds of corn.

And ice cream. The boys could eat about twenty-five gallons of ice cream in a week, which the galley's cooks kept stored in walk-in freezers. Their favorite flavors were peppermint and tropical passion. Ice cream was so loved by sailors that mess-hall cooks ran an ice cream parlor aboard the *Indy*, called a "gedunk" stand. In the military, everything had a nickname. A beer parlor was called a "slop chute." Candy bars were named "pogey bait." A Dear John letter was also known as a "green banana," and the advance of a sailor's pay was called a "dead horse." But the men of the USS *Indianapolis* had no easy slang to describe the way most of them felt about leaving San Francisco.

UNDER the feet of marine private Giles McCoy, the ship's gray, steel quarterdeck, located in the middle of the ship, hummed. The low-wave frequency came up through his bones, shook him, told him: something's in the wind today, boy.

At Mare Island, after Captain McVay's announcement that they would sail this morning to Hunters Point, marine captain Edward Parke had gathered his detachment of thirty-nine marines and explained that at Hunters Point they were about to assume special guard duties of the utmost importance.

An imposing man in his early thirties, with sandy hair, a barrel chest, and blue eyes that some of his men said pierced like daggers (more than one thought he bore a striking resemblance to Burt Lancaster), Parke had said nothing more; that was all they would need to know.

A marine detachment aboard a navy ship sleeps in its own separate compartment—away from the ship's crew—and operates the onboard brig, or jail; fires the guns during battle; and provides all-around security for the ship. As part of this group, Private McCoy was eager for the opportunity to be part of something big. He looked up to Captain Parke, a hero who had fought at Guadalcanal and earned the Purple Heart. Parke sometimes let him tag along on liberty; before setting out for a night on the town, he would unpin his insignia identifying him as an officer but then warn McCoy: "Don't think this means I'll cut you any slack back on the ship. Because I won't." McCoy felt he always knew where he stood with Parke.

After docking at Hunters Point, McCoy stood belowdecks in his tiny compartment before a stainless-steel mirror—on warships, broken glass is a hazard—staring at the face that had become his own during his thirteen-month tour of duty. At eighteen, he had the sharp eyes of a boy but the quick grimace of an old man. He fastidiously dry-shaved, ran a comb through his black wavy hair, did a quick re-buff of his duty shoes, and bounded up the ladder, or stairs, topside for duty.

Usually, Hunters Point harbored some fifteen warships, all in various stages of repair and resupply. But this morning the shipyard was empty; only a few seagulls screeched into the pale blue sky. Accompanying them were the musical lap and ping of black water against the *Indy*'s gray, steel hull. Along the rail of the ship, the crew milled and stared at the wharf, as if trying to read signals from the silent tableau of warehouses, camouflaged trucks, and empty piers.

Approaching Captain Parke, McCoy requested an inspection of his appearance before assuming duty. Parke checked the razor creases in McCoy's pants, the angle of his cover, or hat, atop his head.

"You may proceed, McCoy."

"Yes, sir!"

A dock crew had wheeled a gangway up to the *Indy*'s quarter-deck, which served as its main entry and exit. McCoy stepped down and assumed his position of duty: chest out, hands at his sides, a loaded Colt .45 hanging from his canvas duty belt, one round in the chamber.

Until given further orders, he was to let no man onto the ship who was not authorized. He was scheduled to get off duty at noon; because of the mid-morning relocation to Hunters Point, his watch was slightly abbreviated. He hoped the cargo came on before he was relieved, however.

The *Indy* was operating in a battle-ready state known as Condition Able, which meant that the boys were on watch for four hours and then off for four, an exhausting, relentless schedule that left little time for sleep and induced in the boys a dreamlike state of jittery wakefulness. And yet, McCoy felt lucky to be aboard the *Indy*. On a ship, marines liked to say, no one was ever shooting at you, at least at close range. The competitiveness between the two military branches was good-hearted but persistent. Sailors called marines "gyrenes," and marines called sailors "swabbies." New officers were mocked as "shave-tails." (There was no end to the nicknames: engineers were called "snipes"; the bridge crew was known as "skivvy wavers," because they waved flags while executing semaphore, a silent means of communication between ships at sea; and members of gunnery crews were called "gunneys.")

But as sailors liked to tell those who thought navy life was comfortable, "When the battle-shit hits the fan on a ship, you can't dig a hole and hide. You have to stand and take it."

Private McCoy had been pulling temporary guard duty at the main entrance gate on Mare Island when he received the call to return. It was a job he liked; he enjoyed the way the amputees, many of them his age and veterans of the invasion of Iwo Jima that had taken place almost five months earlier, hooted and hollered as they raced their wheelchairs down the steep hill leading from the hospital to the guard shack.

He was easy on them when they tried smuggling booze into the marine barracks. They hid the bottles in the hollow of their fake legs, and McCoy could hear them clunking around inside—step, shuffle, clunk-step—as they approached.

"For crissakes," he told them, "why don't you wrap those things in towels? Your sergeant catches you, you'll be court-martialed!" They smiled, and he let them pass.

McCoy marveled at how these boys had accepted the awful things that had happened to them in war; he wondered how he would react in a similar situation. He hoped he wouldn't have to find out.

But McCoy had faith in his ship. The *Indy* was a vessel on which he was proud to serve—the honored flagship of the U.S. Navy's Fifth Fleet, which was under the command of Admiral Raymond Spruance. The *Indy* was a heavy cruiser, a fast thoroughbred of the sea, whose job it was to run and gun enemy emplacements on land and blow enemy planes from the sky. She was a floating city, with her own water plant, laundry, tailor, butcher, bakery, dentist's office, photo lab, and enough weaponry to lay siege to downtown San Francisco.

The first time Private McCoy rounded the corner at the Mare Island navy yard and saw the *Indy,* he was awestruck. God, he thought, now that's a ship!

She towered 133 feet from her waterline to the tip of her radar antennae, called "bedsprings" because of their appearance, and she cast an alluring silhouette. McCoy couldn't help thinking that if she were a woman—and sailors have traditionally thought of their ships as women—she'd be wearing a gray dress cut low in the back and looking coyly over a cocked shoulder. But there was a saying about ships like the *Indy:* "She wears paint, but she carries powder"—meaning gunpowder. Translation: she was not a lady to be trifled with.

Commissioned in 1932, she had been chosen by Roosevelt as his ship of state. He liked to stand at the stern on her wide fantail, above the massive, churning propellers, while smoking a cigar and watching the New York skyline drift by during a ceremonial review of America's naval fleet. From her deck, he also toured South America, docking in Buenos Aires and Rio de Janeiro, on a prewar "good neighbor" tour. (During the trip, Roosevelt dined on fresh venison and watched Laurel and Hardy's *Our Relations* on a movie screen painted on one of the ship's bulkheads especially for the occasion.) The *Indy* trained at war exercises off the coast of Chile and became the flagship of the navy's scouting fleet. With her hull painted bone-white, her afterdecks spanned by sparkling awnings, an aura of luck and privilege had enveloped the ship.

McCoy loved to boast that at 610 feet long, she was the size of nearly two football fields, but she was smaller and nimbler than battleships, like the USS *South Dakota,* whose job it was to bomb enemy inshore installations with their gargantuan 16-inch guns.

The *Indy* was bigger and better armed than destroyers, which hunted submarines with underwater sonar gear and provided at-sea security for ships like the *Indianapolis*. In battle formation, a cruiser flanked the more ponderous aircraft carriers and battleships and directed anti-aircraft fire at enemy planes, while the flotilla itself was prowled by vigilant destroyer escorts. Ever since the seventeenth century, navies had relied on ships that could strike quickly, raid enemy lines, draw fire, and then muster the speed to sail away before being sunk, leaving the heavy work of shore destruction to battleships. At her top speed of 32.75 knots, few ships, enemy or friendly, could keep up with the USS *Indianapolis*.

Yet, as McCoy understood, what a cruiser gives up for its astonishing speed is armor: the *Indy* was protected midships with only three to four inches of steel (battleships carried an average of thirteen inches), while her decks were laid with two inches. In her day, she had been the queen of President Franklin Delano Roosevelt's naval fleet. But on this morning in July, she was considered old, past her prime. Newer cruisers were not as beautiful, but they were bigger, faster, and better armored.

AROUND 2 p.m., the PA crackled to life, calling all hands to their stations.

Dr. Haynes, standing on the forecastle deck, located on the bow, could see planes circling overhead in tight patterns, keeping careful watch. The dock was lined with some ten marines carrying automatic weapons. Whatever was coming on board, Haynes figured it was hot property. The tall physician waited, pensively smoking his cigar.

Shortly, two army trucks thundered to a stop on the wharf, and a detachment of armed marines silently stepped down. Haynes watched as the canvas flaps on the rear of the trucks were parted. Two large items emerged: the first was an enormous wooden crate, measuring some five feet high, five feet wide, and fifteen feet long. Then came a metal canister, painted black, about knee-high and eighteen inches wide. Two marines struggled to lift it down from the truck.

A line from a crane aboard the *Indy* snaked down above the crate, which was secured with straps. Haynes's eyes followed the crate as it was lifted skyward and set securely in the port hangar, a fifty-square-foot-wide area normally used for observation planes. There the crate was lashed down.

Following a marine guard, the bearers of the ominous-looking receptacle struggled up the gangway. The heavy canister hung between them on a metal pole.* They marched with it to the flag lieutenant's cabin located in a part of the ship near the bow called officers' country, a place strictly off-limits to enlisted men. (The flag lieutenant, a member of Admiral Spruance's staff, was absent from the ship.) Accompanying them were two army officers, Major Robert Furman and Captain James Nolan, who announced themselves as artillery officers. Haynes didn't recognize them. He thought they were nervous-looking men—Nolan, in particular.

---

* One crew member describes not just a single black canister being unloaded from an army truck, but two of these receptacles, which he and another sailor struggled to carry up the gangway to the *Indy*. This is contradicted, however, by other eyewitness accounts, including that of Dr. Haynes.

In general, confusion has surrounded the details of the actual loading. At least two previous accountings of the *Indianapolis* disaster describe this mysterious cargo being loaded on July 16, which contradicts Captain McVay's own narrative of the event written nearly two months after his rescue.

A few minutes later, Captain Nolan reported to Captain McVay on the bridge. He explained that with the aid of the ship's welder, they had fastened the canister to the deck of the flag lieutenant's cabin, and that it had been padlocked. Nolan would hold the key throughout the ship's journey.

McVay thought for a moment and said, "I didn't think we were going to use biological warfare in this war." He was clearly fishing for further information.

Captain Nolan left the bridge without explanation.

LOOKING down from the bridge, about forty-five feet above the main deck, Captain McVay surveyed the ship's state of disarray. A noontime farewell luncheon held on board with his officers and their wives had gone off hurriedly but without a hitch; now, with the cargo safely loaded, he could at last turn his attention to more pressing concerns, such as his ship's seaworthiness.

What the captain didn't know was that another cruiser, the USS *Pensacola,* which had been moored next to the *Indianapolis* at Mare Island's Pier 22S, had originally been chosen to set sail in their stead. But a week earlier, after an overhaul and refitting, she had failed her sea trials when her engines had quit in especially rough seas. Immediately, a search had begun for a replacement ship. And the spotlight had fallen on the *Indy.*

Before the surprise orders were given, it had been assumed that she would spend at least another six weeks of repair in the yard, followed by two weeks of sea trials to complete necessary shakedowns. Much still remained to be tested, such as the calibration of her radar range finders, firing drills for her main battery of 8-inch guns, automatic weapons tracking drills, intraship flag drills, voice radio drills, coding board drills, and anti-aircraft tracking drills. Belowdecks, yard welders were still at work mending the ship's steel frames.

Even under McVay's previous sailing orders, which had him leaving San Francisco in another two months, the repairs had been running behind schedule. And the end results of some of these repairs were uncertain.

One of the ship's major problems, leading to the removal of one of the plane-launching catapults, had been solved, although never explained. After the catapult's removal, however, the ship had developed a curious, albeit slight, three-degree list, or tilt, toward its lighter side. (If she was going to list, it should have been in the direction of the now heavier side.) The condition had been corrected by shifting freight and by the added weight of the oncoming fuel. McVay was also worried about the ship's water condensers, supposedly repaired since they were damaged in the kamikaze attack; they were malfunctioning again. The condensers were used to make steam to run the *Indy*'s four turbine engines. Because they weren't working to capacity, Captain McVay had posted an alert on board that all potable water had to be reserved for the engines. The crew was not allowed one drink from the scuttlebutts, or drinking fountains, dotted around the ship. But still, in the midst of all the activity on board, it was possible no one was paying attention to the alert.

Of his crew, more than 250 of the 1,195 men were new to the ship, some fresh from boot camp and training school. How would these green hands perform in the open sea? Or battle? Of McVay's eighty officers, thirty-five were also new—at least one had graduated just weeks earlier from the Naval Academy in Annapolis. The navy had a nickname for the fresh Officer

Candidate School graduates: they were called "ninety-day won-ders." The captain estimated that 25 percent of his crew was inexperienced, and he knew it would be a challenge to sharpen them into naval fighters before joining the invasion's task force.

As the afternoon wore on, McVay could see nothing but prob-lems. Until yesterday, the ship hadn't even been loaded with her complement of required life vests; then a double order arrived—nearly 2,500 vests. With available storage space tight, where was he supposed to stow all the extras? And to make matters worse, earlier, before announcing this special mission, naval command had ordered the *Indy* to taxi nearly 100 extra navy personnel to Pearl Harbor for further assignment; now these men were show-ing up with seabags in hand, looking for berths. McVay, frustrated by the increasingly crowded conditions aboard ship, worried about his ability to run his new crew through their regular battle drills once at sea. It was a madhouse.

It was going to be a long night.

FOR the crew, the night ahead was filled with possibility. The sudden order to sail affected the boys in odd ways. Sailor Bob Gause, from Tarpon Springs, Florida, hatched a scheme to sneak off the ship to see his wife one last time. As a quartermaster, he had been so busy on the bridge during the last few days' prepara-tion that he hadn't even had time to tell her the ship was sailing.

Others were bolder in their plans. Sailor Ed Brown had been plotting his escape since morning, when the captain first an-nounced that all liberties were canceled. Brown, from Sioux Falls, South Dakota, felt he had always been lucky—he never failed to find a way to get around things. He joined the navy in 1944 and left for boot camp an hour after playing his last high school basketball game. He and his father had had to hurry to make it to the train station to catch the troop train passing through; there wouldn't be another for a week.

As the train pulled away, his father ran alongside shouting, "Now, son, I gotta tell you about the birds and bees! I forgot to tell you about the birds and bees!"

"What, Dad!"

And his dad cupped his hands and said, "You're gonna meet some women, and the only thing they want is your money!"

Brown shrugged, confused. "Okay, Dad. Bye. Tell Mom I love her."

He sat down, wondering, "What the hell's he talking about? I don't even have any money."

Four months later, he was aboard the *Indianapolis*, and he thought he understood what his father had meant about the birds and bees. While the *Indy* was in overhaul these past two months, he had met a girl and they had made plans to go dancing tonight at the Club Lido.

Down in his compartment, four decks below the bridge where McVay stood fretting about the problems of the ship, Brown now stripped and dressed in his navy blues—blue woolen pants and a jumper, the standard uniform for a sailor on liberty—and then over these he pulled on his dungarees and denim work shirt.

Racing up the ladder topside, Brown grabbed a garbage can from the hangar deck and walked down the gangway, trying to appear at ease under his uncomfortable bundle of clothing. His ruse worked; to anyone watching, he looked like a sailor on work detail dumping the ship's trash.

Once he was on the wharf, he cut behind a warehouse building and tore off his dungarees and shirt and stuffed them in the trash can, covering them with newspaper. And then he sprinted through the yard's main gate and stuck out his thumb for a ride into San Francisco. He was free!

But things did not come off quite as he expected.

MONDAY, JULY 16, 1945

AT around 5 a.m. Monday morning, the shrill blast of the boatswain's pipe came over the ship's PA. Rolling over and scratching, naked or dressed in skivvies, the boys whose turn it was to go on duty grumpily set to getting the ship ready to sail.

Lines were sprung from the bow and stern, and navy tugs prepared to back out of the harbor with the *Indy* in tow. On the wharf, a lone figure came running, his hand waving wildly; it was Ed Brown.

"What the hell are you doing off the ship!" yelled an officer standing at the top of the gangway. The tugs had now started the lean against the hawsers—the *Indy* was pulling away.

The officer was so flustered by the sight of Brown pulling his sailor suit from a trash can that he could barely speak. He watched in astonishment as Brown stuffed his clothes under his arm and sprinted up the gangway, judged the six feet between him and the departing ship, and jumped. In another five seconds, he would have missed it altogether.

AS the security detail of planes appeared in the pale blue sky, the *Indy* moved out into the harbor. Around them, navy patrol boats prowled in crossing patterns, keeping a respectful distance. But then, at 6:30 a.m., the *Indy* did something unexpected. She halted, as if waiting—but for what, it wasn't exactly clear.

One thousand miles to the east, on an expanse of scrubby desert in New Mexico, a tremendous flash filled the morning sky. It was an explosion of improbable magnitude, vaporizing the 100-foot tower from which it emanated. The searing blast turned the desert sand beneath it into glass. In high school textbooks, this moment would come to be known as the Trinity test; it was the first explosion of a nuclear device in the history of the world.

The men aboard the *Indianapolis* knew nothing of this explosion. But shortly after the ship paused, a marine delivered a message by motor launch. It was presented to Dr. Haynes, who, as a senior medical officer of Admiral Spruance's flagship staff, was authorized to open it.

Haynes quickly perused the message, then took it to the captain on the bridge. It read: INDIANAPOLIS UNDER ORDERS OF COMMANDER IN CHIEF AND MUST NOT BE DIVERTED FROM ITS MISSION FOR ANY REASON.

Essentially, President Harry S. Truman was ordering the ship ahead at any cost.

Captain McVay appeared neither pleased nor anxious. He gathered his officers and informed them, "Gentlemen, our mission is secret. I cannot tell you the mission, but every hour we save will shorten the war by that much." He also told them that in the event of a sinking, the black canister, which had been loaded on board with such care the previous afternoon, was to be placed in its own raft and set adrift. Only after doing this were the men on board to tend to their own safety.

McVay rang the engine room. Soon the propellers caught the

water—the whole ship began to quake. It was like the movement of a freight train, imperceptible at first, but communicating power, the promise of speed.

LASHED to the port hangar deck, the large, wooden box rode easily as the *Indy*'s nose swung for the Golden Gate Bridge. The box was made of plywood and one-by-fours and resembled a heavily constructed packing crate; the screws were all counter-sunk and sealed carefully with red wax to prevent tampering. An area of thirty feet by thirty feet was cordoned off around it with red tape.

In the middle of the space, Private McCoy stood guard. He had orders to consider the watch "live ammunition duty," which meant that he was to keep one round in the chamber of his .45 at all times. He was to use the weapon if necessary. It seemed silly—who was he going to shoot? He knew all these guys. He watched as the crew pressed to the tape, peering in, guessing out loud about the crate's contents. They imagined it was everything from Rita Hayworth's underwear to gold bullion.

Behind McCoy, inside the wooden crate, sat the integral components of the atomic bomb known as "Little Boy." In the canister welded to the flag lieutenant's cabin was the carefully packed uranium-235, totaling half the fissible amount available in the United States at the time, its value estimated at $300 million. In twenty-one days, the bomb would be dropped on Hiroshima.

The contents of the crate were known to only a handful of people: President Truman and Winston Churchill; Robert Oppenheimer and his closest colleagues at the Manhattan Project; and Captain James Nolan and Major Robert Furman, who were now aboard the *Indy*. In reality, Nolan was a radiologist and Furman an engineer engaged in top-secret weapons intelligence.

For Nolan and Furman, the past three days had been an intense ordeal as they moved the bomb—what Oppenheimer and others bemusedly called "the gadget"—by a secret, plainclothes convoy from Los Alamos, New Mexico, to Kirtland Army Air Force base in Albuquerque, where the black canister was given its own parachute and set aboard a transport plane on a seat between Nolan and Furman. After landing at San Francisco's Hamilton Field, each stoplight and intersection along the route to Hunters Point had been timed and mapped in advance to ensure a safe, predictable arrival. Nolan and Furman had slept near the gadget with loaded .45s in a safe house at Hunters Point, their fake artillery uniforms laid out and ready for the dawn departure.

Now, as the *Indy* began steaming for the open ocean, Truman was with Churchill in Potsdam, a suburb of Berlin. He was about to deliver the Potsdam Declaration to Japan: surrender, or be annihilated. Earlier, the USS *Indianapolis* had paused after leaving the wharf to await the test results of this instrument of annihilation; if it had failed, she would have been ordered back to the pier.

But the Trinity test had succeeded, and, by 8:30 a.m. on July 16, 1945, Captain Charles Butler McVay had cleared the San Francisco harbor and was sailing to war

CHAPTER TWO

Good-Bye, Golden Gate

Whenever the *Indy* sailed under the Golden Gate, we used to say,
"Going out to sea was the worst of hell."
And coming back—that was the best of hell.

—BOB MCGUIGGAN,
seaman first-class, USS *Indianapolis*

Sailing to Tinian Island, South Pacific Ocean

———————

FOR every sailor, passing under the Golden Gate bridge was a solemn moment. Silently eyeing its ochre spans, the boys wondered if they would ever lay eyes on it again. Down on the fantail, on the ship's stern, headquarters for the enlisted men, some of the boys formed a betting pool: anybody who wanted could throw in a buck to wager on the next time they'd see the Golden Gate. Ed Brown, having successfully avoided the brig, was in the middle of the action, his white sailor's hat filled with bills.

"The Golden Gate in '48!" he said.

"I say '47!" said another sailor.

"Ah, you're all crazy, this war won't be over for another ten years." The boys booed.

Bob Gause was standing at the wheel as the ship made her way out of San Francisco Bay. Beside him was Captain McVay, looking stern, unflappable.

When Gause looked up at the bridge, his blood ran cold. There on the span, although he could barely make her out, was his wife. And she was waving! Beside her were other wives, also signaling their regretful good-byes. Gause couldn't believe it. Hunched down, he glanced out of the corner of his eye to see if the captain was looking in the same direction, too. The last thing he wanted was for McVay to growl, "Say, Gause, you see all those women up there? I wonder who they're waving at."

The sailor would have to tell the truth. And that could get him court-martialed. He'd violated navy orders by letting his wife know when the *Indy* was leaving. A poster he'd seen in San

41

Francisco, depicting a drowned sailor, had said it best. Its caption read: A CARELESS WORD . . . A NEEDLESS LOSS. Another had admonished: CARELESS TALK GOT THERE FIRST.

Gause didn't breathe easy until the ship had completely cleared the bridge and the beautiful structure was fading off the stern.

MCVAY'S orders for this mission remained sealed in an envelope he'd kept locked in a vault in his cabin. Following the schedule he'd been issued, he waited until he was the specified distance from land before tearing open the document.

Then he picked up the microphone on the open bridge: "Men, this is a speed run to the island of Tinian, where we are to deliver the cargo. We can't lose time. All hands be sharp. That is all."

Coxswain Mike Kuryla now opened the PA's line to enlisted men's country, which included everything to the rear of the number-one smokestack and the captain's bridge. This area was about 300 feet long and 60 feet wide, terminating at the stern of the ship. As a coxswain, it was Kuryla's job to handle the ship's landing lines and craft, as well as pipe messages. He wore a seven-inch silver pipe on a lanyard around his neck. Positioning his mouth close to the small metal screen mounted in a wooden control board located on the quarterdeck, he gave the pipe a blow.

"Now hear this, now hear this! Work party lay to, clean and sweep all decks and ladders!"

Then the fun began. But to get the boys to work, Kuryla had to catch them first. The old salts on board were the best at avoiding duties with their games of hide-and-seek. Kuryla knew exactly where to look; preferred hiding places included bulkhead corners or the turrets of the ship's 8-inch guns.

"Come on, sailor, grab a broom and get to work!" Kuryla said when he managed to squeeze the bums out of hiding. "Now don't give me any guff," he'd roar. Kuryla, a building contractor's son from Chicago, was just nineteen, but his experience and attitude more than compensated for his youth. As he rounded up the boys, the work division brought the deck to life with hoses, mops, and swabs, scrubbing dirt and salt from all painted surfaces. The navy was fanatical about cleanliness, and there was a lot of ground to cover. In all, it would take a man ten minutes at a dog-walking pace to travel the entire 610 feet of the deck, all of which was painted gray, including the two heavy, seven-foot-long anchors set high in the bow like the eyes of a curious gargoyle.

Anyone watching the crew work could have gotten a glimpse of America: there were boys who hailed from Texas ranches, Greek neighborhoods in Chicago, sprawling cities, and remote villages no one had ever heard of. As was the tradition, all the sailors wore handmade knives in scabbards at their sides. They were dressed in dungarees, denim shirts, and black boots called boondockers, their white pillbox hats rolled over their foreheads.

The crew swept and hosed the deck forward from the fantail, past the rear 8-inch gun turret. Some skirted to the rail, past the 5-inch and 40 mm and 20 mm gun decks hanging high overhead from the ship's framework like steel lily pads. Under Kuryla's watchful eyes, others moved past the number-two smokestack and the two airplane hangars surrounding it, to the quarterdeck. It was one of the *Indy*'s social hubs, like the fantail and mess halls belowdecks.

Beyond the quarterdeck was officers' country, with its four levels in ascending order: communications platform, signal bridge, navigation bridge, and fire control station. Captain McVay usually resided in command on the navigation bridge. His realm overlooked the bow, where two more turrets of 8-inch guns sat, their nearly forty-foot barrels poking out to sea. Underneath the four bridges were the officers' sleeping quarters and wardroom; nearby stood the code room and radio shack 1, also known as Radio Central, which received incoming messages from Honolulu twenty-four hours a day. Here, seated around a half-moon-shaped desk spanning the ten-foot room, men sat at keyboards, listening through headphones while typing minute-by-minute incoming messages from commands spread across the Pacific. The nimble accuracy of these men was so valuable that they were exempted from operating the guns.

Behind the number-two smokestack stood emergency radio shack 2, its transmitters warmed up and ready in case Radio Central was knocked out of commission.

Below the main deck, there were two more main levels, airless hells lit by hundreds of bulbs nestled in wire cages. Directly below the fantail was the brig, where Private McCoy, when he wasn't standing duty at the secret crate, guarded prisoners. There were currently two fellows in the brig, cooks who had gotten drunk on liberty and gone AWOL in San Francisco, a rather frequent occurrence.

From the fantail, it was about a three-minute walk to the middle of the ship, where, on the lower levels, the majority of the 1,114 enlisted men bunked in some 25 compartments arranged in rows like combs in a vast, steamy hive. The compartments consisted of narrow passageways just big enough for two men to pass each other brushing shoulders. Bunks rose from floor to ceiling on both sides and were chained against the wall when not in use. A boy assigned a top bunk practically had to throw himself six feet into the air and somehow manage to move sideways at the same time, inserting himself in the slot that was his home. Lying on his pillow, the overhead, or ceiling, was only twelve inches from his nose. He usually fell asleep staring at a picture of a Vargas girl torn from the latest *Argosy* magazine.

The mess halls—there were two main ones for the enlisted crew—were a thirty-second walk from the sleeping compartments. The largest one was forty by sixty feet and loud as a gymnasium. Next door was the gedunk stand, and next to that was the post office, where mail went after its delivery by passing ships or by airdrop from planes. Letters from home were, unfortunately, often months old. Ed Brown, while shelling the island of Saipan, received his invitation to his high school graduation six months late. He wrote back, "Thanks, but I won't be able to make it."

Past the post office, heading toward the bow, were the ship's dentist office, a library stocked with detective novels and aging *National Geographic* magazines, and a photo lab for developing battle reconnaissance photos taken by the observation planes. Least favorite for the ship's sometimes recalcitrant cleaners was the bathroom, or head, a charmless spot with twenty-foot-long troughs flowing with seawater along each wall. On top of some were communal wooden benches with holes cut out for sitting. (Senior officers had private toilets and showers.)

Below the crew's head were the engine rooms, and, like the radio shacks, these were separated—one located fore and the other aft—by boiler rooms. The division was a safeguard; if one of the areas was blown up, there would be a reserve.

Topside, rising from the deck were two 100-foot observation

towers called "sky aft" and "sky forward"; they were connected by phone to the bridge, which was manned with "telephone talkers." Their job was to keep communications open with McVay throughout the various gun stations.

Positioned strategically around the deck were stacks of life rafts, four high. Two wooden lifeboats rested in stanchions near the stern, and hanging on the bulkheads were twenty-four floater nets. There was enough lifesaving equipment to handle over 1,500 men. Clearly, for the men aboard, though, the quickest and easiest way off the ship in case of emergency was with an inflatable life belt or a life vest; these were stored in hanging bags tacked along the bulkhead running the length of the ship, and each man kept one within easy reach on a hook next to his bunk.

In case of attack, the favored contingency plan was rescue from nearby escorting vessels, such as the destroyers that had generally accompanied the *Indy* on her previous three years of battle duty. This afternoon, however, she traveled alone, as she was well over 6,000 miles behind front lines.

CAPTAIN McVay was tense but composed as he stood watch on the bridge. Already, the day had brought a bit of excitement, the kind of circumstance that he had to try to avoid to get the ship to Tinian on schedule. Within several hours of clearing the Golden Gate, the *Indianapolis* had run into rough seas, with swells of fifteen feet. The ride had been a bone-jarring ballet of dips and vaults. The ship's eight White-Forster boilers were driving four sets of Parsons turbines (each engine block measured about ten feet long and five feet high), and the ship, which weighed as much as a ten-story office building, was pushing 107,000 horsepower.

But it was not fast enough for McVay. He rang the engineer for more speed, and the *Indy* jumped to twenty-eight knots. Her four massive propellers, each one spanning fifteen feet, began striping the indigo sea with a wake as wide as an eight-lane highway.

By sunset, she had made 350 miles, excellent time.

But McVay couldn't relax. The captain's head was filled with potential problems. For starters, there was the obvious concern of maintaining the secrecy of his mission, and all that this involved. Until reaching Tinian, his ship would be traveling under radio silence, which could only be broken in the event of trouble. Because the *Indy* was traveling so fast, McVay had to keep a close eye on fuel consumption, rendering the voyage a racy balancing act between speed and conservation.

Although McVay was encouraged by the time he was making, his executive officer had now informed him that the water condensers were still malfunctioning. All hands, McVay announced, were ordered to shower with salt water. Every ounce of freshwater was needed to pour into the boilers.

Still, McVay tried to be his usual self, a man who liked to describe his ship as a "happy ship," and whose easygoing nature was extraordinary for a naval captain. Most commanders, enlisted men joked, were either big SOBs or little SOBs. McVay, however, was neither. He was known for his egalitarian spirit and for his graciousness. Sometimes, while anchored in a harbor, he instigated skeet-shooting sessions off the *Indy*'s fantail. Out of nowhere, his voice would sound over the PA: "Anyone interested in fishing, join me at the bow." When new crew members came aboard, he made an effort to greet them by name, saying, "Welcome, sailor. We're going to have a happy cruise."

But the stakes of this tour were high. If he succeeded in this voyage, delivering the cargo safely and quickly, it was possible that Charles McVay, completing the arc of a thus far stellar career, would make admiral. It was possible that he might actually surpass the accomplishments of his family.

McVay's grandfather, the first Charles McVay, president of the Pittsburgh Trust Company, had financially supported the Naval Academy during its lean years after the Civil War. McVay's celebrated father, Admiral Charles McVay Jr., had commanded the Asiatic Fleet during World War I. He was a stern taskmaster, who had retired in 1932 to Washington, D.C., after an illustrious forty-two-year naval career. An 1890 graduate of the Naval Academy, he had taken the school's motto—"God, Country, and Regiment"—to heart. He had drilled these values, in turn, into his son.

And the son had been a good student. Charles Butler McVay III had graduated as an ensign in 1919. He was fluent in French and had completed a Naval War College correspondence course in international law. He served with distinction in several navy commands, working aboard twelve ships in the Atlantic and Pacific. In 1943, he was awarded a Silver Star while acting as executive officer aboard the cruiser *Cleveland* in the Battle of the Solomon Islands. After this, he was appointed chairman of the Joint Intelligence Staff in the Office of Vice Chief of Naval Operations in Washington, D.C. His assignment to the *Indianapolis* in November 1944 was his first as a captain.

In many ways, McVay was a study in contradictions. Although at times he was quite outgoing, there was sometimes a shyness about him, which people would mistake for arrogance. The captain's temper could flare on occasion, but he rarely held a grudge. McVay was cut from the cloth of a schooled navy tradition yet remained simpatico with his enlisted crew, many of whom had quit high school to join the navy. With his broad smile and chiseled features, women found him irresistible; men were drawn to his sense of jocular bravado. He was known to love a good bourbon once the ship's engines had been shut down. But never before.

ON the second day out from San Francisco, McVay ordered General Quarters, or GQ, otherwise known as battle stations. When the announcement was signaled over the PA, every man was expected to jump up from the toilet or from sleep and run to his station. This morning the crew responded admirably, beginning without delay to fire the guns in a live-ammunition drill.

The *Indy* was capable of shooting more than 500 rounds of 5-inch gun ammunition in under six minutes. If all nine barrels on the ship's three 8-inch gun turrets were fired simultaneously, the recoil could turn the *Indy* on its side. The concussion from a single weapon had once ripped the shirt off the back of a crew member who was standing too close. It had taken a week for his hearing to return.

The *Indy* carried four different kinds of guns. The big 8-inchers were capable of lobbing 250-pound shells eighteen miles, while the 5-inchers shot barrages of armor-piercing shells and could take out Japanese pillboxes (gun emplacements) eight miles from shore. The 40 mm and the 20 mm deck guns were used for the close-in work of shooting at attacking Japanese planes.

The guns could be operated by tracking devices called fire-control directors located on stanchions rising high above the deck. They could also be maneuvered with eye and hand—"local control"—using a crew of as many as twenty. This included "loaders," "levelers," and "trainers," who moved the guns left and right and up and down by spinning large steel wheels, and "fuse-setters," who prepared the shells—some with proximity fuses—for firing. It was a team sport.

Usually, during normal battle training, a plane was ordered to fly past the ship at a designated distance towing a sleeve, a 150-foot streamer resembling a windsock, which trailed behind on 500 yards of wire. After estimating the distance of the plane and its speed, the crews were able to sight their guns. Gun crews often aimed for the towing wire, slightly ahead of the sleeve, and often succeeded in breaking it. This was a way to halt the ordeal until a new wire was rigged. The crews usually claimed they'd just aimed badly, but got chewed out by the officers anyway. The victors—the crew with the most direct fire—did, however, win trips to the gedunk stand.

Today's practice, which did not involve the sleeve but was a simpler shooting exercise, had a guest judge. Major Furman had torn himself away from the uranium canister long enough to officiate. Furman, who had studied gunnery at Princeton before the war, had a fairly good understanding of the process. But his colleague Captain Nolan, a radiologist by training, was having a harder time passing himself off as an army officer. When asked the size of the guns he'd shot in the army, Nolan held up his hand, as if measuring the size of a fish, and replied, "Oh, about like this." He seemed to have little grasp of the power of the guns that surrounded him.

His less-than-experienced eye didn't matter much this morning. The shooting was uniformly mediocre. One ensign, one of the green hands, missed every assigned range and distance.

McVay, hardly reassured, was reminded yet again of just how much work there was to do. Later that day, his tension turned to anger when a fire broke out belowdecks. His mood didn't improve when he discovered that the blaze had been caused by some of the extra crew members, who had carelessly stacked suitcases against a smokestack.

The following day, the seas were calm. McVay's outlook improved when he was able to push the *Indy*'s engines close to their limits, to an average speed of twenty-nine knots. The roar beneath decks in the engine rooms was like a tornado's. The ship quaked with the violence of its spinning propellers.

IN the years following her peacetime commissioning in 1932, it seemed that the ship that Charles Butler McVay now worried over and prayed for would never see any war action. But her fate, along with many of the lives now on board, changed on December 7, 1941.

Japan, which began its all-out war against China in 1937, was expanding its colonial empire in search of needed oil deposits and metals. When President Roosevelt stopped the export of U.S. resources in 1941, Japan had a choice. Its leaders could agree to American demands that it cease expansion into the Dutch West Indies and the Philippines. Or they could declare war.

The *Indy* was delivering supplies and troops to Johnston Island, several hundred miles southwest of Pearl Harbor, when Japanese pilots bombed the Pacific Fleet on that terrible Sunday. An urgent bulletin was beamed to the *Indy;* WE ARE AT WAR WITH JAPAN—THIS IS OFFICIAL. In response, the ship threw everything that was flammable—including FDR's stateroom furniture—overboard and steamed deep into the Pacific on an unsuccessful search-and-destroy mission directed at retreating Japanese forces. She then turned her attention to bombarding Japanese troops beached in the Aleutian Islands. This was followed by duty in the 1942 Battle of the Coral Sea. For her valorous service she was awarded her first battle star, one of ten she would collect in the next four years, a laudable achievement of service.

By 1942, however, as the Japanese attempted to fight their way island-to-island from Asia to Hawaii, the commander in chief of the Japanese fleet, Admiral Isoroku Yamamoto, had told his superiors that after Pearl Harbor it would have six months to "run wild" over American forces. After the U.S. victory in June at the battle of Midway, which made a hero out of spry, fifty-five-year-old Admiral Raymond Spruance—to whom the *Indy*'s fate would soon be tied—the prediction seemed to be coming true. America's worst defeat came two months later at the battle of Savo Island in the Solomons east of New Guinea. Japanese forces sank four cruisers (one Australian) and one destroyer, killing 1,270 men.

By 1943, the Allied plan for defeating the Japanese had evolved into two distinct approaches: naval commander in chief Admiral Chester Nimitz (with Spruance under his command) would sail with his forces west from Pearl Harbor and meet General Douglas MacArthur's army marching toward the invasion of the Japanese-held Philippines.

Later that year, Admiral Spruance declared the *Indy* his flagship, the command center for the enormous resources of the Fifth Fleet. Spruance liked the *Indy*'s speed, and he liked her age. He reasoned that if his presence was needed in an emerging hot zone, she could be withdrawn from battle without disrupting the battle plan.

Over the course of the next two years, the *Indy* saw vicious fighting. At Tarawa, in November 1943, her crew spent long hours pulling the dead bodies of American troops aboard with boat hooks but suffered no casualties of their own. During the Battle of the Philippine Sea in June 1944, the *Indy*, as the Fifth Fleet's flagship, played a major role; in all, U.S. forces "splashed"—or downed—410 Japanese planes during this battle.

The *Indy* continued to be a very lucky ship, emerging as one of the navy's most proficient fighting machines. She evaded submarine attack (with help from accompanying destroyers), enemy battleship bombardment, and onshore fire. (She was once hit by a shore-launched shell but it failed to explode.) By the time Captain McVay took command in November 1944, the USS *Indianapolis* had earned eight battle stars. McVay took the ship to even greater heights of valor, as the war reached a feverish, homicidal pitch.

In contrast to the war in Europe, where even the Nazis observed cease-fires and flags of truce, the Pacific campaign had taken on a surreal quality. Japanese soldiers disemboweled themselves at the sight of approaching marines rather than be captured. This sense of desperation only increased as the U.S. invasion of the Japanese islands of Kyushu and its close neighbor Honshu (where the capital of Tokyo is located) neared.

DR. Lewis Haynes came aboard the *Indy* in July 1944, and he immediately found a home where he could hone his medical skill. He had joined the navy in peacetime, in 1939, after finishing his medical schooling at Northwestern University. As a boy growing up in northern Michigan, he had watched his father practice dentistry and decided he wanted to be a surgeon.

In high school, Haynes held the state record for the 440-yard dash, and he loved to hunt grouse and fish for brook trout along the Manistee River. Michigan was wild country, and he knew it well. But when he joined the navy, he was rarely on land anymore, and to his surprise he found that he loved ship life, treasuring the camaraderie that developed among officers. Under Captain Mc-Vay, the *Indy* was more than the sum of its firepower and speed; it was a friendly city of more than 1,000 sailors. And Haynes watched herd over these boys.

The doctor had an innocent fascination with the latest shipboard gossip—what sailors called "the poop." Every week, in the officers' wardroom—reminiscent of a sparse hotel lobby, complete with magazines (usually outdated), and a worn leather couch—Haynes and his fellow officers roasted one another, attempting good-naturedly to add levity to the grim business of war. The officers at the dinner table, pushing away their dessert plates of lemon pie or ice cream, took pleasure in addressing the sharp-witted doctor as "Dr. Seezall Tellzall."

But duty came before play for Haynes. He loved losing himself in his work. When he concentrated during surgery, the blood and screams in the operating room faded. He was no longer surrounded by boys exploded to pieces. Facing him, instead, were challenges that engaged and absorbed, and which he prayed his medical training could conquer. By February of 1945, as the horrors of the war multiplied, Haynes's talents—and his capacity to distance himself—were sorely tested.

He was on alert when the USS *Indianapolis* sailed with Admiral Spruance into the Battle of Iwo Jima on February 19, 1945—D-Day on the island. Their objective was the bombardment of the 21,000 Japanese dug deep into the coral tunnels braiding the volcanic island. Down in the *Indy*'s sick bay, the physician cared for the wounded men continually hoisted aboard from landing craft trafficking back and forth from the beach. His surgical theater contained four operating tables and was supplied with anesthetics including drop-ether and Novocain for spinals and locals. He used the latest cutting instruments, sterilized by autoclave. It was all operated by an auxiliary generator in case the ship suffered main-power loss, and it was also the only compartment in the ship that was air-conditioned.

In less than three months, B-29 Superfortress bombers would have leveled fifty-six square miles of Tokyo and countless other cities—Osaka, Kawasaki, and Yokohama. Light, wooden Japanese dwellings would be destroyed in the firestorms, and by July 1945, all but 200,000 of Tokyo's 8 million residents were forced to abandon the capital. Even now, as the Japanese struggled fiercely to maintain control of Iwo Jima, it was becoming increasingly clear that Japan's war machinery was literally running on fumes. Out of desperation, and lacking sufficient aircraft and adequately trained pilots with which to battle the well-equipped U.S. aircraft carriers, the Japanese command created the kamikaze pilot. It named their suicide planes "divine wind."*

While Haynes worked nonstop through this storm of lead and diving planes, the *Indianapolis* managed to survive untouched.

DURING the buildup to the invasion of Okinawa the following month, the war had grown even more desperate, and Private

---

* The term *kamikaze* arises from two thirteenth-century battles that outnumbered Japanese warriors fought against Kublai Khan, whose 40,000 troops, after conquering Korea and China, had landed at Kyushu. During the first battle, a storm sunk 200 of the invader's 900 ships, and Khan retreated. Seven years later, however, he returned, this time with over 140,000 troops and 4,400 ships. Again his fleet was devastated by a storm whose "divine winds" sunk nearly all his ships. The Japanese believed that these winds had been sent by the gods.

Giles McCoy's thoughts turned increasingly toward home. Born in the old river city of St. Louis, Missouri, McCoy had been just a freshman in high school when the Japanese navy attacked Pearl Harbor. He had heard the news booming from his father's radio in his living room. McCoy had wanted to enlist immediately after graduation, but because he was only seventeen, he wasn't eligible without a parent's signature. (The standard age of induction was eighteen.) His mother reluctantly signed for him.

His mother was his best friend and confidante, a woman who could beat him at wiffle ball and Ping-Pong. She liked to laugh at silly things. She would roll a napkin into a ball and try to toss it into a glass on the kitchen counter. While McCoy's sisters did their homework and his father read the newspaper, she would close the kitchen door, hand him the napkin, and say, "All right, son, let's see how good you are tonight." They could play that game for hours.

Tatie McCoy was full of life and pithy sayings. Early on, she gave McCoy a piece of advice he had never forgotten. "Just because I brought you into this world," she told him, "doesn't mean anything's going to be easy. You'll have to work for everything you get." He credited her words with getting him through Okinawa.

Okinawa was Japan's Alamo, the only island standing between American forces and the final assault on Tokyo. Called Operation Iceberg, the U.S. attack on Okinawa was equal in scope to the invasion of Normandy one year earlier. The *New York Times* would call this siege, the final naval battle of World War II, the "most intense and famous in military history." In total, the Japanese launched nearly 2,000 kamikaze planes at a fleet of 1,500 American ships—the most powerful armada ever amassed. The pilots, often dressed in ceremonial robes and clutching dolls given to them by their daughters, were relentless—the sky rained suicide planes (each attack averaged 150 kamikazes). Watching in awe as they spiraled out of the sky through rising fountains of lead and shrapnel, McCoy felt both his hatred and respect for the Japanese increase exponentially.

He was bent to his work with a fierce will, sweating through the thin, cotton face mask he wore as protection against the muzzle blasts of the 5-inch gun he was manning. Its barrel poured flak barrages into the sky. Wearing heavy asbestos gloves pulled to his elbows, McCoy was supposed to catch the empty, heavy brass shell casings as they rolled smoking from the gun. The muzzle flash from the gun burned his face even through the protective mask. He heard the kamikaze roaring toward the *Indy* before he saw it.

"Bogey! Bogey! Bogey!" cried one of the boys on deck assigned to watch the sky for attackers through special glasses resembling welder's goggles. It emerged out of the blinding sun, as was the usual strategy of kamikaze pilots. On the fantail, the 20 mm anti-aircraft guns opened up. McCoy watched as the red tracers arced skyward toward the Japanese plane and on up. But the kamikaze pilot, moving fast, was closing in. There was no time for further fire. Captain McVay ordered the *Indy* into a hard emergency turn.

McCoy was petrified. All around him men were ducking for cover, but he found himself unable to move. For a split second, it seemed that the descending plane might miss the ship, which was heeling under the strain of its turn.

But then the plane hit. The Japanese pilot dropped a 500-pound, armor-piercing bomb, which plummeted through the ship's decks, ripping holes as it fell, passing directly through the enlisted men's mess room and through a dining room table where a sailor sat eating. The bomb, as it passed, broke the boy's legs and lacerated the hull of the ship. The explosion loosened rivets on the ship and filled the mess hall with boiled beans.

McCoy had run to the smoldering hulk of the plane and, with the help of other men, began rocking it off the ship, fearful that it would burst into flames. Staring through the cracked canopy, McCoy caught a glimpse of the pilot embedded on his control console before the plane slid into the sea.

Belowdecks, fuel oil filled one of the engine rooms, drowning some of the men trapped there. Seawater flooded exploded compartments and threatened to sink the ship. Damage control crews set to work "dogging down" a system of watertight hatches and valves, and after a tense twenty minutes, the blown-up areas were secured. In a triumph of nerves and procedure over mayhem, the *Indy* was saved.

McVay received a message from naval command that read: CONGRATULATIONS ON YOUR EXCELLENT DAMAGE CONTROL. YOUR MEN DID AN OUTSTANDING JOB.* As a reward for that performance, the boys had been sent to an R&R camp on the island of Ulithi—an idyllic place nicknamed "You-like-it-here" located 400 miles southwest of Guam—where they enjoyed the three *B*s of a contented sailor's life: beaches, baseball, and beer, and imbibed a concoction called Torpedo Juice, made from Royal Crown cola and the industrial-grade alcohol used to propel U.S. submarines' torpedoes. It was potent stuff and gave some of the crew splitting headaches.

---

* Generally speaking, however, the navy suffered its worst losses of the war at Okinawa, with 9,700 casualties, 4,907 of which were fatal.

Now, three days away from San Francisco, McCoy tried to forget the images of Okinawa as the *Indy* rounded the volcanic black hump of Diamond Head. He wondered what the future—the invasion of Japan—held in store for him. The damn thing was sure to be a bloodbath, and most of his shipmates believed they wouldn't make it. But he had to. For his mother. And his father. McCoy and his dad had never really had much of a friendship. The McCoy family had been comfortable through the depression because Giles McCoy Sr. worked twelve-hour days as a successful butter salesman. He would come home at night, listen to *Fibber McGee and Molly* on the radio, and drift off to sleep. In truth, his son didn't know him that well.

The night before McCoy was to ship out by troop train for boot camp in San Diego, his friends threw him a beer party. Two boys sped into the yard, throwing gravel onto Mr. McCoy's flower beds. He was angry; it was clear the boys had been drinking. But McCoy knew that his father was upset over more than the beer. His dad had served in World War I and had a vivid bayonet scar on his side to prove it. McCoy sensed his father was scared for him.

He told McCoy, "You're not going anywhere with those boys."

McCoy was shocked. "But, Dad! This party is for me. I'll be all right."

"You're not going."

McCoy took a breath and said, "Well, Dad, I am."

He had never spoken to his father that way before, had never disobeyed him. He surprised even himself. He stepped off the porch and started walking to the car. The next thing he knew, his father was running up beside him. He suddenly reached out and hit McCoy in the back of his head, knocking him across the lawn.

McCoy couldn't believe it. He got up and walked toward his

father, leaned into him, looked him in the eye. He said, "Boy, you should never have done that. That was the wrong thing to do." And then he walked away.

When McCoy came back that night from the party, his mother met him at the door. She asked him how he was going to get to the train station the next day.

"I'll walk," said McCoy.

"Why don't you have your dad take you?"

"I don't want him to."

But in the morning McCoy's father was already up and waiting. They drove to the train station in silence. At the door, McCoy got out first. He'd decided he'd at least say good-bye to his dad. As he came around the car, he saw his father was crying, tears streaming down his face.

He said, "I don't want you to leave like this."

"I don't want to either." The two hugged, and McCoy told his father, "I'll try to come back, I really will!"

"You better."

And then McCoy walked to the station. When he looked back, he could see his father sitting in the car, staring ahead through the windshield. He watched as he draped his arms over the steering wheel and dropped his head, his body heaving as he sobbed.

This was an image that McCoy had kept with him. It wouldn't go away. It patrolled his mind as he heard the PA system announce triumphantly: "We have just set a record!"

The cruise to Pearl Harbor had been more than 2,405 miles, and it was a feat the crew accomplished without incident in an astounding 74.5 hours.* The boys sent up a cheer, hats flying. Then they hurriedly dressed in their navy whites, thinking they'd

---

* It set a record that remains unbroken today.

be allowed off the ship for liberty. They took turns giving each other the once-over—if you weren't presentable at inspection, you couldn't leave the ship. Some of the boys even gave each other quick, on-the-spot haircuts.

McCoy wasn't the only one disappointed when he heard McVay announce that there would be no liberty. Instead, the captain off-loaded his passengers, refueled the ship, and five hours later turned back to sea, to Tinian. The island still lay 3,300 miles ahead, deep in the West Pacific. There was no time to rest.

On July 21, the ship crossed the international date line, which was usually cause for celebration in a sailor's life, especially if he was a green hand and had never made the transit into the "Golden Dragon's domain." This time, however, there was no ceremony; the new recruits on the *Indy*—dubbed "polliwogs" for the occasion—were informed that today's crossing would be noted in their records. Their next step in becoming true men of the salt would be initiation into "King Neptune's domain."

McCoy was disappointed in the lack of formality, but he understood the need to press the *Indy* on her mission. And perhaps, for the green hands' sake, it was just as well. The induction into King Neptune's domain, for example, which was carried out when a ship crossed the equator, could be a daunting affair. On one navy ship, the induction, which was meant to strengthen esprit among the boys, involved older officers ordering the green hands to strip and, while dressed only in black neckties, push a peanut across the deck with their noses. Next they met King Neptune himself, usually a fat crew member whose belly had been covered in shaving cream, and which the polliwogs rubbed their faces in: this was called "kissing the royal pudding." Finally, the recruits entered the King's Chamber, which was actually an artillery target sleeve filled with garbage. Only after passing through the ripened mess did the polliwogs emerge as hardened shellbacks, initiated members of King Neptune's domain.

In general, this leg of the voyage had been efficient but uneventful. Seven days after leaving Pearl Harbor, on July 26, Charles Butler McVay and the crew of the *Indy* rode into Tinian at flank—or full—speed, the ship's gargantuan propellers spinning in a molten whir. As the ship dropped anchor, a flotilla of boats bore down on them in greeting. The *Indy* had made it.

Private McCoy was still wondering if he would make it back to St. Louis.

CHAPTER THREE

The First Domino

Whenever I was traveling alone, I always had the feeling,
"Suppose we go down and we can't get a message off?
What will happen then?"

—CHARLES BUTLER MCVAY,
captain, USS *Indianapolis*

The South Pacific

THE boats present at the anchoring of the *Indianapolis* in Tinian included an impressive gathering of officers from the military, about thirty men in all. While it may have struck some as strange that so many high-ranking officers were on hand, the island did remain a strategic location. It was from here that many of the B-29 Superfortresses took off for bombing raids on Japan. Private McCoy, standing on the quarterdeck, had never seen anything like this spectacle.

Looking out at the island a half mile distant through heavy, rubber-coated binoculars, he saw a devastated wasteland. Tinian Island, a mere ten miles by five miles, was, at the time, the largest airbase in the world. A small city carved from coral and palm trees, it was shaped like the island of Manhattan. McCoy knew that naval command had jokingly named its main thoroughfare of crushed coral and limestone after Broadway. Riverside Drive ran along the western shore of the island, and the airfield used by the B-29 Superfortresses was located at Ninetieth Street just east of Eighth Avenue.

The airfield consisted of four paved runways, each nearly two miles long and wide as a ten-lane highway. In the hills, it was said, several hundred renegade Japanese troops remained on patrol, sniping at passing jeeps.

McCoy had never been to Tinian before. But he had heard the stories of the bombardment that had taken place in July 1944, when Dr. Haynes had been aboard with Admiral Spruance, and the *Indy* had taken part in leveling the island. The *Indy*, along with the rest of the Fifth Fleet, had given the place a "Spruance haircut." Hardly a bush or palm tree now remained.

McCoy could see the burned hulks of B-29s. Capable of carrying a ten-ton load of bombs, the enormous planes, with wingspans of over 141 feet, needed every yard of the runways to lift off into the thick, tropical air. Those that hadn't made it sometimes exploded in showers of burning napalm.

About ten men from the flotilla of boats now boarded the *Indy*. McCoy watched as shipfitters emerged from officers' country with the black canister. The wooden crate was removed next, this time with the use of the ship's crane perched atop the hangar deck. Ed Brown was at the controls, with executive officer Joseph "Red" Flynn directing the delicate task. Just for a laugh, Brown let the lever slip on the crane's control bar, and the crate began a heart-stopping plummet for the deck of the landing barge rocking fifty feet below. Brown then applied the brake. The gathered officers went berserk. McCoy smiled, but executive officer Flynn, looking like his nerves were shot, softly muttered, "Brown, tell those officers to shove off."

Brown expertly lowered the crate the rest of the way to the barge. Even though they had no idea what it was they had carried, they knew this: their mission was complete. McVay and the boys of the *Indy* let out a cheer.

Private McCoy noticed Captain Nolan and Major Furman searching the crowd, but it was unclear whether they found what—or whom—they were looking for.* McCoy had heard that

---

* The two officers were seeking a knowing face that could tell them if the Trinity test had been successful. When the *Indy* paused before leaving San Francisco, not even Nolan or Furman knew why; the reason was only disclosed later in the postmortem of the atomic effort.

the voyage had been difficult for Nolan, who spent much of his time seasick in his cabin. All in all, he had seemed a suspicious character.*

Moments later, scanning the shore with his binoculars, Mc-Coy followed the wooden crate and canister as they were transferred by another crane to a waiting flatbed truck. The cargo was quickly covered with a tarp, and the truck picked its way carefully over the jungle track toward a staging area called North Field.

HER cargo unloaded, the *Indy* could now return to her life as a regular fighting ship preparing for the seemingly distant invasion of Japan.

Tinian lay in what was now called the backwater of the war. Tokyo, on the Japanese island of Honshu, was 1,600 miles to the north. Everything north of an imaginary line drawn across the Philippine Sea between Tinian and Leyte, 1,500 miles west of Tinian, was considered the forward area, or war zone. Iwo Jima and Okinawa lay in this area, but they had been secured and were held by occupying U.S. troops; the sea around them, however, was still patrolled by Japanese submarines.

The transition from backwater to war zone was murky, and it was difficult to say exactly when a ship might sail from relative security into imminent danger. Japanese submarines did not pay attention to imaginary lines of safety.

As the unloading of the bomb was taking place, new orders

---

* In fact, Nolan was spending a good deal of time in the flag lieutenant's cabin, where, with the use of a Geiger counter he kept hidden from the crew, he measured the canister for possible radiation emissions. There were none.

for the *Indy* had arrived through the radios aboard ship and were decrypted by the code room. The source was the advance headquarters of the Commander in Chief, Pacific Fleet, otherwise known as CINCPAC, which fell under the direction of Fleet Admiral Chester Nimitz. McVay's orders were simple: from Tinian, he was to proceed to Guam, a 120-mile cruise to the south, where he would report to the naval base for his further routing orders, or "road map," to Leyte. After arriving in Leyte, he was to report by coded message to Vice Admiral Jesse Oldendorf, commander of Task Force 95, announcing his arrival and readiness to rejoin the Pacific Fleet. Oldendorf, one of the war's most decorated officers, who had gained fame at the 1944 Battle of Leyte Gulf, was aboard his cruiser, the *Omaha*, and patrolling the coast of Japan, 1,500 miles to the north of Leyte, in preparation for the invasion.

But before joining Oldendorf and his warships, the *Indy* would engage in seventeen days of drills and gunnery practice and General Quarters. McVay, now free of his extra passengers and duties, would finally be able to train his men.

In Leyte, McVay was to report to Rear Admiral Lynde McCormick, Oldendorf's immediate subordinate officer, who was anchored there aboard the battleship *Idaho*. McCormick, an expert in logistics and a recipient of two gold stars and the Legion of Merit, would lead McVay and his crew in preparatory exercises.

Six hours after arriving at Tinian, the *Indy* pulled anchor, and a smiling McVay, pleased with his new plans, pointed the ship to sea, south for Guam.

As McVay sailed this night, however, the well-laid plan was already going awry.

Copies of the orders directing him to report to Oldendorf and then McCormick were radioed to eight different commands: Fleet Admiral Nimitz and Admiral Spruance, both on Guam; the port directors on Tinian and Guam; the commander of the Mariana Islands, Vice Admiral George Murray, who was also in charge of overall naval operations in Guam and Tinian; Rear Admiral McCormick; Vice Admiral Oldendorf; and CINCPAC at Pearl Harbor. This broadcast was standard procedure, intended to keep relevant parties abreast of events.

However, when a member of McCormick's radio staff aboard the *Idaho* received the message, he decoded the name of the addressee incorrectly. Since the message appeared to be addressed not to McCormick but to another commander, the staff member stopped deciphering it altogether. He never decoded the body of the message, which described McVay's arrival, and which had been marked "restricted," meaning it was not a "classified" or high-priority communication.

As a result, Rear Admiral McCormick did not know to expect the arrival of the USS *Indianapolis* at Leyte.

The other addressees, including Oldendorf, received the information more or less as planned. But the message didn't include the date of the *Indy*'s arrival. That would be communicated in a future dispatch.

EN route to Guam, Captain McVay was able to run his crew through anti-aircraft drills, which went well. He then readied himself to report to the port director for his new routing orders. Nearing the island on July 27, the *Indy* paused at the mouth of Apra Harbor. The ship waited as a tugboat pulled back on long cables attached to an underwater net, meant to keep enemy subs from entering, strung across the harbor's mouth. Another tug circled behind the *Indy*, dragging in her wake sonar gear to make certain no submarines were following the ship. Once inside the harbor, the tugs pulled the net closed and the *Indy* anchored. While fuel tankers and supply ships pulled alongside the *Indy*, a motor launch arrived and McVay was ferried to shore.

Guam was a bustling island of nearly 500,000 troops. Japanese forces had captured the island in December 1941, and the United States had retaken it two and a half years later after three weeks of bloody fighting. During the invasions of Iwo Jima and Okinawa, transport ships carrying thousands of troops had left this harbor day and night for a week, bound for the beachheads more than 1,200 miles to the north.

Currently anchored in the harbor were twenty ships of various classes—cruisers, destroyers, and transports. Also dotting the green lagoon were vessels damaged during kamikaze attacks and waiting for repair in the island's dry docks. One disabled ship had been commandeered as a floating barracks for troops.

Guam had about it a sunny, makeshift feel. At its palm-fringed beach, flyboys sat at wooden tables drinking large, green cans of beer, which had been cooled to icy perfection by flying them around in an airplane for three hours at freezing altitudes.

Testing his land legs, McVay requested a driver and a jeep—officers never drove themselves. Soon he was being whisked along a freshly paved road that hugged the shore, past thatch huts that housed the island's few remaining natives. Continuing on, the captain breezed through the bombed remains of the island, which had been flattened during the U.S. invasion. The road climbed above the sea, and McVay's jeep stopped atop what was called CINCPAC Hill, command center for the Pacific war theater.

CINCPAC headquarters was a two-story wooden building fronted by a flagpole and surrounded by flower beds. It overlooked the sea and harbor, and reclined against a hillside jungle. Circling the HQ were metal Quonset huts painted green; they housed the offices of Admiral Nimitz's support staff.

At HQ, McVay met Nimitz's assistant chief of staff, Commodore James Carter. Straight off, he asked if he and his ship could undertake gunnery training at Guam rather than wait for his scheduled session at Leyte. McVay was feeling the pressure of time; he wished to sharpen his crew immediately. Carter informed McVay that training was no longer offered at Guam, but that he could begin it at Leyte.

McVay was frustrated. At this rate, he remarked, his boys would probably receive their training off the coast of Tokyo, during the invasion. After the rather brief and unsatisfying meeting, he joined Admiral Spruance for lunch in the officers' mess, in one of the Quonset huts. McVay had not seen Spruance since the kamikaze attack off Okinawa nearly four months earlier. Spruance had left the wounded ship promptly to continue overseeing the naval bombardment from the deck of the USS *New Mexico*, which had become his temporary flagship.

Spruance was relaxed about the war's present state of affairs but reticent to talk details. He disclosed only that for the moment, the invasion plans were progressing smoothly. He and his staff were preparing for the year's end assault on Kyushu, which they hoped would result in the surrender of Japan.*

---

* Spruance, although he may have known of McVay's special delivery mission to Tinian, most likely wasn't privy to the existence of the atomic bomb. Two days before

Essentially, there were two battle plans being waged to win the war at this time. The first involved the deployment of an estimated 1 million American troops to the shores of Japan. The second, the top-secret Operation Centerboard, consisted of dropping the bomb, the exact outcome of which was uncertain.

Sworn into office three months earlier after the sudden death of Roosevelt, President Truman had only recently been apprised of the project involving Little Boy and Fat Man. (Fat Man had been lightheartedly named in honor of Winston Churchill, a proponent of the Manhattan Project, and Little Boy's original nickname was "Thin Man," in honor of Roosevelt. It was changed to "Little Boy" when the design of its "barrel" was shortened.) General MacArthur, commander of all U.S. Army forces in the Pacific theater, would only be informed by the first of August. Throughout its development, the Manhattan Project had been kept in the shadows of the larger invasion plans, which were given the code names Olympic and Coronet.

As they ate, the admiral noticed the captain's concern about getting his men readied, and he attempted to reassure McVay. He told him that there was no need to hurry the training exercises at Leyte. Spruance added that he might send for the ship at some point during the sessions to pick up part of his flag staff in Manila, north of Leyte in the Philippines. He himself planned to come back aboard in the fall and then meet with Vice Admiral Oldendorf off the coast of Japan in preparation for the invasion.

After lunch, McVay was driven back down the hill to the port

---

this conversation Admiral Nimitz—Spruance's superior officer—had had his first glimpse of the awesome power of the weapon when he watched a film of the Trinity test. He'd been shown the footage by Captain Parsons, the officer who had given McVay his secret, hurried orders to sail two weeks earlier in San Francisco.

director's office on Apra Harbor. The building, blazingly hot in the tropical sun, sat twenty feet from the water's edge. Inside, the busy office was feebly cooled by electric fans hanging from the wall. It was filled with some fifteen enlisted men and officers answering telephones and struggling under a barrage of incoming routing orders and coded dispatches. The office was a clearinghouse for forwarded orders coming from CINCPAC HQ, where McVay had just had lunch, to the island's naval base, which handled the actual implementation of the CINCPAC directives.

McVay exchanged pleasantries with one of the convoy routing officers under the command of Lieutenant Joseph Waldron. In the past ten months, the office had routed an estimated 5,000 ships, a heady pace under any circumstances. Routing orders, a ship's road map, directed her along specific, approved ocean routes. McVay's seemed simple enough. He told the officer that he wanted to arrive off Leyte in the dawn hours to practice anti-aircraft firing. (Low-light conditions would make it easier to see the tracer rounds and judge the accuracy of the gun crews' shooting.)

McVay was told that if he left the next day, Saturday, July 28, he could arrive on the morning of Monday, July 30, assuming he maintained an average speed of 25 knots (about 29 mph). McVay considered it, but was concerned about the state of his ship's engines after the punishing high-speed run from San Francisco. He didn't want to push his luck. So the two men agreed that the ship should aim to arrive off Leyte on Tuesday morning. That was doable if she maintained a slower speed of 15.7 knots. McVay was agreeable to this pace, which was the SOA, or Standard Speed of Advance.

He was then instructed to follow what was known as the Peddie convoy route, which ran from Guam to Leyte. A journey of

1,300 miles, it had been used throughout the three and a half years of the Pacific campaign and was considered a routine transit.

McVay and the *Indianapolis* were about to sail from the Marianas Sea Frontier into the Philippine Sea Frontier, and it was like passing between two different worlds. A ship moved from one frontier to another by crossing the Chop, a boundary marked by the 130-degree line of longitude. Clear as this delineation was, there was a complicating factor: communications in this area were often confused by a political battle between Admiral Nimitz and General MacArthur, who were locked in a struggle to control the navy. MacArthur, in charge of the Seventh Fleet, wanted to unite it with the army. Nimitz, commander of the Pacific Fleet, wanted to remain autonomous. In the end, Nimitz had been given control of the entire Pacific naval operation, but friction between the two military titans still existed. Information about a ship's whereabouts, or other crucial facts, sometimes got lost in the fallout. This could mean trouble for the *Indianapolis*, which sometimes relied on the presence of carefully timed escorts to protect her from enemy submarines and spirit her out of danger.

The *Indy* had no sonar gear; detecting subs was not her job. The task of hunting enemy subs was left to destroyers, which bombed them with fifty-five-gallon drums of a highly explosive gel called Torpex. The depth charges, or "ash cans," as they were called, generally did not blow up a sub—they usually weren't accurate enough—but rather surrounded it in clouds of sonic concussions, which succeeded in shaking the sub until it sank.

When, in the course of the talk, McVay requested an escort for his crossing to Leyte, Lieutenant Waldron, the ranking convoy routing officer (who by this point had joined the meeting), picked up the phone. He placed a call to the office of Captain

Oliver Naquin, surface operations officer. Waldron inquired of the officer on duty whether there was an escort leaving for Leyte, with whom the *Indianapolis* might tag along. Waldron was told that none was necessary, and that all battle-ready destroyers were already deployed in assisting the continuing B-29 raids on Japan, picking up downed pilots. They were also needed to escort transports delivering fresh troops to the forward area of Okinawa.

The *Indy* had traveled on her own before, and at this point in the war, naval command assumed that she could travel safely in the backwater unescorted.

When Waldron hung up and informed McVay that no escort was necessary, McVay accepted the news easily. He then asked about intelligence reports concerning enemy traffic along the Peddie route. He was told that such a report would be prepared. It would accompany his routing orders once they had been typed up. After agreeing that his navigator would retrieve both later that night, McVay left the office, confident that the *Indy*'s upcoming voyage would be smooth.

AFTER McVay's navigator returned to the port director's office and picked up the routing orders and intelligence report, he came back to the ship, where McVay gathered the officers and told them, "We are going to Leyte to prepare for the invasion of Kyushu." The island was Japan's southernmost home island, located about 500 miles from Tokyo. This was a clear indication that the *Indy* would be in the thick of the action.

He also announced that they would be traveling without an escort. Dr. Haynes, like McVay, took the news in stride. "Here we go again," one of the officers said. Haynes remembered the time, earlier in the war, when the *Indy*, with Admiral Spruance aboard, had sailed the 1,000 miles from Iwo Jima to Okinawa without an escort. The energetic Spruance was always commanding the ship on sudden orders to the next crisis.

When McVay next met with his navigator and executive officer Flynn they reviewed the ship's orders. McVay learned that he was to follow a "zigzag" course during daylight hours, and at night, at his discretion, during periods of good visibility. Zigzagging was a defensive maneuver—the thinking being that if a moving target is hard to hit, an erratically moving target is even more elusive. In truth, the maneuver was of negligible value but was required by navy regulations.

The intelligence report seemed to contain nothing unusual. It stated that three submarines had been reported sighted in the Peddie area, two of them unconfirmed as actual enemy. Of these, one was a report of a "sound contact" only and the other was of an unidentified ship spotting a "possible" periscope. The remaining and most credible sighting was already nearly a week old. The *Indy*'s navigator had already received the information from what was called the Blue Summaries, intelligence dispatches sent out weekly by the fleet command at Pearl Harbor.

But neither the report prepared for Captain McVay nor the Blue Summaries included two crucial pieces of information.

Three days earlier, on July 24, as the *Indy* was sailing to Tinian, the USS *Underhill*, a destroyer escort, had been sunk by a Japanese kaiten—a manned torpedo suicide craft—while sailing from Okinawa to Leyte in a convoy of fifteen ships. One hundred and twelve men had died, and another 109 were rescued by the convoy. The kaiten had been released by a large Japanese patrol sub, and the *Underhill*, upon spotting it, had defensively (and, in retrospect, mistakenly) rammed it, causing the explosion.

McVay's intelligence report also neglected to mention the fact that the Tamon group was known to be operating in waters around the Peddie route, the same path the *Indy* was about to sail to Leyte. Commodore James Carter, with whom McVay had met at CINCPAC headquarters, knew about the *Underhill* sinking and the Tamon submarines, but he did not mention either to McVay. He didn't customarily discuss intelligence matters with captains. But he assumed that McVay would be apprised of the situation when he received his routing orders.

Captain McVay, however, was not apprised of the situation. This is because the existence of the Tamon submarines had been deduced by ULTRA, an extremely top-secret code-breaking program that had operated to brilliant effect throughout the war. The operation was composed of heavily guarded decoding headquarters at Pearl Harbor and Washington, D.C., where men sat at typing consoles, headphones clamped to their ears, transcribing Japanese radio messages. The Japanese sent their messages in a code created by a cipher machine American intelligence officers had nicknamed PURPLE; the Americans fed the intercepted communications into a decrypting machine of the same name. These machines used a series of "telephone stepping switches" in an incredibly complex decryption process involving thousands of computations to spit out decoded versions of the intercepted Japanese messages. These decoded messages were called MAGIC, and the men who operated the machines were known as Magicians.

ULTRA had been used during the Battle of Midway to pinpoint and annihilate Japanese naval forces. Several days after the battle, however, U.S. newspapers reported that American forces had learned the positions of the Japanese ships and troops, and the effect was disastrous. Within the week, the Japanese changed their encrypting system, completely beggaring the effectiveness of the ciphering machine and forcing the ULTRA program to re-crack the new Japanese system of encryption. U.S. military command determined that the secrecy of ULTRA would thereafter be maintained at all costs. This included the decision to avoid sinking certain ships when the navy knew their precise whereabouts. The hope was to lull the Japanese navy into a sense of security.

But as a result of these security measures, McVay was left in the dark about what lay ahead of him down the Peddie route.

Lieutenant Waldron, the convoy and routing officer who had given McVay his routing orders and intelligence report, did not have access to such intelligence; culpability for the lapse in communication rested with the office Waldron called during his meeting with McVay—the headquarters of the Marianas command, and with Captain Naquin. Naquin was privy to the intelligence gathered by the ULTRA operation, but not to the existence of the operation itself. That is, he received his intelligence reports without knowing how they had been formed. He knew that Japanese submarines were operating along the Peddie route. He was also aware of the July 24 sinking of the *Underhill* in proximity to this route.

Naquin's job was to reformulate sensitive intelligence so it could be used by officers without arousing suspicions among the enemy that it had been intercepted. Because the integrity of ULTRA was so highly guarded, access to it in its raw data form was restricted to officers higher in rank than captain; McVay was therefore not eligible. But if Admiral Spruance had been aboard the *Indy*, the ULTRA intelligence would have been included in the routing orders issued to her.*

McVay was simply, irrevocably, out of the loop.

Sixty feet below the swirling ink of the Pacific's surface, in a state-of-the-art Japanese submarine, Lieutenant Commander Mochitsura Hashimoto fretted. During his four years at sea, the thirty-six-year-old submarine captain had yet to sink even one enemy ship. Now, Hashimoto knew, the war effort was verging on defeat, and he feared he might return home without a single kill. He had erected a Shinto shrine aboard the sub, and he prayed to it daily so that his luck might soon change.

The *I-58* was one of six Japanese submarines still operational in the nation's collapsing navy, part of the renowned Tamon group of subs. It had launched from a naval base on the coast of Japan near Kure, on the same day Captain McVay set sail from San Francisco.

Hashimoto's sub carried the latest in torpedo technology. (In this area of naval warfare, the Japanese had exceeded the American effort until the last months of the war.) The *I-58* was 356 feet long and carried a seaplane as well as a deck-mounted machine gun for, among other things, sweeping the water clear of the torpedoed enemy's survivors. Run by two 4,700-horsepower diesel engines, she could cruise 21,000 miles without refueling, pushing

---

* Clarification as to why Naquin didn't recast this important intelligence in a form McVay might have used disappeared at his death in 1989. In his lifetime he would never fully explain why he didn't communicate at least a portion of his intelligence, except to say that the *Indianapolis'* s risk of enemy submarine attack seemed of "very low order." In short, his was a judgment call.

fifteen knots on the surface. Submerged, the sub moved at a fast clip of seven knots. Her sausage shape was coated in a rubber girdle that distorted her echo pattern and tended to confuse American navy sonar listeners. They sometimes mistook her for a submerged whale.

On board were nineteen oxygen-powered magnetic torpedoes, and six kaitens—kamikaze-like torpedoes piloted by crewmen grateful for the honor. These sacrificial warriors would climb into the forty-eight-foot metal tubes, seat themselves in canvas chairs before a steering wheel and guidance instruments—a compass, Swiss clock, and radio—and wait to hear the fatal word: *Fire!* Released from the metal bands clamping it to the sub, the kaiten began rocketing toward eternity. With a top speed of twenty knots and a range of twenty-seven miles, it was quite a sight, although it regularly missed its target as the pilot struggled to keep the speeding missile on course.

When he was successful—the kaiten was tipped with a magnetic warhead designed to explode within twenty-five feet of any metal hull—the pilot was vaporized upon impact, often in midprayer. (It was impossible for a submerged "mother" sub to retrieve a kaiten, and if the pilot missed his target, he eventually ran out of fuel, and, gliding to the ocean bottom, was fatally crushed by the immense pressure.)

On the night of Saturday, July 28, the kaiten pilots were anxious for their moment of glory. But Hashimoto, peering through the periscope, scanned the night horizon of a choppy Pacific and found it blank.

For the past ten days he'd been cruising steadily south from Kure, on the Japanese mainland, without sighting a target. He had spent today on the surface in hot and squally weather, rocking in the swell, considering his next move. Stationed at the critical crossroads of the Peddie-Leyte route, he was sure a ship would pass.

Six hundred and fifty miles away, at 9 a.m. the USS *Indianapolis* had pulled away from the harbor at Apra, headed for Leyte.

THE USS *Indianapolis* cruised briskly at seventeen knots through a rough sea, under a scattering of bleached clouds. Eight hours after leaving Guam, she sailed beyond the reach of any immediate help she might need. By nightfall, she was beyond a point of no return. Whatever happened next, she would have to fend for herself.

As he stood on the bridge, his feet spread wide as the ship rolled beneath him, Captain McVay's sole concern was to stay the course. He would deliver his crew and ship safely to Leyte, report to Admiral McCormick for gunnery practice, and then get back into the war with Admiral Oldendorf.

McVay lived in a world of absolutes. At the end of the day, at the end of the voyage, and at the end of the war, it was all about life or death. Ships were sinking constantly in battle, and the possibility haunted McVay. One well-known disaster involved the torpedoing of the escort carrier *Liscome Bay* by the Japanese in 1943. The ship sank in twenty minutes, and the attack had killed 644 men. The carriers *Yorktown* and *Wasp* had been torpedoed in June and September 1942, respectively, and were total losses. These were the kinds of stories a captain did not enjoy thinking about.

McVay had spent most of the day in the cramped space suspended high above the ship, monitoring the navigation and communications equipment. Per orders, he followed a strict zig-zag course. In the "sky aft" and "sky forward" watch towers, boys were posted on the lookout for any sign of enemy planes or submarines. Nothing was in sight.

Shortly before the *Indy*'s departure from Guam, news of her passage down the Peddie route once again had been transmitted to interested parties, notifying them of her expected arrival in Leyte. It was a repetition of the process that had taken place on July 26 when she left Tinian. This time, however, Rear Admiral McCormick, whom McVay was to meet in Leyte for gunnery practice, *did* receive and correctly decode the message alerting him to the *Indy*'s arrival.

But since McCormick hadn't received the first message, sent two days earlier, he was confused. In the first place, he was uncertain as to why the *Indianapolis* was reporting to him. Further, because she was the flagship of the Fifth Fleet, he assumed she would be diverted north to replace another cruiser, the USS *Portland*, that had recently been taken out of service. McCormick doubted the *Indy* would ever make landfall at Leyte. Her arrival, from his point of view, was a nonissue.

Elsewhere, there were problems with the second message. Admiral Oldendorf, aboard the *Omaha*, did not receive it. The message made it as far as a dispatch station on Okinawa and then disappeared. Oldendorf had received the first bulletin concerning the *Indy*'s itinerary, but that bulletin had not included the date of her anticipated arrival. Oldendorf knew that Captain McVay would be reporting to him, but he didn't know *when* to expect him.

The effect of this double error in communication was simple: the two people to whom McVay was to report did not possess enough information to determine if he was late. As he sailed to Leyte, Captain McVay was, essentially, a man headed nowhere.

THE voyage was going well and the spirits of the crew were high as lines and matériel were made shipshape and remaining provisions were stored. Coxswain Mike Kuryla liked watching the crew chiefs as they stood on the fantail in the morning, drinking coffee from their huge bowls, thumbs tucked inside the rim. Life at sea seemed lively, delightful even. Down in one of the mess halls, Mc-Coy listened to records played by the ship's onboard disc jockey, a boy from Chicago whose mother always sent him the newest records from the States. Playing lately was Benny Goodman's "Let's Dance." Sometimes, McCoy listened as Tokyo Rose butted in over the mess hall's speakers, her mysterious voice spooking him all the way from Japan, saying, "We know you're out there, sailor boy. We know where you are. Don't you wish you could go home?"

On Sunday morning, July 29, the crew labored through church services in the open air of the main deck, squinting in the glare. The bitter equatorial sun soared straight up from the sea each dawn and dove into the western horizon promptly at six. The neighborly feeling among the boys was strong: first to attend were the Catholics, who then relieved the Protestants from work details so they could attend their service. Father Conway's gentle voice led the Catholic services, and his trusted friend Dr. Haynes directed the Protestant members through old hymns like "The Old Rugged Cross" and "Amazing Grace." McCoy attended the Catholic mass and then spent part of the day chipping old paint from the ship's ladders.

Following church services, the Sunday morning ban on smoking was lifted, and men dispersed to their various divisions to perform deck duties. After a chicken dinner—the best meal of the week, complete with strawberry shortcake—some gathered on the quarterdeck and threw around a medicine ball for exercise. Others jumped rope or sparred at boxing, refereed by Father Conway. Some sat around the quarterdeck splicing decorative lengths of rope as souvenirs, while a few of the boys learned how to crochet pillowcases.

At some point during the early evening, after a brilliant sunset, they passed over one of the deepest spots on earth. They were some 300 miles from the nearest landfall, and a gray scrim of clouds draped the horizon. The section of the Pacific Ocean they were traveling through is known as the Philippine Sea. It is an area east and northeast of the Philippines but still far from dangerous waters close to Japan.

To navigate, the ship's crew was using a series of position fixes made by an ancient method called dead reckoning. This involved tracking a course by multiplying the time spent traveling by speed. Essentially, it was a way of getting where you needed to go by knowing where you had been. Astro-fixes were made by shooting Venus, Saturn, and Mars, which were visible just before sunrise, with a sextant and finding the set of corresponding codes in a book kept on the navigator's bridge. In many ways, the dark night the *Indy* was traveling through could have been any night in the nineteenth century. The *Indy*'s surface radar, nicknamed "Sugar George," was only good for twelve- to fourteen-mile distances, and her air radar, called "Sky Search," was generally undependable. Sometimes it could pick out a bogey (an unidentified aircraft) 100 miles distant; at other times it didn't screen anything until the object was within shouting distance.*

After dark, the boys watched a movie on the starboard hangar deck (the components of Little Boy had occupied the port side hangar). At 9 p.m., "Taps" was sounded by bugle, some boys humming the words:

> *Day is done*
> *Gone the sun*
> *From the hills*
> *From the lake*
> *From the skies*
> *All is well*
> *Safely rest*
> *God is nigh.*

The chief petty officer patrolled the decks looking for opened portholes leaking light into the night, and the announcement came over the PA that the "smoking lamp is now out topside." The red glow of cigarettes showed up too clearly at night; submarines could spot them.

And subs were on everyone's minds. Down in the officers' wardroom, the navigator had announced earlier that a merchant ship called *Wild Hunter* had spotted on July 28 what she thought was a periscope. A destroyer escort had been launched from Guam to investigate the report, but found nothing. The navigator

---

* Indeed, while "Loran A" navigation was possible for about 50 to 60 percent of the Guam–Leyte route (loran navigation, still popular today, uses a series of ground waves sent from onshore radio antennae to fix a ship's position), dead reckoning was both an art and the *Indy*'s default choice of travel. Today's weekend boater equipped with a Global Positioning System has more sophisticated navigational equipment than the *Indy*'s.

also remarked that the *Indy* would be passing the spot of the sighting late in the night. The men joked that surely the *Indy*'s destroyer escort would sink the sub. They laughed and finished their game of bridge.

Sometime between 7:30 and 8 p.m., Captain McVay had given the command to cease zigzagging. His orders explicitly stated that he could do this at his discretion during times of poor visibility. The sea was running rough, with a long ground swell, and the sky was hung with low, heavy clouds, which smothered a thin strip of pale moon. At times, it was so dark that men on the bridge had to announce themselves by name.

McVay's decision was also supported by the intelligence report, which reassured him that his route along the Peddie corridor was clear of enemy traffic.

Shortly after 10:30 p.m. McVay stepped off the bridge into the humid night air along its walkway. Belowdecks, the ship was an inferno, radiating the heat it had absorbed throughout the day, as the temperature soared well above 95 degrees. In the engine room alone, temperatures regularly exceeded 120 degrees; all hatches and doors had been opened to draw the precious salt breezes inside.

In the crew's quarters, temperatures were barely more comfortable, and many of the men chose to sleep topside, where the night air hovered in the mid-eighties. They traipsed across the deck with blanket and shoes in hand in search of relief from the humidity and heat. Some of the boys crawled underneath the massive gun turrets, where they curled up against the cool steel sides of the makeshift caves. Trailing behind them was a phosphorescent wake, faintly flickering against the ship's hull as it sailed through the dark.

The *Indianapolis* was traveling in what was called "yoke modified" position. The most secure position was known as Zed, which meant that all hatches and doors had been dogged—sealed off—making the compartments impermeable. "Yoke modified" described a more relaxed state of sailing and was acceptable in waters where there was little perceived threat of enemy attack. It left the ship's interior spaces dangerously vulnerable. With the hatches opened, the otherwise watertight compartments could be breached in seconds.

At least 300 boys were scattered across the deck in the dark, turning restlessly, searching for sleep. McVay could hear them talking softly, or snoring, or dreaming aloud, set against the steady *shoosh* of the enormous steel bow parting the black sea. He stayed on deck for about fifteen minutes.

By 11 p.m., the ship was buttoned up for the night, cruising in Condition Able. Shortly thereafter, Captain McVay retired to his battle cabin, where he slept during times of combat vigilance. The size of a large garden shed, it was located immediately behind the charthouse on the navigation bridge. If he was needed, he could be summoned either by a quick knock at his door or through what was called a "talking tube." The tube, which connected him to the bridge, pointed directly toward his ear.

The officer of the deck, in charge of the eight-to-midnight watch, was to respond to any change in their situation. If the weather and visibility improved, he was to resume zigzagging and notify the captain immediately.

In his hot, cramped cabin, McVay stripped naked and climbed into his bed. Beneath him, the ship hummed and throbbed, beating its way west through the murky dark, and soon he was fast asleep.

PART TWO

Sunk

CHAPTER FOUR

The Burning Sea

Buddy, you could hear it—it was just a rumble, you [could] just hear everything blasting. Underneath this deck, it was just like fireworks. You ever hear fireworks when they *posh . . . posh . . .* and then all of a sudden: *pa, pa, pa!* Everything was *exploding.* That concussion just ripped that ship from one end to the other. Those were armor-piercing shells that were going off in there. Well, how in the world could that ship survive?

—RICHARD STEPHENS,
seaman second-class, USS *Indianapolis*

SUNDAY, JULY 29–MONDAY, JULY 30, 1945

The Philippine Sea

———

ABOUT twelve miles from where the USS *Indianapolis* cruised, Lieutenant Commander Hashimoto had been awakened by a subordinate officer, per orders. It was time to begin night maneuvers.

Hashimoto put on his soiled, damp uniform, laced his boots, and walked through the narrow passage of his sub, anxious about what the night might bring. At 11 p.m., he ordered the men to their night-action stations, then raised the night periscope—built specifically to magnify targets in low light—and swung the serpentlike head of the instrument in a sweeping arc. Earlier, the *I-58*'s sonar man had picked up something, which he had finally identified as the sound of rattling dishes. And this rattling was increasing, coming closer.*

On the surface of the sea, the metal periscope poked through; painted gray, it blended perfectly with the murkiness of the night and choppy dishwater sea. Yet the horizon was empty. Not a ship in sight. Hashimoto ordered the *I-58* topside for a more thorough look. The boat jumped to life.

The crew blew the main ballast, releasing forced air into the tanks and jettisoning the water she had drawn upon diving three and a half hours earlier. The sub drifted silently to the surface and broke through, tons of water streaming from her gray, bulbous shape.

* As later explained by Goro Yamada, a petty officer aboard the *I-58*, the sub's sonar man had identified the sound of "clinking dishes" from about 20 kilometers, or 12.5 miles away. The sound, according to Yamada, was emanating from one of the galleys on board the USS *Indianapolis*.

The crew screwed open the conning tower hatch, and the submarine's navigator climbed topside to survey the nightscape. Fresh air poured down the opening into the sub, relieving the stifling onboard conditions. The sub's bridge was built forward on the ship, near the bow. It served as a lookout point whenever she cruised the surface. The crew stood on its metal platform, surrounded by a chest-high shield that protected them from enemy fire. The navigator scoped the horizon silently through binoculars.

Suddenly he yelled, "Bearing red, nine-zero degrees. A possible enemy ship!"

The announcement was a shock. Hashimoto had studied the same horizon but had missed the ship shrouded in darkness. The excited sub captain sprinted up the ladder onto the bridge. But he couldn't tell what he was looking at. The target was some six miles away. It was just a smudge atop the water. Hashimoto ordered the sub into a dive. The hatch was sealed, the ballast vents were opened, and the tanks began sucking in several tons of water. The sub slipped beneath the surface.

The hunt was on.

Down below, at his periscope, Hashimoto set about the task of working up his firing solution. This involved figuring his distance from the target, its speed, and direction. It was a tense, complicated business; each minute that elapsed gave the target more time to escape. The lieutenant commander was looking for an intercept point at which he could aim his torpedoes. As he tracked the target, he kept his eye to the periscope, determined not to lose sight of it. He had no idea if the target was also being followed by a destroyer escort.

At 11:39 p.m., six of the *I-58*'s torpedoes were ordered loaded and ready to fire. One pilot seated himself in a kaiten, while another was ordered to stand by.

Hashimoto crept ahead at a quiet three knots.

He couldn't believe his luck.

ON board the *Indy*, the boys were playing craps and poker, reading paperback novels, making coffee, sleeping, and writing letters home. Father Conway, meeting with a sailor in his makeshift confessional in the ship's library, ordered the boy to write his mother. "I got a letter from her, and she said you weren't writing," he admonished. "You're gonna write her right now. We'll mail it from Leyte." The usually gentle priest, who liked spending time with enlisted men more than officers, handed the boy paper and pencil. The kid complied and bent to his missive as the ship rocked through the steaming tropical night.

The boys confided in Father Conway. During the battles at Iwo Jima and Okinawa, most of them had been scared out of their wits, suffering from stomach ailments and bad cases of nerves. As the kamikazes dove at the ships, the boys cried out from their battle stations for the kind priest. He had moved from gun mount to gun mount, reassuring each sailor. Most of the time, the boys wanted on-the-spot absolution for their sins. "Jeez, Father," they'd say. "My last liberty didn't go too well, if you know what I mean. And I think I gotta couple things to get off my chest."

"Yes, son. Go ahead." And then, as the firing guns rocked the ship, the sailor would confess his sins of drinking or fornication or stealing.

Conway, thirty-seven, was relentless and fearless in his duty. Once, while saying mass, battle stations had been called suddenly, and the astute father shouted out, "Bless us all, boys! And give 'em hell!" The boys loved him for this. He was a priest, it was true, but he was a priest with grit. He wasn't what the boys called "namby pamby." The guy had real backbone.

Down in the sleeping compartment that contained the brig, Private McCoy was guarding two prisoners. He had come on duty early; it had been too hot to sleep in his own compartment, where the other marines were bunked. The space was solid steel, painted gray, and it had felt like a tomb. Rather than lie there in the heat, McCoy had thought, What the hell—he'd do the poor sailor doing guard in the brig a favor and relieve him early. McCoy had gone to one of the mess halls, where he poured a cup of coffee, and then continued on to the brig. The coffee was so hot it made his eyes sting. But he needed something to stay awake.

The narrow compartment stank of sweaty men and dirty socks and occupied the last eighteen feet of the fantail, with bunks stacked four high on opposing walls. At the forward end stood a ladder that led topside, the only way in and out of the place. To the left of the ladder were the two jail cells.

McCoy stepped quietly across the metal deck, careful not to wake the boys, mainly the ship's green hands, who had to sleep here. This place was even hotter and stickier than his own compartment. McCoy tried to look on the bright side, as his mother had often told him to do; he figured that at least the misery of heat would keep him awake during the four boring hours of his guard duty.

McCoy watched the sailors he was supposed to keep an eye on turn restlessly in their bunks. He felt sorry for the two cooks he'd

SUNK

guarded since the ship's departure from San Francisco. They
were serving a two-week sentence, ostensibly living on a diet of
bread and water. But their buddies from the kitchen were always
bringing them sandwiches and pie. McCoy generally looked the
other way. He didn't think he had to be a hardhead. These were
pretty good fellows: they'd just had too much to drink. In Mc-
Coy's mind, the only bad guys were the Japanese.

Swish ping, swish ping, came the relentless pounding of the
sea against the hull. McCoy hoped to hell he made it out of this
war alive. He had another two years in his hitch to go. Around his
neck he wore a string of rosary beads given to him by his mom.

He shone the light on the cooks, checking to make sure they
hadn't hung themselves out of boredom. One stirred.

"Hey, marine," he said. "Could you turn that vent this way?"
The air vent snaked through the ship from the deck, providing
scant, but precious, relief.

"No problem, sailor," said McCoy, turning the swivel toward
the prisoner. He could feel a faint blast himself as he leaned up
against a bunk. On the other side of the bulkhead he could hear
the steady thrum of the ship's propellers. He and the boys in the
brig were at the waterline, baking in a damn floating oven.

When he got off duty at 4 a.m., he would have two hours to call
his own. He planned to chuck down more coffee to stay awake for
dawn calisthenics. At 8 a.m., he'd be back down in the brig, on
duty again.

IN the forward part of the ship, Dr. Lewis Haynes stood in a
doorway to the wardroom, watching a lively game of bridge.
Haynes was exhausted. He'd given 1,000 cholera inoculations to

97

the crew that day in preparation for the coming invasion. There was no telling what diseases the wounded prisoners coming off the beach might bring to the ship.

Haynes knew some of the boys were nervous about the future. They talked to him about lots of things. Mostly, they chatted about problems at home with girlfriends or fiancées. A boy could be wrecked by a "green banana" from his sweetheart telling him she was seeing another guy. And aboard ship, there was no way to get rid of the hurt. Or the longing.

One of the card players looked up to ask if Haynes wanted to be dealt in. Haynes thought a moment, then responded: "Naw, you men go ahead. I'm a damn lousy card player." Then he turned away and continued down the passageway to his cabin.

Next door to Haynes was the ship's dentist, Dr. Earl Henry, who was already asleep. Back in his native Tennessee, Henry was renowned for his bird portraits. Haynes had bought several of the paintings and had them shipped back to his wife. At the Friday night talent shows that Father Conway organized, Dr. Henry did bird calls in between skits where the boys performed in drag or sang barbershop quartet tunes.

Haynes drew the curtain to his berth, stripped, and pulled on white cotton pajama pants. Tomorrow would be a busy day. He would be up at reveille to inspect the mess halls and the crew's living quarters with the captain. Then he'd attend to the sick crew, half of whom weren't really sick; they only wanted to be excused from deck duty. When Haynes found a boy who was goldbricking, he'd bark, "Don't give me that shit!" and send him back to work. Still, he couldn't help but smile at the ingenuity of some of the boys' imagined stomachaches and muscle sprains.

Earlier in the voyage, Haynes had performed an emergency appendectomy on a stout young sailor named Harold Schechterle, who definitely was not a goldbricker. With just a local anesthetic, the procedure had gone beautifully. When it was over, Lew had jokingly told the boy, "Okay, Schechterle, you're all set. Now get your ass back on duty."

The kid had leapt off the table, new stitches and all, and was about to run through the door. Haynes was horrified. "Schechterle! I was just kidding! Now you take it easy, son. You're going to heal up fine."

Alone in his berth, recalling the incident, Haynes laughed to himself. Then, his day finally done, he slid beneath the sheets and fell asleep almost instantly.

IN sky aft, Ensign Harlan Twible, twenty-three, just two weeks out of the Naval Academy, stood in the elevated metal crow's nest eighty feet off the main deck, watching the night sky. Heavy clouds scudded across the moon. It was what the boys called a "peekaboo night"; right now Twible couldn't see his hand in front of his face.

Twible was standing watch with Leland Clinton. The two had gotten friendly during the past two weeks. Clinton was a farmer's son from the Midwest; Twible's parents were Irish mill workers from Massachusetts. Getting into the academy had been a dream come true for Twible. As an ensign, he was at the bottom of the officer ratings, but he was determined to work his way up.

Using a telephone, he could communicate with the bridge. If he spotted a plane or torpedo, he could quickly ring the news through, and the general alarm for battle stations would be called. But now he saw nothing but a confused sea, with long, deep swells rolling across the ocean from the northeast. Since July 27, a typhoon had been moving southwest from Okinawa, and it was gathering strength.

About twenty men were stationed around the ship in similar positions of vigilance, each overlooking a separate quadrant of the ship's horizon. There were four officers on duty on the bridge. The officer of the deck, Lieutenant John Orr, was in charge of communication with Captain McVay if any changes were needed in the ship's maneuvers. McVay was especially reliant on Lieutenant Orr's command, and as OOD, Orr was eager to continue proving himself to the captain. He had also been battle hardened, having survived a torpedoing while serving aboard a destroyer in Ormoc Bay off Leyte.

The supervisor of the night's watch, thirty-seven-year-old Lieutenant Commander K. C. Moore, was charged with keeping an overall eye on both Orr and the operation of the bridge and engine rooms. Moore checked the night watches and lookouts about the ship and found all of them alert.

THREE miles away and closing in on the *Indy*, Lieutenant Commander Hashimoto studied the blurred outline of the ship through the periscope. Hashimoto racked his brain trying to accurately identify the vessel. It was crucial. Lying open on a table near the periscope was a book of U.S. warship silhouettes that provided intelligence necessary to correctly identify battleships, carriers, and cruisers. The book also presented important information about each ship's speed and capabilities.

Hashimoto knew the ship wasn't friendly, because he'd been kept apprised of Japanese naval movement through coded dispatches. It had to be the enemy, but what kind? He studied the approaching shape through the periscope. Destroyer? Battleship? Why was it headed straight at him? He wondered if it was a destroyer hunting him.

He ordered his sub on a new course heading to port, or to his left. Through the periscope, the bridge and superstructure of the ship became more clearly visible as a triangle shape. Now the ID could be made. Hashimoto surmised that this target was of the battleship class. He announced this as the sub's sonar man tuned in to the sound of the approaching ship's engine revolutions. Hashimoto counted the revolutions for one minute, calculating the target's speed.

It was twenty knots.* He next swung his sub into position to meet the *Indy* broadside for the kill shot. From this vantage, he could see that his target, illuminated by the sliver of moon peeking through the clouds, was indeed a large warship. She was huge.

As the attack procedure progressed, the four kaiten pilots became more and more adamant that one of them be launched. But in the excitement of the sudden rush to identify the ship, Hashimoto had actually forgotten about them. He now told the pilots that because of the conditions, with the target closing in, it would be nearly impossible to miss the kill; their lives would be wasted unnecessarily if he used them.

Then, with his eye pressed to the rubber cup of the periscope, Hashimoto gave the order to fire. It was 12:04 a.m.

The first torpedo shot from a forward tube of the sub and

---

* The *Indy* was actually traveling at seventeen knots under a staggered engine pattern, meaning that her four propellers were moving at different rpm rates. This was standard practice, used precisely to confuse the kind of hydrophone readings Hashimoto had just taken.

quickly accelerated to a cruising speed of forty-eight knots, or about as fast as a racing greyhound. It traveled at a depth of thirteen feet, leaving behind a swirling wake.

The torpedo carried 1,210 pounds of explosives and was configured with a preset firing range of 1,640 yards, a little under a mile. This was enough firepower to take out an entire city block. Hashimoto fired six of these, and they left the ship at three-second intervals, in a widening fan of white lines.

IT took less than a minute for two of the torpedoes to intercept the *Indianapolis*.

At 12:05 a.m. all hell broke loose.

The first torpedo hit the forward starboard, or right, side and tore part of the bow away. Men were thrown fifteen feet in the air. Those who weren't blown in two landed on their feet, stunned, their ears ringing.

The second explosion occurred closer to midship and was even more massive.*

The sea itself seemed to be burning. The first torpedo had smashed one gas tank containing 3,500 gallons of high-octane aviation fuel, igniting a burning river that reduced the bulkheads and doors to red-hot slabs of steel. The fuel incinerated everything in its path. The number-one smokestack, acting as a chimney for the inferno raging below, belched a volcanic streamer of fire that shot several hundred feet into the air, littering the ship with sparks and cinders.

The second torpedo had pierced the four-inch steel armor be-

---

* The remaining four torpedoes were not accounted for; presumably they missed their target.

low the bridge, slightly aft of officers' country. Also hit were the *Indy*'s boiler rooms, which provided steam to the ship's forward engine room, called engine room 1, and the powder magazine for the 8-inch guns. Both torpedoes had smashed into the starboard side of the ship, actually lifting the ship off the water and whipping it to the left, onto a new course slightly to the south. The *Indianapolis* paused like a large beast struck between the ribs, then settled back in the water, plowing ahead at seventeen knots. With her bow damaged, she began scooping up seawater by the ton.

It was 12:06 a.m.—just a minute after the torpedoing. The ship had been cut nearly in half. All compartments and crew forward of the number-one smokestack were struggling for life. Those areas aft of the stack, including the quarterdeck, the hangar deck, radio shack 2, and engine room 2, as well as compartments belowdecks such as the gedunk stand, the post office, and the mess halls, initially were relatively untouched by the explosions. Within minutes, though, this situation changed. Soon the armory, library, log room, and marine compartment were in flames, the mess halls choked with smoke and dust. The ship began to slightly list, or tilt, to her starboard side. She had only minutes left afloat, and those aboard her had seconds to decide their fate.

All communications and electrical power in the forward part of the ship were dead, and it was impossible to talk with any crew in the engine rooms. It was a critical moment: it was imperative to shut the engines down to halt her forward movement and the flood of water she was taking on as she steamed ahead.

Down in engine room 1, near the number-one smokestack and the point of impact, sparks flew from the ventilation ducts and showered the compartment. Machinist's mate William Nightingale, on midnight watch, stumbled among the turbine engines as they choked and died. The lights went out, and the room filled with smoke. The emergency generators, needed to provide auxiliary power, sputtered and then quit. Nightingale, with the aid of a flashlight, watched the boilers' steam pressure drop as thick black fuel oil and seawater started pouring through the hatch.

He now realized just how horribly the ship had been damaged. Two of the engines controlled the "outboard" propellers (located one each on the far port and starboard sides). When this engine went down, the propellers had stopped turning. If the ship had been torpedoed, as Nightingale sensed it had been, it seemed important to keep her moving, away from the oncoming sub. But there was nothing he could do here, and he hurried from the compartment, heading aft to engine room 2.

Chief engineer Richard Redmayne, Nightingale's superior officer, had been in the officers' head, standing at the toilet, when the explosion shook the compartment. The torpedo hit less than thirty feet away, and Redmayne smelled smoke and heard flames licking the starboard passageway on the other side of the door. Steeling himself, he ran out through the blazing gauntlet and stumbled, badly burned, through fallen debris and billowing smoke to engine room 2, located behind the number-two smokestack, about 300 feet from the bow. There he found everything in working order.

All the generators around him were operating and supplying power. From midships back, the ship generally had power and lights, supplied by the auxiliary diesel generators that had started flickering automatically. Redmayne tried to use the telegraph and found it dead. He wanted desperately to contact the bridge for a report and further orders. But that was impossible. He tried pumping fuel oil to the port-side tanks to halt the ship's list, but this did nothing to solve the problem.

The stunned and terrified man didn't have the slightest idea of the bedlam in engine room 1. He wasn't even sure what had caused the explosions. Reading his gauges, he discovered that the vacuum power was dropping in the engine that controlled one of the "inboard" propellers (located one each on the ship's port and starboard sides, and flanked by the "outboard" propellers), but that the other was still turning. Redmayne believed the ship mustn't stop if she'd been torpedoed. Since he couldn't consult with Captain McVay or the damage control officer, he had to make a judgment call. He ordered the remaining propeller fired up to 160 rpms.

UP in his battle cabin, Captain McVay had been lifted straight off his bed and slammed to the floor. Rising, he stumbled through clouds of white smoke, his throat scorched from the acrid odor of the burning ship. Immediately, he kicked into battle mode and began collecting himself within a whirlwind of conflicting thoughts. Had they been hit by a kamikaze? Run into a floating mine? Were they under attack? The ship's tremorous vibrations reminded the experienced captain of the kamikaze attack off Okinawa.

McVay quickly ruled out mines because he remembered they were too far out to sea for the Japanese to have strewn the water with the deadly floating spheres. He thought he detected a whipping sensation, as if the ship were shaking from side to side. He reasoned that the shaking of the deck and bulkheads was too violent for a single kamikaze plane to have caused.

The only rational explanation was that they'd been torpedoed. McVay had never encountered this precise kind of disaster before, but he knew his duties. He had three pressing jobs: assess the damage, take care of it, and engage the enemy—if indeed they were in battle. Most dreaded of all was the possibility that he would have to give the call to abandon ship if the damage was beyond control. But for now, his first concern was to get off distress messages detailing the ship's condition and position. He stumbled nude and barefoot from his cabin to the bridge.

In times of stress and battle, a captain aboard his ship is like a king, to which all stations must report the extent of damages along with their prognoses. When McVay walked onto the twenty-foot-wide bridge platform, he found it in chaos. The darkness was so thick that the men had to identify themselves by name. McVay knew he needed to establish order by determining the extent of the damage. He looked for his damage control officer, K. C. Moore, but couldn't find him.

What McVay didn't know was that the water mains used for fighting fire had been ruined. Damage control efforts had proved impotent against the spreading inferno. On the quarterdeck, crews lugged heavy hoses across what remained of the forward deck and screwed them into hydrants, only to throw the valves open and find they had no water pressure. Other crew members, under Moore's direction, were operating a series of valves spaced throughout the ship that opened and closed certain compartments; these could be filled and emptied with sea ballast in an attempt to balance the ship's list. So far, these measures, along with the dogging of the hatches of the blown area, were failing to halt the flooding or slow the increasing list of the *Indianapolis*.

On the bridge, McVay turned to the matter of getting off a distress signal. He ordered Commander John Janney belowdecks to radio shack 1. It was imperative that their latitude and longitude positions be broadcast repeatedly. *Get the message out that we've been torpedoed*, he told his trusted navigator, *and that we need assistance, on the double*. Janney raced from the bridge; McVay would never see him again.

McVay next yelled for his officer of the deck, Lieutenant Orr, and the young officer snapped to attention at his captain's side. The twenty-two-year-old Annapolis graduate was deeply upset, knowing that as the *Indy* continued sailing, she was rapidly taking on water. He calmed himself enough to explain that because the electrical system was out, he couldn't talk with the engine room. "I have tried to stop the engines," he told McVay. "I don't know whether the order has ever gotten through."

McVay took the news in; this was the first report he'd heard of the ship's condition, and he was still undecided about its severity. Judging from the slight list and the probability that the back half of the ship hadn't suffered any damage at all, it seemed likely that the *Indy* could be saved.

McVay rushed back to his battle cabin, where he grabbed his khaki and captain's hat, and returned to his command post, dressing as he awaited Janney. Shortly, Bob Gause entered the dark, smoke-filled bridge. (Gause's bunk was midships, right over the powder magazine that had blown the ship apart. But he hadn't been in his bunk; a bad case of boils had led him to sleep on a bare cot in the catapult tower that loomed over the quarterdeck, port side.) There he found McVay, with gunnery officer Stanley Lipski, leaning out over the storm railing. Lipski had been horribly burned; it was amazing that he was even alive. His hands had been cooked down to tendons; and his eyes were burned to two blackened holes. Somehow, feeling his way along the bulkhead and the lifeline skirting the ship, he had made his way by memory to the bridge.

McVay was glad to see Gause, whom he affectionately called "Conch" (Gause was from Florida). He had last seen the quartermaster at 9 p.m., when they exchanged the night order book. Now that seemed like years ago. McVay asked Gause if he had any idea what had happened to Commander Janney.

"Captain," Gause said, "there is no radio shack 1. It's all blown to hell." McVay was surprised. The situation was sounding more disastrous by the minute.

The ship was crawling with men—there had to be at least 900—in various stages of order and entropy. All awaited the next order. A majority of the boys were still under the impression that this was an air battle. They thought maybe they'd been hit by a Betty—a Japanese plane that released armor-piercing bombs. Or maybe they'd been shelled by an enemy battleship. Who knew?

THE *Indy* was now perched at a fifteen-degree list to the right, which gave the deck a slight uphill climb. With one propeller still turning, she was plowing ahead now at about twelve knots, or fourteen miles per hour, and the list was increasing by the minute. With her bow torn off, the front of the ship resembled a mangled snout rooting ahead through the sea, gulping water. The massive incoming tide was punching through auxiliary bulkheads, taking on a life of its own, roaring back through the ship toward the stern, seeking out all dry places.

Already roughly 100 men were dead—burned, blown up, or drowned. Most of those sleeping forward of the 8-inch guns on the bow had been vaporized. The bodies that remained were charred beyond recognition. The survivors stumbled back from the forward part of the ship onto a deck covered with an inch of blood, their skin smoking in the hot night. Crew members sleeping belowdecks in the final 115 feet from the forward turret to the bow also had died instantly. These boys had been trapped in passageways and quarters by walls of fire that advanced toward them and sucked the air from their lungs.

Lieutenant Commander K. C. Moore had been running through the ship, trying to secure the most badly breached compartments. The key was to stop the flooding before it pulled the ship underwater, but the damage control officer was having trouble finding any repair parties to aid him. As the water poured in, the boys who had managed to survive the explosions tried stealing up ladders to the deck. They found themselves turned back by fires raging above them. Others, racing through the narrow passageways toward the dogged hatches of the stern, were trapped by the accumulating water, flattened against the bulkheads as the ship continued its starboard lean, the nose pointing toward the ocean floor.

Damage control was of no use; the second torpedo had torn open a gaping hole forty feet in diameter in the broad side of the ship. Thousands of gallons of fuel oil were pouring out, trailing the ship like a liquid scarf. Desks, mattresses, books, papers, clothing, bodies, and pieces of bodies were sucked out through the hole as the contents of the ship were exchanged for the incoming breach of the sea.

Topside, those sailors forward of the bridge, nearest the bow, saw that the deck was mangled. They also noticed that the steel plating was split in places and that smoke and flames were pouring from these fissures. Boys standing or lying on the deck in various stages of pain and disbelief were being seared on the superheated steel. The night was filled with screams and explosions that faded over the water, traveling a mile—maybe two.

The *Indy* was alone, cut off, struggling to stay afloat.

MCVAY was still anxiously awaiting a report from radio shack 1. His hope was that if Radio Central was blown, emergency radio 2 could broadcast their location. McVay's thoughts were interrupted by Moore, who busted onto the bridge. Out of breath, clearly upset, the damage control officer informed the captain that the ship's forward compartments were flooding quickly. "We're badly damaged, sir," he announced. "Do you want to call for abandon ship?"

It was now around 12:11 a.m. and the ship had slowed to about nine knots, or ten miles per hour. Since the explosions, her forward momentum and her remaining power had managed to push her about one mile across the ocean.

For the life of him, McVay couldn't figure out why their condition was going bad so quickly. But he had little time to react. He had two things on his mind: that the damage sustained by the kamikaze attack four months earlier off Okinawa had initially seemed far worse, and that to call abandon ship if the *Indy* was salvageable could lead to possible court-martial. He simply couldn't believe that the damage could be so severe, given the short time frame. It defied reason, and his experience. At Okinawa, the USS *Franklin* had been turned into a broiling inferno by the attack of a bomber, but it had managed to stay afloat. The crew had even been able to jump from her listing, burning decks onto a destroyer pulled up alongside. McVay had reason to believe that he could still save the *Indy*.

"Maybe we can hold her," he told Moore. "Go back below and take one more look and report back to me immediately." The man hurried belowdecks to check the situation again. It was the last McVay would see of him.

Almost immediately, his executive officer, Commander Joseph Flynn, the ship's second in command, arrived and briefed him on the ship's worsening situation. The ship was now listing at a perilous angle. Below McVay and Flynn, the wounded boys who were strong enough tried to compensate for the deck's list by walking hand over hand along the ship's lifelines. Those too badly injured stumbled and crashed into bulkheads. Or kept rolling, cartwheeling into the sea.

The executive officer told McVay that the *Indy* was flooding fast. Then came the final blow: "We are definitely going down. I suggest that we abandon ship."

McVay was stunned. However, he trusted Flynn's report. Combined with his damage control officer's earlier assessment, it convinced McVay that there was nothing else to be done.

"Okay, Red," he announced. "Pass the word to abandon ship." Just eight minutes had passed since the torpedoes struck.

THE *Indy* was indeed going down.

The ship was slowing, but not quickly enough, and she was still taking on water. With the bow damaged, the remaining forward part of the ship, about 150 feet, was weakening, threatening to blow off under the force of the water rushing against it. The ship rumbled and groaned as it punched through the heavy, fifteen-foot swells. Belowdecks, the boys heard roars like thunder as machinery and equipment smashed into bulkheads and other compartments were breached by the powerful sea.

Normally, the announcement McVay was about to make would come over the ship's PA, but the PA was gone, along with electricity to the power lines. Moving quickly to the bridge's port wing, he cupped his hands to his mouth and yelled down to the several hundred boys gathered at the rail below, "Abandon ship!"

The order passed like a fever through the crew. In the confusion, the ship's bugler thought that he was being commanded to actually leave the ship. So, instead of picking up his bugle, he dashed from the bridge and began making his way off the *Indy*.

Commander Lipski, meanwhile, had somehow endured the excruciating pain of his wounds and made his sightless way down several ladders to the quarterdeck to order the sailors gathered there to get off the ship. The boys were in line four deep at the port rail as the deck slowly raised and tilted higher and higher above the water. Since the first moment of impact, they had been congregating at the stern, instinctively fleeing the smoke, fire, and explosions at the bow. Some of the terrified boys had even taken it upon themselves earlier to abandon ship without any official confirmation of the order.*

Now they began jumping off one by one, then they began to go in droves, jumping in a wave that swept toward the stern of the ship. Although almost all had life preservers, some were too terrified to jump and stood frozen—they were pushed from be-

---

* A small portion of the crew actually decided to leave the ship within minutes of the torpedoing, leaping from both the port and starboard sides. These early jumpers, finding themselves alone in the sea, would try later to connect with larger groups once the ship had gone down. However, the majority of the approximately 900 crew members who got off the ship did so in the final minutes of the sinking.

hind and dropped out of sight into the sea. Like a crowd trying to
rush a gate, some 400 crew members crowded the rail at the port
stern. A young lieutenant who hadn't heard the order to abandon
ship had been trying to hold the boys at bay, screaming, "Don't
jump yet!"

Now he gave up and was nearly crushed as the boys struggled
to climb onto the rail and steady themselves. They stepped off
into space and plummeted close to eighty feet, screaming as they
dropped into the dark sea below.

The abandon ship procedure, at least as it is practiced in the
pages of *The Bluejackets' Manual*, is an orderly affair. But by and
large, the survival training in boot camp had been lackluster (some
of the boys hadn't even learned to swim), and in the chaos and
confusion—exacerbated by the loss of the PA system—approved
procedures for leaving the *Indy* were forgotten or at best carried
out in haphazard fashion. All of this was compounded by the fact
that during the ship's high-speed run to Tinian, the green hands
on board hadn't had much time to practice any of the abandon
ship procedures.

In the theoretical process, life rafts and motor launches are
dropped into the water. Then rope ladders and nets are lowered over the side of the ship, providing access to the life rafts,
which are stowed with various lifesaving provisions. Survival
gear in 1945 included mess utensils; first aid kits; flare guns
called Very pistols, complete with illuminating rounds called
star shells; signal flags; a metal signal reflecting mirror; and rifles
and ammunition.

On the *Indy*, the two motor-launch whaleboats, stationed near
the stern—each twenty-six feet long and intended to carry twenty-
two men—had been undamaged by the torpedoing. Nearby, stacked

like giant pieces of gray bread, were about seven of the thirty-five cork and canvas-covered rafts, each able to hold twenty-five men. (These were distributed in equal numbers around the ship, but those at the bow had been rendered useless.)

Each craft was supposed to be outfitted with bread sealed in watertight cans and potable water in wooden beakers, or kegs, in three-, five-, and eight-gallon denominations. Abandon ship provisions also allowed each sailor one pound of hard bread and 3.4 pounds of canned meat (Spam), as well as one whole gallon of water. Each whaleboat was also meant to be equipped with a boat chest containing a hatchet, a hammer, a screwdriver, pliers, sailmaker's needles, lamp wicks, sail twine, a seven-inch fishing reel with line and assorted hooks and sinkers, lanterns, oil, and matches.

Of the thirty-five life rafts stacked on board, about twelve made it off the ship, and these carried few of the specified provisions. In the hubbub of the *Indy*'s quick departure from Hunters Point, some of the water kegs apparently had not been filled, and in many of those that had not been recently replenished, the existing water had turned foul in the wooden containers. Few boat chests had been loaded into the life rafts.

On the other hand, luck had been with the boys of the *Indy* two weeks earlier, back in Hunters Point, when the double or-der of life vests had been delivered. These 2,500 life vests—along with a large number of life belts—were everywhere, stored in bags fastened around the ship's bulkheads, and in boxes strategically located at points of disembarkation. As the ship tilted beneath their feet, the boys clamored to reach them.

CAPTAIN McVay worried that the distress messages from radio shacks 1 and 2 hadn't gotten off. In a sense, everything rode on these messages; the crew's survival depended on getting help as quickly as possible. In a little less than thirty-six hours, when the ship didn't arrive in Leyte, no doubt she would be reported missing, but McVay was concerned that many of the injured would not be able to survive the wait. He walked from the bridge to the ladder leading to the main deck and started down. He wanted to see for himself, up close, just what the hell had happened to his ship. The torpedoing still boggled him. Just as he reached the communications deck, the ship violently wrenched to sixty degrees. Below him, on the starboard side, he spied sailors preparing to jump overboard without life jackets.

"No, boys!" he yelled. "Don't go over unless you have one of these!" He pointed frantically at his own jacket. It was too late—the boys were leaping anyway. Nearby, seaman Jack Cassidy, an eighteen-year-old bookie's son from West Springfield, Massachusetts, looked up from the deck where he knelt, to see McVay silhouetted by flames erupting from the bow. Their eyes locked for a moment. McVay cried out, "God bless you!"

Within seconds, the *Indy* rolled to ninety degrees. McVay jumped to the forecastle deck and crawled up to the rail. He did some quick calculations in his head—it was clear the radio shack was unreachable and, in fact, was in imminent danger of flooding. The back portion of the ship, from the bridge to the stern, was crawling with men. McVay started walking aft.

This was a perilous journey, and he teetered along the shuddering rail of the overturned ship. Fifty feet of her red keel were visible, and her port rail was pointing at the sky. McVay was walking a balance beam into total darkness.

The boys still inside the ship—an estimated 100 or so—found themselves walking on the bulkheads or crushed by loose machinery and equipment sent flying. The deck had suddenly disappeared from beneath them. Men trapped on the lower starboard rail tried desperately to climb the deck to the higher port side. They lifted themselves hand over hand using railings, ladders, and stray lines, much like men scaling a sheer cliff face.

THROUGHOUT the ship, the boys had reacted in a variety of ways to the sinking. Some had rushed to their bunks and quickly finished letters home; one sailor paused in his berth to clip his toenails; another made a sandwich and quickly swallowed it whole, followed by a glass of water. On the signal bridge, a few sailors were hurriedly stuffing classified documents into a weighted bag and preparing to throw it over the side. The bag would sink and keep the intelligence out of the enemy's hands. But as the ship's tilt grew more pronounced, the boys gave up and simply stuck it under a desk and ran from the room. It was clear to them that soon *nothing* around them would still be floating.

Jack Cassidy was hacking frantically at the plaster cast on his leg with a knife. He'd wrenched it in gunnery practice during the journey from Pearl Harbor. With a final slice, the cast slid off, and he climbed up the deck to the high port side. Standing on the rail, Cassidy looked forward to the bow and saw dead bodies strewn about the bent metal plates. He leaped, flinging himself as far from the ship as he was able. Naked except for a thin pair of worn dungaree shorts, Cassidy clutched a rubber life belt that he hadn't had time to blow up. He hit the water and began swimming. Then curiosity got the better of him; he turned and saw the ship flaring with explosions that moved through the forward sections in an eerie strobe effect.

At the hangar deck, Ed Brown stood ready to jump when a buddy he'd met up with at the Club Lido the night before sailing yelled, "Don't jump, dammit—the fall will kill you!"

"Do we have any choice?" Brown asked. And he leaped. He hit the water and started swimming away, turning his head as he stroked, to see at least forty-five more boys following. He couldn't make out his friend.

Back on board, boys with knives slashed at bags of kapok life jackets and floater nets. Trying to free one of the *Indy*'s twenty-six-foot whaleboats, a sailor was crushed as the deck slid beneath him and he found himself pinned to the ship's bulkhead under the heavy wooden craft. Mike Kuryla worked at the *Indy*'s second motor launch, but the increasing list made this impossible; he couldn't manage to pull the release pin securing it to the stanchion. He was forced to give up. Finding a bag of life vests hanging nearby, he emptied the netting and, shouting that he had life preservers for all who still needed them, began handing them out by the armful.

At this point, about eleven minutes had passed since the torpedoes struck, and the boys leaving on the high, port side were sliding down the long expanse of exposed hull, which was mercifully clear of barnacles as a result of the *Indy*'s extensive overhaul in San Francisco. They entered the water with a splash, screaming as they dropped.

On the low side of the ship, the starboard rail was now level with the water itself, and the boys on this side could walk off like swimmers stepping into a pool. Some stepped off without even getting their hair wet. They settled with the lightest of splashes and began swimming away.

It was here, depending on which side they left the ship, that the crew began to seal different fates for themselves. Those who departed from the port side entered a sea nearly devoid of any lifesaving equipment. Because the ship was heeling to the right, or starboard, all the lifesaving gear was sliding down the deck and into the sea in that direction. The boys leaving the *Indy* from the lower rail bobbed along a pitching swell littered with empty powder cans, wooden desk chairs and desks, papers, and crates of potatoes and carrots. Loose life vests and rafts were also floating in the water off this low side. The boys needed to work fast, collecting what they could before swimming as far as possible away from the ship, whose burning hulk was now threatening to roll over on top of them.

Regardless of which side of the ship they exited, the boys were swimming directly into the poisonous field of black fuel oil spewing from the ship's exploded hull. It was sticky as molasses, and they couldn't avoid swallowing it as they paddled around in the heavy swells. It smothered them in a noxious blanket, clogging their eyes, ears, and mouths, eating away with acid intensity at all their sensitive membranes.

Many simply drifted in shock. All that was visible of their blackened faces was the whites of their eyes and their red, screaming mouths.

Chaos was at full fiery whirl.

CHAPTER FIVE

Abandon Ship

I jumped and I swam. I looked back
and the ship stood right on end, and there must have been
300 sailors standin' on the fantail, and it just went under.
And they drifted off like a bunch of flies.

—ROBERT GAUSE,
quartermaster first-class, USS *Indianapolis*

MONDAY, JULY 30, 1945

MCCOY knew something very bad had happened, but because there was no smoke, fire, or loss of electricity in the brig, it was hard to figure out what exactly was going on. He was completely unaware of the terror unfolding in the forward area of the ship. Before the hit, McCoy, dressed in a green T-shirt and fatigues, had been standing beneath the air vent that rose through the bulkheads, angling for the coolest sip of salt breeze, lulled by the steady rhythm of the massive, brass propellers turning on the other side of the bulkhead. Then *Wham!*

The lights had blacked out, and the compartment rung like a gong. McCoy had been tossed fifteen feet across the brig to an opposite wall, where he hit a bunk. This set into motion a chain reaction of bunks falling to the floor. McCoy ended up pinned with an unconscious boy's body draped across his legs. After he rolled him off, he stood up and felt for broken bones. He was fine.

McCoy's first thought was that the *Indy* had been rammed by a Japanese destroyer. Or that maybe the ship had hit a mine. He had no idea. One thing he *was* sure of: his first order of duty was to help the wounded out of the sleeping compartment adjoining the brig, then hurry to his battle station at the 5-inch gun located aft on the ship. All around him, sailors were screaming out in pain. McCoy searched around the pitch-dark interior, found a big nine-volt-cell battle light, and played it over the gray metal walls of the compartment.

About thirty enlisted men had been thrown from their bunks into a tangle on the deck. In the pale beam of his light, McCoy could see the fall had knocked a few of them out. He knelt and felt for pulses, and tried shaking them back to consciousness. It was no good—they were out cold. There would be time to move them later; McCoy guessed that damage control crews on the main deck were busy fighting fires and, he hoped, winning the battle while the hatches were closed and flooding compartments contained.

But it was the closing of the hatches that worried McCoy. He didn't want to be in this compartment if an order was given to dog them. He knew he had to move fast.

Behind him, the two prisoners yelled to be let out of their cells, and McCoy quickly fumbled for the key and released them. All three turned their attention to the wounded. Some had broken legs, arms, and ribs. About twenty of the thirty boys were now stirring, writhing, and begging McCoy to move the bunks off of them.

McCoy and the cooks, breathing heavily in the foul heat, began untangling their crewmen and escorting them up the steep, metal ladder through the hatch—the only way out. It was hard work, and they were frantic to keep moving as quickly as possible. About eight minutes after the explosion, a chief petty officer appeared in the black square of night filling the open hatch. McCoy could see he was agitated.

"We're gonna have to dog this hatch, Private!"

"But there's men still down here!"

"Well, get 'em out!"

This was what every sailor feared: that the boys who couldn't be moved would be entombed forever within the ship.

They upped their pace, but by the time the chief petty officer reappeared McCoy guessed that there were nine boys still in the compartment. The cooks dashed up the ladder and disappeared into the night. Looking up the rungs leading to the hatch, McCoy could see the night sky pinned with clouds. He couldn't bear the thought of leaving the compartment. Sensing that their fate was being settled, the boys left behind cried: "Don't leave us. Don't leave us."

McCoy barked, "I'm coming!" at the chief petty officer and, with a sick feeling, ran up the ladder without looking back. A few seconds later, he heard the clang of the hatch closing and the metallic whir of wheels spinning shut. Then came the rasp of the pin as it was inserted into the locked position.

The men trapped inside were screaming, but the sound was tinny and faint. McCoy knew the night was just beginning.

Reaching the main deck, he steadied himself on the high port rail, then he started to the bow, intent on reaching his gun mount on the starboard side near the hangar deck. He saw boys scrambling across the pitched deck, faces burned and blackened, wailing. They seemed out of their minds. *This is my home*, he thought.

But the damn thing was falling apart right under his feet. He wondered what had happened to Captain Parke and the other marines.* McCoy could hear the ship hiss as it sank; it was a terrible, high-pitched sound.

Looking down, he realized he was wearing only one shoe— he was holding the other. He quickly jammed it on his foot and inched along the rail, found a life vest, and snatched it up without stopping. He could feel the ship shaking beneath him as explosions sounded throughout her interior. It was like riding a

---

* At least one-quarter of the thirty-nine-man marine detachment were killed instantly in the torpedoing. As McCoy was climbing the ladder from the brig, in fact, his bunk and the entire sleeping area were in flames. Had he not relieved the brig watch ahead of schedule, he would have been incinerated with the others in the blast.

thunderhead. Ahead, he could see that the bow was completely under water. The ship's rails were driving through the sea. It was then that he realized that the *Indy* was really going to sink. The deck gave one final turn, and the port rail pointed directly at the sky. Slipping, McCoy grabbed the loose ends of some wiring, wrapped it around his fists, and began climbing up a tilted gun mount.

He pulled himself over the splinter shield, a large square plate of steel that protected the gunners, and stood on top of it. *It's now or never*, he thought, and he stepped off onto the side of the ship and began walking down the metal hull, converging with a swarm of about thirty boys, all headed for the sea. McCoy dropped into a crouch, sat down, lifted his feet, and slid across the keel. With a splash, he hit the water and was smothered in the blanket of leaking fuel oil.

He surfaced, gagging, shook his head, then tried wiping his eyes, but this only smeared more oil into them. And then he began to swim. Looking over his shoulder, he could see one of the ship's inboard propellers still spinning. Men were jumping off the stern, screaming as they dropped. They hit the blades and were thrown into the air. One minute they were dropping straight for the sea; the next, they were flying sideways, wailing as they flew out into the darkness.

ASLEEP in his private berth in the forward part of the ship, Dr. Lewis Haynes had been knocked high into the air when the first torpedo hit, landing on the edge of his small Formica desk. He'd just managed to stand up on wobbly legs when the second explosion knocked him down again. This time, he heard his hands sizzling on the hot metal deck. *Christ, I better get the shit out of here,* he thought as he grabbed his life jacket from its hook by the door. Then he took one last look at the framed picture of his wife and hurried through the curtain into the passageway, where he was greeted by the sound of tortured screaming.

Haynes paused to try to locate the source: it was Lieutenant Commander Henry, the dentist, next door. Haynes was paralyzed by the sounds of mortal agony; it was clear that the man was burning up in his room. He started in Henry's direction but stopped. He knew there was nothing he could do. Haynes guessed that Henry's berth had taken the brunt of whatever had struck the ship. With the dentist's screams still in his ears, he pushed on down the passage.

There he met Lieutenant Commander Ken Stout, who emerged from smoke gathering in thick plumes along the ceiling of the hall. "Look out, Lew!" Stout yelled, and Haynes lifted his hands to his face just before the tremendous burst of a flash fire—*fwoom!*—scoured the hall. Haynes heard the snap and fizzle of wires shorting out; farther away, near the bow, there were more explosions. For a moment, Haynes believed he was on fire himself, so intense was the heat and pain.

The fire had, in fact, singed Haynes's hair, forehead, and hands, giving him what he knew from experience were third-degree burns. When he was able to open his eyes, Stout had disappeared. All that remained was the harsh scent of burned skin.

The explosion had blown open the hatch to the powder magazine for the 8-inch guns on the main deck. (An elevator in the magazine was used to lift shells and powder up to the turret.)

Haynes stared at the shells, transfixed. Their thin coating of protective oil was burning, and the casings were flickering like candles.

Stepping through the smoke, he headed toward the officers' wardroom. He was trying to reach the quarterdeck, his battle station, anxious to get to work and do what he could for the injured. Stumbling into the wardroom, he was overcome by the noxious smoke of the gray paint burning off the bulkheads. The room was filled with a red haze. In one corner, a man was trying to beat out a fire burning in a pile of rags on the floor. Barely able to see, Haynes felt his way along the hot bulkheads with his burned hands, trying to find a way out toward the stern. Then he tripped over a chair, grabbed at the air, and collapsed into a sitting position.

He looked around the room. He was dying now, and he knew it. In spite of his fear, he had no desire to move farther, to safety. He slumped over, feeling nothing.

Looming over him suddenly was a person—another officer, equally dazed, who screamed, "My God, I'm fainting," then tripped over the chair that had waylaid Haynes. The officer— Haynes couldn't identify him—fell across his legs and came to rest in his lap.

Instantly Haynes stood up, as if waking from a bad dream. He had no idea where he was. The unconscious officer tumbled to the floor, and Haynes stepped over him, hearing a voice in a corner of the room calling out, "Open a porthole! For crissakes, somebody open a porthole!"

A porthole? Yes! That might be a good idea. The notion wormed its way into the doctor's consciousness as he lurched across the room, bumping into furniture. Finding one open, Haynes jammed his head through. The relief was instant; he drew in the humid night air with deep, invigorating breaths. Then, looking down, he saw the gaping hole in the ship's side, and a steady stream of debris exiting it.

Something wet slapped him in the face. It was a rope. It occurred to him that he might be able to wiggle out the porthole and climb the line up the side of the ship to safety. It was not an easy move, especially given his shoulder, which was killing him, and his aching hands. But it was the only way out. He would have to try.

The doctor grabbed the rim of the porthole. First he stuck his right arm and shoulder through and kicked with his feet, like a man swimming in air. This eased him through the opening enough so that he could then squeeze his left arm through. He could now see the sea roaring below. Salt spray mixed with oil splashed up onto his face, and he tasted the putrid tang. Carefully, he twisted around so that he was lying on his back in the porthole, then eased himself into a seated position.

He gripped the line. The pain in his hands was excruciating. Looking up, he could see a climb of about five feet to the deck above. He gritted his teeth and began pulling, rising hand over hand. As he neared the top, the screaming from the quarterdeck grew louder. He hoisted himself to the lifelines and stepped through them.

The scene was horrifying: spread before him were several dozen wounded boys in various stages of delirium, some burned beyond recognition. Several were walking about in a daze, clothes scorched from their bodies, hair smoking. One man held up his arms, and Haynes saw the burned flesh hanging down in ghostly streamers. Walking closer, he saw that this was the very same officer who earlier had asked him to play a hand of bridge. A light breeze picked up the streamers of flesh, and they fluttered behind the man like wings. "Don't touch me! Don't touch me!" he was yelling.

Do something—do anything, Haynes thought. But what? These men needed a hospital—many of them, he saw, would shortly die from their wounds. During abandon ship drills, the wounded had been instructed to gather on the quarterdeck, and Haynes saw that his pharmacist's mate, John Schmueck, had pulled some cots from one of the hangars and was lifting those who could be moved onto them. He'd also found a first aid box. When Haynes joined him, Schmueck handed over a stethoscope and a packet of morphine syrettes. The boys were in such bad shape that Haynes quickly began shooting them up with the painkiller without asking questions or performing even cursory examinations.

When he started to run out of morphine and then gauze bandages, he ordered a sailor to retrieve some supplies from the sick bay. The sailor ran to the ladder at the end of the quarterdeck, took one look down, and sprinted back to Haynes. "There ain't no sick bay," he shouted. Water was rising up the passage. An officer rushed up to Haynes's side. "You better get some life vests on these men, Doc!" he screamed through the smoke.

Dropping their syringes and rolls of bandages, Haynes and Schmueck ran across the deck and up a ladder to the next deck, which led to the number-one smokestack and several gun mounts. Here, boys were cutting down life vests and passing them out to a constant flow of men. Haynes grabbed as many as he could, and then he and Schmueck ran back down the ladder to their writhing patients.

Haynes approached the burned man with the wings for skin. As he loosely tied the canvas straps around the man, he kept telling him, "I have to do this. I have to do this. Oh Christ, I have to do this." The man screamed as Haynes pulled the vest snug. And then Haynes turned his attention to the next wounded man. Working steadily by the weak light of an intermittent moon, he tried his best as his heart broke.

What happened next was almost too much to bear, but he watched without averting his eyes. The hangar was by now filled with cots containing patients, and as the ship lurched to starboard, these men began sliding down the deck—first one at a time, then in groups. Gaining speed, they crashed into the water. Haynes watched as one man wearing a leg cast clawed at the air and then sank without a sound.

The helpless doctor crawled up the quarterdeck, which by now was listing at about sixty degrees, and grabbed at the life-lines. Nearby, about twenty steps away, a life raft and floater net were fastened to the bulkhead. The latter, made of heavy twine, was edged with thick cork floats. The weight of the net and the raft bore down toward the starboard rail, away from him, and he could lift neither. He was panicked, thinking of the lives he might save if he could free them both. But he couldn't. There was nothing left to do but leave the ship.

He started slowly walking down the gray hull, amid a frightened crowd of boys, their screams and shouts rising and falling like a stunned choir's. After about fifteen steps, Haynes reached the bulbous keel. There was nothing but blackness before him. Here and there, little bouquets of flame twisted on the water.

And then Haynes jumped.

Quickly, he began stroking away. When he turned to look back, the stern of the ship was pointing almost straight up at the sky. He saw boys standing motionless on one of the giant, stilled propellers on the port side, like figurines perched atop a beastly flower made of brass—riding the ship into the sea.

AS the *Indy* sank, distress signals giving her longitude and latitude positions were broadcast on frequencies monitored by ships at sea and onshore stations. Radioman J. J. Moran had entered radio shack 1 after the torpedoing, and begun keying out messages. XRAY VICTOR MIKE LOVE, read one, WE HAVE BEEN HIT BY TORPEDOES. NEED IMMEDIATE ASSISTANCE.

It seemed doubtful that there was power enough to successfully transmit these pleas for help. In fact, he was working with a dead key. Radio shack 1, normally used to send messages, had borne the brunt of the second torpedo. The cables connecting the transmitters to the transmitting keys had been severed. Inside the shack, the heavy radio equipment rocked in its stanchions. One of the bulky transmitters tipped forward and crashed onto the deck.

Radio shack 2, located several hundred feet away, near the stern, under the number 2 smokestack, had remained up and running after the hit. All the lights were on, and the room was crowded with about fifteen radio crew members.

Radio technician Jack Miner—fresh from Yale University and nine months of rigorous training in radio and radar electronics—had only been aboard the *Indy* two weeks. Miner entered radio shack 2 shortly after the torpedoing to find his superior officer, chief radio electrician L. T. Woods, trying to improvise sending a signal on equipment that wasn't normally meant for the job. Woods grabbed Miner by the shoulders and positioned him squarely in front of one of the transmitters. It was black, about as big as a refrigerator, and filled with hundreds of foot-long vacuum tubes. Woods ordered Miner to warm up this transmitter, then went to work on one nearby, which operated on another frequency.

Once Miner had warmed up his equipment, he watched as Woods found a solution to the problem. Sticking out from the front of Woods's transmitter was a toggle resembling a light switch, and Woods knew that if he flipped it up and down, he could send a series of binary signals—on-off, on-off—similar to the keying of the telegraph pad. Because the switch didn't automatically spring back once it had been pressed down, Woods had to flip it in a staccato series of clicks.

Miner was amazed by Woods's calmness. He watched the red, hair-thin needle in the meter monitor jump with each flip of the toggle switch. This meant that power was circling through the transmitter and traveling from the cables to the antennae. Woods keyed for about two minutes, clicking out the SOS and the ship's coordinates.

The crew was so intent on the work that they completely lost track of the ship's increasingly starboard list. When Miner broke himself away from the red-needle trance, he realized that the radio shack was heeled on its side at a steep angle. He and Woods kept falling downward into the machinery. Miner knew that if the room tipped any more, the two of them would be doing push-ups against the bulkhead. Woods finally yelled, "Okay, abandon ship!"

Miner stepped out of the room to find the port rail pointing up at the sky. Shit, he thought, he was on the ship's low side; he remembered from boot camp that he had to get off the ship from the higher rail. Leaving from the low side meant risking having the *Indy* fall on top of him if he didn't swim away fast enough, and it made him more vulnerable to the suction's tendrils the ship would create as it sank. As a sailor crabwalked past him heading for the port rail, Miner grabbed his legs and cried out, "Let me pull up where you are!" But the panicked sailor kicked at Miner's hands and knocked him free. He went tumbling down the deck and sailed over the top of the lifelines, which were just inches from the water.

Suddenly he was surrounded by darkness, as if the ship had rolled over on top of him. He thrust his hands up and yelled, "No!" He'd surfaced with his head in a metal mop bucket. Miner couldn't believe it. He almost had to laugh: *The whole Pacific Ocean, and I come up in a bucket!* He chucked it aside. And then he began swimming, hard. He was confident that a distress message had left the ship, and he told himself that rescue had to be on its way.

IN fact, in a radio shack on the island of Leyte, about 650 miles to the west, the message had gotten through. It was received by a sailor named Clair B. Young, on security duty near the sleeping quarters of one Commodore Jacob Jacobson, the ranking officer of the Leyte naval operating base at Tacloban.

Sometime after midnight, a messenger arrived at the post with a dispatch. Young read the message by flashlight and quickly realized that it needed to be brought to the commodore's immediate attention. The message announced that the USS *Indianapolis* had been torpedoed, and gave her co-ordinate positions. Young hurried inside Jacobson's hut, which was perched on a hill overlooking Leyte Harbor.

Jacobson was asleep under an umbrella of mosquito netting. Young turned his flashlight on the commodore's face and announced, "I have a radio message for you, sir." Jacobson roused himself and, rising on one elbow, read the message by the flashlight's beam.

"Do you have a reply, sir?" Young finally asked.

"No reply at this time," the man said. "If any further messages are received, notify me at once." He sent Young away. Confused, the sailor returned to his post. No effort was made either to confirm or to deny the SOS's legitimacy.[*]

A second message was also received at Leyte, according to a sailor named Donald Allen. Allen was serving as a jeep driver for the acting commander of the Philippine Sea Frontier, Commodore Norman Gillette. From his office in Tolosa, twelve miles south of Tacloban, Gillette oversaw all naval operations on the island.

Shortly after midnight on July 30, a radioman in the officer of the day's Quonset hut, where Allen was standing guard duty, announced that he had just received a distress message from the *Indy* that listed her coordinates. In response, an officer on duty then dispatched two fast, oceangoing navy tugs from the Leyte harbor, bound for the site of the sinking.

At the time, Commodore Gillette himself was playing bridge on the nearby island of Samar, north of Leyte, with a group of officers. According to Allen, later that night, upon hearing that the tugs had been dispatched without his authority, Gillette recalled them to the harbor, even though they had completed about seven

---

[*] Several days later, Young would notice that the *Indy* had been assigned a berth in the Leyte harbor. He would notice as well that she hadn't yet shown up in that berth. Remembering the radio message, he was puzzled but said nothing because, as he later explained, he knew that other people were aware of the SOS, too. In other words, as a lowly enlisted sailor, he felt his hands were tied and that his opinion would matter little.

hours of the twenty-one-hour cruise. No further investigation was made to determine if indeed a ship was sinking.

Finally, a third message was received aboard a landing craft in the Leyte harbor. A sailor named Russell Hetz was on watch when the ship's radio room received an SOS dispatch from a ship claiming to be the USS *Indianapolis*, and then, eight and a half minutes later, Hetz's ship received a duplicate message. The radio crew tried contacting the *Indy* but couldn't get a response. Hetz's vessel forwarded the message "thru chanels [*sic*]" (presumably to the Leyte naval operating base), but it was ignored.*

The prevailing protocol within naval command was that messages that couldn't be confirmed by a reply were to be disregarded as pranks. Such responses were more or less pro forma at this point in the war. The Japanese forces, hoping to confuse U.S. intelligence and draw out search vessels, had made a habit of broadcasting bogus distress signals. Earlier in the war, such a message might have been investigated, but tonight it was written off as a potentially deadly move in the war game.

SHORTLY after the distress calls were sent, Captain McVay found himself alone, leaning against a bulkhead near the port rail. He debated the merits of going down with the ship and considered the immense guilt that he would feel if he were one of the few

---

* Clair Young's account didn't come to light until 1955. That year, after reading a *Los Angeles Times* story and a subsequent *Saturday Evening Post* article about the sinking, Young was surprised to learn that no record existed of anyone receiving the *Indy*'s SOS. Young wrote to the Navy Department, which replied that the *Post* story, in particular, was "an account of an individual survivor, and not sponsored in all its facts and conclusions by the U.S. Navy." Russell Hetz and Donald Allen made their recollections public in 1998/1999, as the survivors were working in Congress to exonerate Captain McVay.

to survive. He also dreaded the drilling he knew he'd face from naval command once he was back on shore. A captain's primary responsibility is his ship's well-being. McVay understood that, ultimately, he was to blame for the screaming and moaning he heard rising in the night. Yet the sinking had been so quick that he still couldn't understand it. All the normal response systems had collapsed almost immediately. It was all like a nightmare he couldn't wake from.

He climbed onto the rail and stood perched above the Pacific. Well, he thought, this is the end of me. Without warning, he was brushed off the ship by a tall wave moving along the submerging rails. Looking up from the water, he could see a propeller overhead, and it looked as if the ship might fall on top of him. And then he started swimming through the hot, spilled oil, feeling it burn the back of his neck. He heard a swishing sound, and when he turned, his ship was gone.

I T would later be estimated that 300 men died immediately during the torpedoing and subsequent explosions. Close to 900 made it off the ship.

The boys surrounded the sinking ship in dog-paddling throngs as the *Indy* shook with more explosions and belched fire from her split deck. Since the torpedoes hit, she had plowed ahead for nearly two miles, the forward part of the ship increasingly submerged, and now, in this final moment, she had slowed to about three knots, or three and a half miles per hour. The boys watched with horrified fascination as the ship finally stood straight on end and paused, trembling—the stern pointed directly at the sky— then began to sink, slowly at first, then picking up speed, drawn suddenly into the deep by the nose. Within fifteen seconds, the entire bulk of the ship disappeared. All that remained was a wide swath of debris, about half the length of a football field, boiling with foam. The foam itself hissed, like an immense swarm of bees.

There were no birds in the sky, no wind; only the lapping of the noxious stew of seawater and fuel oil against kapok life vests. There were no stars, just the occasional flash of a crescent moon, like a needle of bone threading its way through a flying curtain of cloud. At times, the exhausted boys floated in complete darkness, unable to discern any horizon at all, the sea rising and falling in heavy swells. At other moments, the boys were lit by a ghostly silver light. The living prayed out loud while the dying screamed.

Beneath the boys, beneath their kicking feet, the ship was falling as if in slow motion, its bow aimed at the bottom of the sea. A porthole or two still glowed from within, the last flickering remnants of the numerous fires raging through her compartments. At some point, the pressure became more than the ship could bear, and the *Indy* began self-destructing under her own weight. Air chambers, bulkheads, gas tanks, and boilers—anything that hadn't exploded—now belched, releasing more gas and debris into the diving ship's slipstream.

Completely submerged, the ship let loose one last tremendous explosion, a resounding *whumpfff*, and the shock waves jellied the warm, black water.

In her final seconds, she reached a terminal velocity of as much as thirty-six feet per second, or about twenty-five miles per hour, just slightly slower than her best flank speed during the run from Hunters Point. She was falling in three and a half miles of water, some of the deepest on the planet, and it took nearly five minutes for her to reach the bottom, a place so remote and dark and cold that in the history of the world no light had ever shone there. As she slammed into the ocean floor in a giant cloud of silt, her steel hull broke into two pieces and gradually rocked to a halt.

It had taken only twelve minutes for the USS *Indianapolis* to vanish.

M^CCOY could feel this last explosion reverberating in his bones, his gut. He was swimming harder than he'd ever swum in his life, trying desperately to flee the ship as she plummeted to the bottom of the sea.

As he swam, he felt something reach out and grab his left leg and tug off his shoe. And then it jerked him backward in his swimming stroke, pulling him underwater, dragging him down deep. The last thing he remembered before blacking out was the rush of water past his face and the sensation that his eyes were ready to pop under the increasing pressure.

When he snapped back to consciousness, he found himself shooting to the surface at great speed, like a man in an express elevator. He was not in an elevator, though. He was in an air bubble, a huge one, and its dry jaws were clamped around the lower half of his body, leaving his head and shoulders sticking out as he rocketed upward.

He erupted with such force that he rose three feet out of the water. With a splash, he fell back into a black world of screaming men. All around him, the sea was littered with crates of potatoes, ammunition cans, stray life vests, and dead bodies.

He looked around and knew he had one decision to make: *Am I gonna live, or will I die?*

One year after its commissioning, the USS *Indianapolis* leaves the Philadelphia Navy Yard, June 1933. *AP/Wide World Photos*

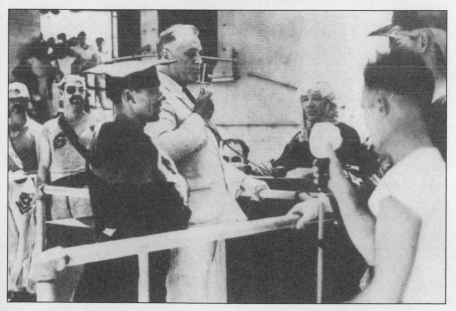

On his way back from South America in 1936, President Roosevelt participates in his ship of state's equator-crossing festivities. Here, he appears before King Neptune's Court, made up of *Indianapolis* crew members. *AP/Wide World Photos*

Burial at sea aboard the *Indianapolis*, August 1942. Tipped into the sea following a twenty-one-gun salute, the body was weighted by a forty-pound ammunition shell; the draped flag was later sent home to the boy's family. *National Archives*

Admiral Raymond Spruance (front row, fifth from left) with his staff aboard the *Indianapolis*, circa 1945. Widely regarded as one of the navy's most brilliant military planners, Spruance commanded the Fifth Fleet from the *Indianapolis*. *Naval History and Heritage Command*

Admiral Ernest King (center) visits the Mariana Islands on board the *Indianapolis*, July 18, 1944, with (left) Admiral Chester W. Nimitz and Admiral Spruance. *Naval History and Heritage Command*

Indianapolis officers on deck in 1945 (front row, left to right): Cmdr. Johns Janney, navigator; Captain McVay; Cmdr. Joseph Flynn, executive officer; Cmdr. Glen de Grave, engineering officer; (back row, left to right): unknown; Lt. Cmdr. K. C. Moore, first lieutenant; Lt. Cmdr. Lewis Haynes, medical officer; Lt. Cmdr. Earl O'Dell Henry, dental officer; Lt. Cmdr. Charles Hayes. De Grave was put ashore at Pearl Harbor prior to the sinking; of the rest of the group, only McVay and Haynes survived. *Courtesy of the collections of Bill Van Daalen and Lewis Haynes*

ABOVE LEFT: Dr. Lewis Haynes, pictured before his tenure aboard the USS *Indianapolis*, circa 1942. At one point during the war, Haynes went thirty-nine months without leave. *Courtesy of the collection of Dr. Lewis Haynes*

ABOVE RIGHT: Marine Corps captain Edward L. Parke stands at attention on the *Indianapolis* quarterdeck as Captain McVay presents him with a Silver Star, awarded for bravery during the battle for Saipan in 1944. *Courtesy of the collection of Giles McCoy*

Commodore Norman Gillette, acting commander for the Philippine Sea Frontier at Leyte, in 1944, ten months before the *Indianapolis* was sunk. Both he and his subordinate Alfred Granum fought the letters of reprimand they received from naval command after McVay's court-martial. *AP/Wide World Photos*

Commodore Jacob H. Jacobson, commandant, Naval Operating Base at Leyte, did not deem it his responsibility to monitor the arrival of the *Indianapolis* at Leyte, and his officers took no action when the ship was discovered to be overdue in port. Jacobson was not reprimanded for his decision, but his subordinates Lt. Cmdr. Sancho and Lt. Gibson were. *National Archives*

Captain Oliver Naquin, Surface Operations Officer, was privy to enemy Japanese submarine activity on the Peddie/Leyte route, as well as the sinking of the USS *Underhill*, yet he failed to warn McVay of possible danger. Although cited in the Navy Inspector General report, Naquin was not censured in the aftermath of the sinking. *AP/Wide World Photos*

July 10, 1945: the USS *Indianapolis* at Mare Island, California, shortly before her final voyage. The ship would be sunk nearly three weeks later after delivering to Tinian Island the components of "Little Boy," the atomic bomb that would be dropped on Hiroshima. *Courtesy of the collection of Giles McCoy*

The *I-58* was part of the Tamon group, the largest and most technologically advanced of Japan's submarines. By mid-1945, however, they were not considered a significant threat, which may have led to a false sense of security within U.S. Naval Command and to the July 30 torpedoing of the *Indianapolis*. *Naval History and Heritage Command*

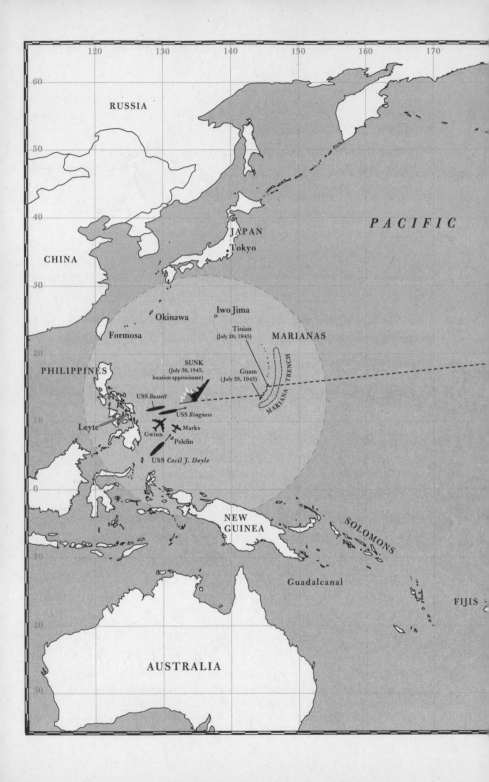

RUSSIA

PACIFIC

JAPAN
Tokyo

CHINA

Iwo Jima

Okinawa

Tinian
(July 26, 1945)

MARIANAS

Formosa

SUNK
(July 30, 1945,
location approximate)

Guam
(July 28, 1945)

PHILIPPINES

MARIANA TRENCH

USS *Bassett*

USS *Ringness*

Leyte

Marks

Gwinn

Peleliu

USS *Cecil J. Doyle*

NEW
GUINEA

SOLOMONS

Guadalcanal

FIJIS

AUSTRALIA

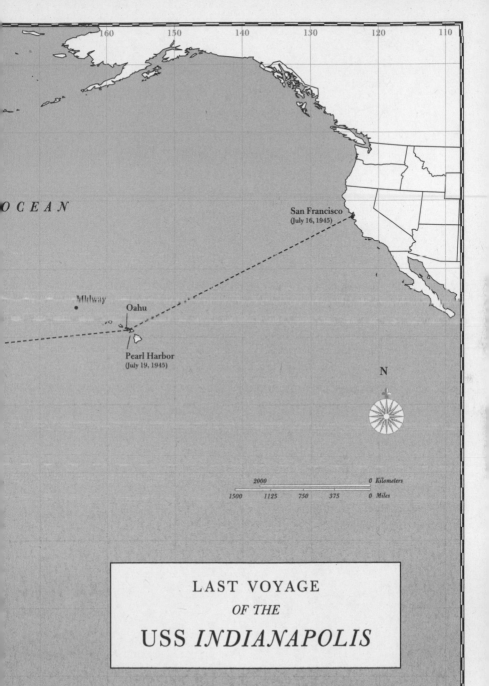

160 150 140 130 120 110

OCEAN

San Francisco
(July 16, 1945)

Midway

Oahu

Pearl Harbor
(July 19, 1945)

N

2000   0 Kilometers
1500   1125   750   375   0 Miles

LAST VOYAGE
OF THE
USS *INDIANAPOLIS*

© James Sinclair

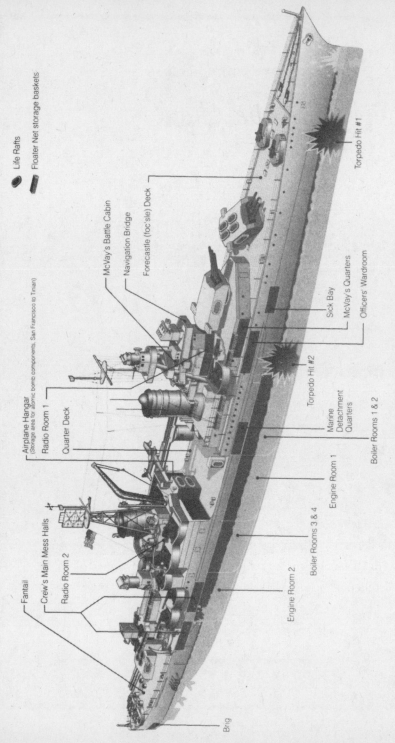

Life Rafts

Floater Net storage baskets

McVay's Battle Cabin

Navigation Bridge

Forecastle (foc'sle) Deck

Torpedo Hit #1

Sick Bay

McVay's Quarters

Officers' Wardroom

Torpedo Hit #2

Marine Detachment Quarters

Boiler Rooms 1 & 2

Engine Room 1

Boiler Rooms 3 & 4

Engine Room 2

Airplane Hangar
(Storage area for atomic bomb components, San Francisco to Tinian)

Radio Room 1

Quarter Deck

Fantail

Crew's Main Mess Halls

Radio Room 2

Brig

Cutaway of the USS *Indianapolis*. Illustration by *Tim Barrons*

CHAPTER SIX

Hope Afloat

———

What did I think about when I was in the water?
I fantasized about meeting my parents at a dim roadside bar
in the north woods of Wisconsin to share the story over a few very
cold beers. I bargained with God. As the days dragged on,
I thought less and less while I dreamed more and more.

—JACK MINER,
radio technician second-class, USS *Indianapolis*

Day One
Monday, July 30, 1945

As they floated through the inky murk of the night, even the most lucid of the *Indy*'s survivors found themselves in an extreme state of disorientation. Without the ship as a point of reference, they had little idea of where they were headed, or how far they had traveled, or how many of their crewmates had made it off alive.

In fact, they were floating now in a slightly southwesterly course, headed in the general direction of Borneo rather than toward their sunken ship's intended destination of Leyte, which lay approximately 650 miles ahead nearly due west. Behind them, maybe another 650 miles to the east, was Guam, their previous port of call. They were drifting through the dead middle of a no-man's-land, a pocket of ocean that spanned some 10,000 square miles.

And they were spread along a roughly three-mile-long line that was lengthening—and widening—by the minute. During the first several hours, the majority of the men had collected in several groups, all scattering in different directions. Each was separated by about a mile of an oily, pitching sea. Initially, no group knew for certain that any other existed, but as time passed, the scared boys would find themselves separated from one cluster and then united with another. Gradually, commands of sorts were evolving.

Dr. Haynes, Captain Parke, and Father Conway found themselves in charge of the largest group of survivors, which consisted solely of boys in life vests and some in inflatable life belts; Haynes

141

would come to think of them as his "swimmers." Along with Parke and Conway, he set about collecting the boys, shouting orders that all sailors within earshot should swim to him. Ed Brown and Bob Gause, hearing the doctor's high-pitched cry, moved toward the sound. Gause was in serious pain, having jumped forty feet from the stern of the ship before she went down, only to hit the massive steel rudder. He didn't think he'd broken any bones, but he could barely swim.

Many of the boys were bleeding, vomiting, and overcome with diarrhea. Quite a few had broken legs and arms; some had fractured backs and skulls. Those too seriously damaged by the explosions had already drowned. Haynes, wearing only his cotton pajama pants and life vest, paddled through the wailing crowd, trying to help. Haynes knew that the boys, when in good health, could live for maybe thirty days without food and perhaps seven without water. But the severely weakened and wounded among them, he guessed, had only hours—some, if lucky, maybe a day or two—before they would be dead. Rescue had to come soon.

About half of the 900 survivors had gotten off the ship with either a life vest or an inflatable life belt. These latter proved worthless as the fuel oil ate into the seams and they started to leak. The boys wearing them began to sink and, if they were too weak to swim, to drown. Those without belts or life vests dog-paddled frantically about, keeping lookouts: whenever a boy died, he was flocked by several others eager to take his vest.

Conway and Haynes spent the bleak early-morning hours swimming back and forth among these terrified crew members, sometimes dragging loners back to the growing mass using an awkward, modified sidestroke. At one point, Parke spotted what looked like a blinking red light. He froze. "Nobody signal back!" he shouted in a hoarse whisper. The marine worried that the light was from the sub that had sunk them. If it found them, they were dead men. They'd be machine-gunned for sure. Then the red light faded. Had it even been real? the boys wondered.

The second-largest group was led by ensign Harlan Twible and chief engineer Richard Redmayne. It numbered about 325 men, most of whom had jumped from the *Indy* after the Haynes group but before McVay and McCoy; unlike the swimmers, the Twible-Redmayne group had left the ship from the flooded rails of the starboard side, which was awash with precious lifesaving equipment. Most of these boys had been lucky enough to grab hold of something: among them, they had five floater nets, four rafts, and a smattering of random supplies. These included some malted milk tablets (meant to slake thirst), biscuits in watertight tins, and a few wooden beakers of potable water. Four of the five floater nets were piled with the wounded, while the fifth was commandeered as a rest station for the healthy. Each net held about fifty men, none very comfortably (this was twice the recommended number). Every shifting body upset the balance of the whole, causing the boys to knock heads and slip under the waves bucking beneath them. It was miserable.

Captain McVay found himself paddling alone through the dark, and it unnerved him. He didn't want to believe that he'd been the only man to survive the sinking, and yet, above the slap and slosh of the waves in his face, he heard no shouts; none of his boys drifted out of the gloom to meet him. At this same time, about a mile away, Private McCoy, clutching a life vest he hadn't had time to put on, was bobbing on the oily tide and vomiting like crazy. He, too, didn't know where the hell he was.

All the groups were traveling in a prevailing westerly equatorial current that was pushing ahead at a steady pace of about one mile an hour. The northeast trade winds were also blowing westerly at an average of 3 knots, or 3.5 miles an hour. The rate of drift was such that the boys would average about twenty-four miles per day. This put the nearest body of land, an island called Mindanao, about three weeks ahead of them.

However, the factor that truly determined each group's direction and speed of travel was something called the Leeway Effect. This phenomenon involves the relationship between exposed body surface, ocean current, and wind. For instance, if a survivor had more of his body submerged in the water than exposed to the wind, the current acted upon him to a greater degree than the trade winds. This meant that those strapped and sunk up to their chests in life vests were typically more affected by the current, while those sitting high in rafts were more forcefully pushed and tugged about by the breezes.

Almost none of the boys adrift knew anything about survival at sea. All were without sails or means to make sails. Only a few of the twelve rafts had functional paddles. No one aboard any craft had a compass. As the boys drifted through the predawn darkness, the temperature was already rising by the hour. No one knew what would happen next, yet most remained hopeful that sometime in the next forty-eight hours this unbelievable ordeal would be over. They believed that when the *Indy* failed to show in Leyte at its scheduled time of arrival the next day, search parties would be dispatched. They told themselves and one another that rescue was imminent. They told themselves they could be in Leyte in less than two days—and out of the water before that. They prayed aloud for this.

RELEASED from the giant air bubble and coughing up stomachfuls of seawater, Private McCoy cursed and struggled to regain his wits. He knew that he was a marine, and that he was expected to be tougher than any of the raw navy kids. If he quit, what would they do?

He tied himself tightly into his life vest and tried his best to assess his situation. He figured that a distress message must have gone out from the ship, but he couldn't imagine that planes would be arriving anytime soon. Up ahead, he could make out a life raft and decided it was a far better place to spend this Monday morning than drifting alone in his life vest. As he prepared to swim to the raft, a shipmate slid up to him, completely taking him by surprise. The boy was in bad shape. He didn't have a life vest, and he was straddling a gunpowder can about the size of a paint bucket. It was the only thing keeping the kid's ass off the cold ocean floor.

McCoy looked at him. "We're gonna have to get you a life vest."

"I know."

"Well, we'll just wait for something to float by."

"Where you headed?"

"Over to that yonder raft."

"No, you stay here," said the boy. "They'll be picking us up any minute."

"Like hell." McCoy, who wished for a moment that he'd let the kid keep believing, took off. He tried stroking through the oil-covered sea to the raft, but the film was at least two inches thick. He could barely push through it in his sodden life vest. *Shit*. He struggled back to the boy, spitting out oil.

"I can't make it," the boy said.

"I see that." At that moment, a dead body drifted out of the darkness and continued past them, as if on a mission of its own. McCoy couldn't tell who it was; the face was smeared with oil. He paused, then gingerly reached out, pulled the corpse close, and removed the dead man's life vest. Then he gave the body a gentle push. It sank beneath the waves and was gone.

McCoy handed the vest to the sailor, and tried to figure out the right next move. He could hear yelling from the direction of the raft; it sounded like a group of guys. "Over here, over here!" they kept shouting. "We got a raft!"

McCoy thought they sounded like they wanted company, and he didn't blame them. As his legs dangled free beneath the surface, he felt that at any second something was about to grab at them again. *To hell with it*, he thought, and tore off his life vest and tossed it to the boy. Then he took an enormous gulp of air and started swimming.

McCoy dove deep and bobbed up every ten feet or so to breathe. He figured it was about 100 yards to the raft, but it was tough going. By the time he'd drawn close, he was gasping and nearly unconscious. His arms flailed until he finally grabbed hold of a line hanging from the craft's side. He hung there, choking on the oil and staring at his hand, as if disembodied from it. Slowly, he watched it open and release the line. Then he began to sink.

It was at this moment that he felt somebody grab him by the hair and yank him aboard. He rolled over, vomiting, and then looked at the horrific-looking collection of boys before him. McCoy was shocked to see one man so badly burned that the skin was stripped from his arms. The boy's pain was so intense that no sound was coming from his open mouth as he stared up at the sky.

McCoy stuck his finger down his own throat and started vomiting again, attempting to purge his system of the fuel oil and seawater. Inhaling the oil's fumes was as bad as swallowing it, and he worried that his lungs were going to collapse.

On the raft were four other boys, all vomiting as well. The raft itself was a six-by-ten-foot rectangle of balsa wood stretched with gray canvas. It was already wrecked. Half the bow was gone, and the wood latticework floor was in pieces. Its floor was suspended off the frame on lines that let it hang about five feet beneath the ocean's surface. McCoy wasn't so much sitting on the thing as he was standing up in it, his arms draped over the side.

The morning's waves raised the broken craft about fifteen feet every ten seconds, then dropped it out from under the boys with its passing. The abrupt motion kept snapping McCoy's head backward as if he was being punched again and again. His legs and arms ached; he felt like he'd been kicked in the chest. The waves were also making some of the boys feel seasick, compounding their oil-induced nausea. McCoy looked around and decided that he'd done a very stupid thing. This was a very bad place to be.

Nobody said anything; the screaming had stopped. McCoy couldn't at first identify any of the boys because they were all smeared with fuel oil. He could barely remember his own name. Gradually, as he wiped the oil from his eyes, he took in the strange scene. In one corner was a tall, rawboned youth by the name of Bob Brundige, a cotton farmer's son from Tennessee who was maybe nineteen. He silently eyed McCoy from behind his black mask of oil. McCoy simply could not bear to look at his baleful eyes.

In another corner of the raft was a thin, soft-spoken sailor from North Carolina named Felton Outland, eighteen and one of the ship's anti-aircraft gunners. Felton had walked off the ship without even getting his hair wet. But then, like McCoy, he'd been sucked deep underwater by the vacuum of the sinking ship—he'd nearly drowned. He was fully dressed, in a long-sleeved denim shirt and dungarees, his white pillbox sailor hat stuffed in one of his pockets. He appeared unhurt.

Also aboard the raft were nineteen-year-old Ed Payne, a farmer's son from Kentucky, and Willis Gray, about twenty-eight, from Chicago. Payne and Gray, shivering in the pitching raft, were dressed only in T-shirts and dungarees. Both had scrambled from their bunks in enlisted men's country and didn't have time to fully dress before jumping off the ship.*

"All right, loosen up," McCoy announced. "We're gonna get picked up in the morning just as soon as they find us missing at Leyte. Okay? So let's keep a sunny side up to this situation!"

Outland pitched in to spread some cheer, but Brundige only grunted. Payne and Gray were busy getting sicker.

Tied to this raft were three more, each tailing the other on ten-foot lines, making a total of seventeen boys in the group. In the raft immediately behind McCoy's was coxswain Mike Kuryla, who had also nearly drowned in the sinking ship's suction. With every passing wave, all four rafts collided and knocked the boys against the rails, or pitched them forward on

---

* A stoic, gentle man who rarely talked about his experience aboard the *Indy*, Felton Outland did not remember in our interview that Ed Payne was aboard the raft; indeed, he remembered another sailor, a ship's cook named David Kemp, as part of this group. When asked, however, if Payne could have been a fellow rafter—as McCoy insisted he was—Outland assented.

the submerged flooring, where they sunk before shooting up again, spluttering.

Kuryla was retching but looked like he felt better than McCoy. Kuryla had found his raft a half hour earlier, and his shouts had helped lead Payne, Outland, Brundige, and Gray to the relative safety of theirs. Kuryla reached over the side and plucked up what looked like a greasy black ball. Rubbing off the covering, he discovered it was an onion coated in fuel. He tucked it inside his vest for safekeeping.

McCoy was able to scavenge a tin of malted milk tablets from a passing wave. But, rooting around in the raft itself, he found nothing useful whatsoever. He badly wanted to get his hands on a signal mirror or some flares. Tied to the rail of the raft in a rope harness was a wooden water beaker, but it was empty, and McCoy guessed it had never been filled before the ship's hurried departure. Ravenous, McCoy tried eating one of the malted milk tablets, but they just made him more thirsty; his lips and tongue were already dry as a bone.

Clearly, things were going from bad to worse. He resolved to take action: he would clean his pistol. Reaching down into the water inside the raft, he found his holster still attached to the belt on his fatigues. He removed the .45 and held it up in the air, shaking the water from the barrel. McCoy could disassemble and put back together the weapon blindfolded, and that was essentially what he tried to do now. He guessed that he and his raftmates would need it sooner or later to signal a passing plane or a rescue ship.

McCoy told everyone to hold out their hands, then placed a gun part in each outstretched palm. Using his T-shirt, he wiped the oil from the receiver and grip—it was a poor cleaning job, at best. When a tin of petroleum jelly floated by, he snatched it and eagerly greased the action on the pistol.

Kuryla couldn't believe it; this crazy marine was cleaning his gun in the middle of the ocean. McCoy racked a round and announced that the gun was clean. Then he spotted something floating on the horizon—something huge and gray. It was heading directly for them.

"You see that?" he asked Kuryla. McCoy became convinced that it was a ship, and he was certain that it was coming to rescue them. He raised his pistol and fired off a shot. The gun's sound was instantly swallowed by the air. McCoy peered anxiously into the dark, hoping to see a return flash from the ship, some signal he'd been spotted. Nothing—he saw nothing.

"What's wrong with these people!" He racked another round, then fired again.

"Sonofabitch! Why don't they see us!" And then McCoy had an awful thought: What if whatever he was shooting at started shooting back? He suddenly realized that the silhouette might be a sub. Or maybe a Japanese destroyer.* McCoy felt dumber than he'd ever felt in his life. He wondered if he had gone out of his head without even knowing it; he knew he had to keep a close check on his feelings, his actions. He felt like throwing up again.

D̲R. Haynes and his group of boys were on the verge of collapse. Herding them together had been painstaking work, and it seemed to Haynes they would never get everybody rounded up. The tire-

---

* In fact, what they were seeing was the Japanese *I-58* that had sunk the *Indy*. Lieutenant Commander Hashimoto would later explain that he had resurfaced in an attempt to confirm a hit. Unable to find anything, he gave up after an hour.

less efforts of Father Conway and Captain Parke aside, the boys were close to scattering in all directions.

"Count off!" Captain Parke bellowed. Parke, the boys had always said aboard ship, might give them hell, but he also gave them credit for their efforts as military men. Slowly at first, they began sounding off, until the number grew to 400. To Haynes, it was an amazing spectacle of command and endurance on Parke's part. The marine then ordered the boys to tie their life jackets together to keep them from drifting apart. It worked. Instinctively, each one wrapped his legs and arms around the boy in front of him. In this way, each one could also lie back on the chest of the boy behind him. Together, they drifted like this, looking up at a blackness that had no shape and that felt nearly suffocating.

In the center of this human ring, Dr. Haynes floated in his life vest. Like most of the men, his face was covered in oil. Many of the sailors didn't recognize him. Soon the cries started out, "Hey, anybody seen a doctor? We need a doctor here!"

Haynes considered the request. He felt curiously ambivalent about announcing himself. He knew it would be much easier to hang back, to slink away into the crowd and shirk the responsibility of treating boys who were really too sick to be helped. The prospect of facing the misery around him without the aid of any medical supplies filled him with dread.

Then he heard a voice: *Your job is to make people better.* It was as if his mother were whispering in his ear. He hadn't thought of her much lately. Now he pictured her with his father in their comfortable house on Fifth Street in Manistee, Michigan. He wondered if she was looking at the lake, and whether it was sunny there. His father would be at his dental practice, filing away on some farmer's teeth. When Haynes snapped out of the reverie, he realized what he needed to do.

A few boys were vomiting so violently that they were actually doing somersaults in the water. Trying to keep calm, Haynes called out: "Here! Right here! Where is the sick sailor?" And then he moved into the throng. About a dozen sailors were holding a body aloft, an incredible feat of strength considering they were all treading water furiously to stay afloat beneath the added weight.

The man in question was in terrible shape. His eyes had been burned away. The flesh on his hands was gone, and what remained were bare tendons. The boys held him in an effort to keep these wounds out of the stinging bath of salt water.

Haynes recognized the man as his good friend and liberty buddy, gunnery officer Stanley Lipski. Miraculously, Lipski had made his way blind from the quarterdeck, off the ship, and into the water. Haynes knew that Lipski's pain must be intolerable—he himself could barely look at his old friend, who was moaning softly. Stanley, he knew, was one tough bird; Haynes also understood that he didn't have long to live. Reluctantly, he turned away to those he could actually help.

The horizon glowed with a faint bloom of sunrise. Dr. Haynes prayed that daylight would comfort the boys.

FLOATING to the northeast of both Haynes and McCoy, Captain McVay was formulating his own plan for survival. Other than the oil in his eyes, he was neither injured nor in other physical distress. He was actually in remarkably good shape. Even his wristwatch was still working perfectly. He was, however, unable to shake the fear that he was the only one to have made it off the ship alive.

Then something nudged him. It was a potato crate. He hopped on top and grasped it between his legs, continuing to scope the horizon. But he still couldn't see any other survivors.

He could hear voices in the distance, though. Two life rafts drifted toward him from the darkness, and he stroked over atop his potato crate. Finding the rafts empty, he climbed aboard one of them and quickly lashed it to the other. Out of the night came a yell: "Help! Anybody out there!"

"Yes! It's the captain here!" Bearing down on the paddle, he rowed ahead to meet three blackened, indistinguishable faces. He pulled a quartermaster named Vincent Allard aboard his own raft, and then hauled the other two sailors into the second.

McVay knew Allard well. At thirty-three, the quartermaster had served on the *Indy* for three years—since the ship's early days of the Aleutian Islands bombardment at the beginning of the Pacific war—under five different captains. A quartermaster served his captain in the daily enforcement of the ship's regulations, and this morning McVay had never been happier to see him.

With Allard were Angelo Galante, twenty, and Ralph Klappa, eighteen: two seamen of the lowest rank. Klappa, in fact, had only come on board the *Indy* in San Francisco. Angelo Galante had been on the ship for just several months. The two boys were true green hands, and McVay feared they were dying. They had apparently swallowed a good deal of salt water and oil, and were vomiting.

Twenty minutes later, some good fortune followed. Out of the early-morning light came another raft. On board was twenty-two-year-old John Spinelli, a cook from New Mexico whose wife had recently given birth to a baby girl. (Spinelli, in fact, had received the order to return to the ship at Mare Island while visiting his wife and new daughter in their hospital room just two days after she was born.) With Spinelli were John Muldoon, a thirty-year-old machinist's mate from New Bedford, Massachusetts, who'd been aboard the *Indy* for over two years; yeoman Otha Havins, twenty-two, and his buddy Jay Glenn, twenty-one, an aviation machinist's mate; and George Kurlick, twenty-two, a fire control man. Kurlick was naked, blanketed only by life vests, but all the others were dressed in their dungarees and denim shirts. And except for the persistent intense stinging in their eyes from the fuel oil, none was seriously injured.

"Boys," McVay said, surveying his motley crew, "is this all that's left of us?" Spinelli didn't have an answer. Only several hours earlier, he'd been playing a little after-hours pinochle with his buddies in the bakeshop, a pan of fresh rolls cooling on the table. And then his world had sunk beneath him. But being in McVay's presence was a huge comfort.

McVay took command of the three rafts, one floater net, and eight sailors—a ragtag flotilla that he intended to lead, nonetheless, with unbending fairness and sturdy naval discipline. "Don't worry," he told the crew, "we will be rescued—don't lose faith. Keep heart."

The words rang hollow; McVay realized that there was no guarantee rescue would come anytime soon. He hoped that the pilots of the tractor planes that he'd requested to meet him for gunnery practice at 6 a.m. on Tuesday, July 31, near Homonhon Island (fifty miles east of Leyte) would report their failure to show.* If they didn't report the ship missing, McVay further reasoned, and if no one had received their SOS, rescue would begin when the *Indy* didn't show up in port at Leyte midday on Tuesday.

With this in mind, he told his group that Thursday seemed the

---

* The tractor planes did not report the *Indy* missing at the appointed hour; it's possible that McVay's request was never carried out.

earliest date they could hope for aid. He confidently announced that it would be ships, not planes, that would find them. "Planes," he explained, "would be flying too high to ever see us."

All the boys, though bone-weary and scared, felt good about their chances.

AT dawn, when the sun launched off the horizon and began its race into the sky, the temperature shot from a nighttime cool of low 80s to over 100 degrees. Just twelve degrees north of the equator, the heat was merciless. The men's exposed heads baked as they squinted in agony and paddled about.

The large group led by Ensign Harlan Twible and Richard Redmayne seemed to have everything it needed to survive—life rafts, floater nets, and food—but lacked cohesion among their ranks. Unlike the group headed by Haynes, Parke, and Father Conway, which was performing as one unit bent on survival, this group was mostly an uneasy collection of alienated souls. Redmayne had been badly burned in the explosions, and although he was an officer, he was not in a position to command.

Ensign Twible tried to compensate, but he was seriously underexperienced. Still, he had taken to heart his Naval Academy training, and he began a close imitation of what he believed an officer's behavior should be. He wasn't trying to fool anyone; he was only trying to keep the men alive and get them organized into some kind of survival plan. Three weeks earlier, he'd been riding a train across the country, freshly graduated from the academy; now more than 300 oil-smeared faces stared back at him as he issued orders. As he told them to tie their life vests together, the blank look in their eyes startled him. Few obeyed.

Then, from within the crowd, a voice said, "You heard the officer. Now do it!" This was Durward Horner, a gunnery captain, one of the old salts who was widely respected by the crew.

Twible spotted one of the sailors holding up a bottle of whiskey. He couldn't believe it—what had the boy been thinking as he struggled to get off the ship? "Toss that out," Twible ordered. "It'll only cause you trouble." The sailor grumpily handed the bottle over and Twible emptied it into the sea.

Jack Miner—minus the bucket that had fallen on his head earlier—was in a daze, but he tried to do as commanded. As Twible was issuing an order to remove shoes so as to swim more easily, Miner looked down and saw something flash beneath his feet. One moment the image was there, and then it was gone. He gave it no more thought.

ABOUT two miles to the south of this group, Dr. Haynes, Captain Parke, and Father Conway were undeterred by the day's scorching heat. One of their boys found a life ring and passed it to Parke, who quickly devised a use for it. Attached to the ring was 200 feet of ship's line. Parke ordered the boys—as many as would fit—to grab hold. As if impelled by an invisible wind, the line began curling around the epicenter of the life ring. With the boys attached, it whirled slowly and in a circular motion, creating a flower of pain, with the most severely wounded caught in the middle.

Captain Parke ordered Haynes into the center among the wounded, while Father Conway paddled the edges, hearing confessions and saying last rites for those too wounded to carry on. About half the boys were naked or dressed only in skivvies, while others wore only a shirt or just their shoes. Some had nothing but a hat. Still, the boys' spirits rose as the day progressed, and they cheerfully cursed their predicament. Having endured the torpedoing, the group was plagued by a strange giddiness. At times, they laughed and shouted over one another's heads like men at a New Year's Eve party; rescue, most were sure, was just a day, maybe two, away.

Around 10 a.m., they unexpectedly drifted free of the vaporous oil slick, and beneath them the sea lit up like an enormous green room. The effect was fantastic. Suddenly they were floating in space, suspended between earth and sky. A complex web of sea life, including giant grouper, man-of-war jellyfish with stinging tentacles, and giant barracudas, twined beneath them.

But the relief was short-lived; the sea also teemed with dozens of probing bacteria and organisms that, as the boys drifted, began gnawing at their flesh. The salt water itself was a caustic brew, consisting of 3.5 percent sodium chloride, and including trace elements of sulphate, magnesium, potassium, bicarbonate, and boric acid. Floating in it was not unlike immersion in a mild acid bath. The boys swallowed small amounts of seawater each time a wave splashed their faces. The high potassium levels in each taste began leaking into their bloodstreams and breaking down their red blood cells, forging the first link in a chain that could, if left unchecked, lead to the onset of anemia and increased physical weakness.

Whenever the boys inhaled any of the salt spray, accidentally aspirating it, it set off what doctors call a "plasma shift" in the lungs. This meant that their lungs were slowly beginning to fill with fluid, the accumulation of which could cause the onset of pulmonary edema; the edema itself would lead to difficulty in breathing, a lowering of the oxygen content in the bloodstream, and finally rapid, irregular heartbeats.

By late morning, the heavy swell dropped, the sea went flat, and the sun began shattering around them in millions of burning medallions across the water. The boys' eyes stung in the glare. For some, the pain was unbearable. Even with their eyes closed, they could still see the sun. Each blink of an eyelid felt like sandpaper dragged over the inflamed cornea. The boys were beginning to suffer the first stages of photophobia.

Dr. Haynes ordered them to tear their clothing in strips and tie them in blindfolds. As they drifted, they now resembled men facing a firing squad. Haynes knew the situation with the sun was bad, but thought it would be controlled if the boys kept their eyes protected. He also noticed that the whites of some of the boys' eyes were swelling from exposure to the salt water. His sense of futility defied his paternal instincts and determination as a doctor. He knew that, by the hour, the boys could turn into physiological time bombs, detonating all around him.

Then he realized that he was no different from the rest.

CAPTAIN McVay and his ragged crew passed Monday morning in relative comfort, all things considered. The nine men hunched down on the edges of their rafts. At some point they discovered that the fuel oil, which had nearly poisoned them, made an excellent sunscreen. McVay ordered them to slather it on any exposed parts of their bodies.

As the day went on, planes buzzed high overhead, some near, some far. In spite of McVay's earlier pronouncement that rescue would in all probability not arrive by air, the planes were a welcome sight and cheered the captain and boys. Whenever one passed, McVay ordered everyone to splash and kick at the water, in a fruitless bid to attract attention. At 1 p.m., McVay spotted what he thought was a twin-engine bomber flying west. He flashed it with a metal signal mirror, but to no avail. At 3 p.m., he saw what he identified as either a B-24 or a B-29 passing to the south. It also failed to respond to the signal mirror. These planes had taken off from Tinian and Okinawa and were almost certainly heading toward the Philippines.

McVay recorded all of these sightings in a makeshift log he crafted out of paper scraps cadged from his crew's wallets. He was determined to carry out his normal duties. He patiently instructed the boys in the use of the signal mirror and the flares. But as more planes passed overhead, these proved of no use. This shocked some of the men, but not the captain.

"It's the same old thing," he announced. "If an aviator doesn't expect to see anything, he doesn't see it. He's too busy flying his plane."

McVay also took an inventory of the boys' rations. He found several cans of Spam and of crackers, a couple of tins of malted milk tablets, a first aid kit, flares, a flare gun, and a fishing kit containing hooks and line. There was enough, he figured, to last ten days at sea. He ordered the crew to stand two-hour watches for rescue planes.

At one point, he spotted a wooden water cask drifting on the tide and hauled it aboard. It was a boon worth its weight in gold, and the boys were overjoyed. Sadly, McVay realized that the wooden keg had cracked. Still, he shook it and heard the jostle of liquid inside. He gingerly lifted it to his lips and sipped. The taste was awful; it contained plain salt water. But sensing how vulnerable the boys were, he lowered the cask and smiled. The water, he told them, was okay, but that they would save it for a time when they really needed a drink. He then encouraged them to keep their eyes peeled for planes.

This was a characteristic moment for the captain. On board the *Indy*, he had once made his reputation with the enlisted men by standing in the sailors' chow line—the officers ate at their own mess—waiting his turn to eat the same "shit on a shingle" served to the lowly seamen. McVay had heard the men complaining about the food; he was determined to taste it himself. After the cook carefully dolloped the slop onto the captain's dented metal tray, McVay sat down and ate. It wasn't terrible. It was mediocre, which in McVay's world may have been an even worse offense. He got up, approached the cooks, and announced: "These men work hard for this ship. You make sure they eat damn well. I don't want to hear any more complaints."

McVay—like Private McCoy and Dr. Haynes floating nearby—was operating on the thinnest fumes of hope. He thought rescue would come. But he was a logical man without illusions. What good would worrying do?

BELOW, drawn up from the deep, perhaps attracted by the booming of the *Indy*'s exploding chambers or lured by the blood trail of the injured and the dead, the boys' greatest fears were coming to life.

By dusk on Monday, hundreds of sharks had encircled them. There were makos, tigers, white-tips, and blues. Rising at the speed of a man at a gentle run, the sharks ascended from the depths of the dark sea to the paler glow of approaching night overhead, toward a sky empty of stars. As the heat of the day tempered into relative cool, the boys, lying in their rafts, hanging from floating nets, and bobbing in life vests, began to feel things bumping from below—nudges and kicks that they mistook for the touch of their comrades treading water.

They nodded off and slept, if their wounds allowed them to rest. They woke often, with a start, staring into the dark, wondering, *Who's there?*

CHAPTER SEVEN

Shark Attack

They stalked for hours, going around and around. And somebody
said, "Those are PT boats!" And another guy said, "No, those
are sharks! It's the wake they make!" Finally, they attacked—they
pulled guys right out of the water. We thrashed, trying to keep 'em
away from us, but they came right into the group. Took the net
and everything right up into the air. Tore guys' limbs off.
The water was bloody.

—GUS KAY,
seaman first-class, USS *Indianapolis*

Day Two
Tuesday, July 31, 1945

THE sharks attacked around dawn on Tuesday.

McCoy looked over his raft's edge and saw them prowling in frenzied schools. Like figures trapped in glass, the huge, gray fish were spiraling to the surface. *Jesus,* he thought, sitting up, *this is getting serious.*

They had begun their attacks late Sunday night, but in the dark, many of the disoriented survivors hadn't really taken notice. Around daybreak on Monday, McCoy had seen a man slumped in his life vest—apparently asleep—suddenly disappear. McCoy waited for the vest to pop back up to the surface, but it never did.

In all likelihood, the sharks now gathered around the boys had been following the *Indy* for days. It is the habit of sharks to track oceangoing vessels and feed on refuse regularly tossed overboard. The *Indy*, made of steel, emitted low-grade electrical currents that may have stimulated and attracted the predators.

Until this point, it seemed, the restless fish had been feeding mostly on the dead, tearing at the bodies as they fell to the ocean floor. Or they had concentrated on lone, straying swimmers. But now the sharks were starting to home in on the large groups that had amassed during the past thirty-six hours. Those sailors who were naked or not fully clothed were at greatest risk of attack. The fish keyed in on color contrasts, such as that between a pale body and a blue sea.

Sharks are some of the oldest predators on the planet, dating back 400 million years, but, perhaps mercifully, many of the sailors hadn't given the possibility of attack a second thought until this morning. Most of these boys—many of whom were away from home for the first time in their lives—had had little contact with the sea, and sharks were the stuff of tall tales. Navy lore abounded with advice about what to do in case of an attack, but who really had paid attention to how to protect themselves? Certainly, the haggard and weakening survivors of the *Indianapolis* were ill-prepared to deal with the danger as the sun began burning off the night's haze.

The truth was, there was nothing naval command could have told the boys about how to handle an actual encounter. Boot-camp training had taught the sailors to thrash the water to frighten the predators away.* In 1943, the navy had set out to develop a shark repellent device known as the Life Jacket Shark Repellent Compound Packet; it was made of black dye, decomposing shark flesh, and ammonium acetate, and was meant to be deployed by a floating sailor from a pocket kept in his flotation vest. The plume of noxious odors and dark color was supposed to shield the luckless swimmer from attack. But none of the *Indy*'s boys were equipped with these devices (which had proved to be useless anyway). All that these men had to combat what sailors call the "hyenas of the sea" were occasional luck, guts, and what remained of their common sense.

No evidence has ever been found that sharks prefer humans to their regular diet of fish. Nor has it been scientifically established that they attack wounded or bleeding people more readily than the unwounded. Biologists are not even sure why sharks at-

---

* Present-day wisdom concludes that a potential attack victim should lie perfectly still, as thrashing may excite the shark into thinking it's spotted wounded prey.

  Accurate data on shark attacks on World War II servicemen may never be known since medical records did not note them. In fact, the navy was sufficiently concerned about loss of morale that it discouraged public mention of the menace.

tack humans, although they do believe that people emit irregular low-level frequencies and odors that resemble those of wounded fish. They are opportunistic eaters (especially the rapacious tiger shark) and have also been known to eat turtles, seagulls, and tin cans. Even submarines have been attacked, and fiber-optic cables on the ocean bed have been bitten and ruined. Other objects found in shark stomachs include a suit of armor, a barrel of nails, a roll of tar paper, coal, raincoats, shoes, plastic bags, goats, sheep, lizards, snakes, chicken, reindeer, and monkeys.

In Dr. Haynes's group this Tuesday, where most were dressed only in their gray life vests, one sailor would wake from sleep, half stupefied and half dreaming, and give a buddy next to him a "good morning" shove. The guy didn't respond. When the sailor pushed again, the friend's body tipped over like a child's toy and bobbed away. He'd been eaten in half, right up to the hem of his life vest.

At one point, Bob Gause swam away from the group to aid an exhausted sailor who was on the verge of drowning. The boy had clearly gone out of his head at the sight of the fish circling below him. He was waving his hands and calling for help. As Gause paddled out, he was intercepted immediately by a large dorsal fin knifing toward him, so he swam as fast as he could back to the group. The boy in distress soon disappeared.

As the shark attacks multiplied, the once optimistic boys were filled with a sense of helplessness. Jack Cassidy came face-to-face with a tiger shark that had been bothering him so long that he had even given it a name: he called the beast Oscar. He swung at it with his homemade knife and buried the blade an inch deep in the fish's tough snout, but Oscar swam away as if only annoyed. Cassidy was furious—he wanted to *kill* the shark—but he was relieved to be left alone.

As the water flashed with twisting tails and dorsal fins, the boys resolved to stay calm, clamping their hands over their ears against the erupting screams, but this resolve vanished when one of the boys was dragged through the water like a fisherman's bobber tugged by a big catfish. The victim, clenched in the uplifted jaws of a shark, was pushed at waist level through the surf, screaming. Others disappeared quietly without a trace, their life vests shooting back to the surface empty, the straps in shreds. As the excited sharks grew more agitated, the attacks intensified in ferocity.

Capable of bursts of speed up to forty-three miles per hour, they were attacking using what is known as "bump and bite maneuvers." The fast, powerful bites of sharks in laboratory pools have been measured at fifteen tons per square inch; their chewing process has been honed to evolutionary perfection. Their jaws, suspended on a length of braided muscle, allow the embedded teeth to rip away chunks of flesh, without releasing their clamp on victims. The bumps stun the prey, while the bites deliver the victims to eternity.

ABOUT twenty-five sharks circled around McCoy's group of rafts. Most, he estimated, measured about ten feet. He watched as they searched the rafts looking for a way in, pursuing them, he realized, the way wolves follow the scent trail of a wounded deer. Because McCoy's raft was broken at the bow, there was, in fact, a gaping entrance. He and his four compatriots bunched together at the far end of the craft as one shark rose up through the broken wooden grating in the floor.

McCoy recoiled as the shark's pointed snout, tipped with large black nasal chambers, jabbed hungrily through the hole. The eyes reminded him of plums. The teeth, about two inches long, were snow-white, protruding from a jaw about two feet wide.

At first McCoy was stunned by his fear. He reached for his .45 in its holster and pulled the trigger, but the gun wouldn't fire. Then he kicked out blindly, trying to drive the fish from the raft with his leg. The rough scaly skin ripped at his bare foot, but he managed to kick the fish in the eye. McCoy was amazed as he watched it thrashing back out of the raft in retreat. Glancing over the side, he watched the shark writhe and spin fifteen feet below him, its spasms magnified by the pure, green lens of the sea. But within seconds another shark came nosing into the raft's opening.

Elsewhere, in Dr. Haynes's group, some of the men went perfectly catatonic during the attacks, while others flailed. Boys at the edges of a floating group fared worse than those in the middle. Clinging to a floater net, one sailor looked down and saw hundreds of sharks circling.

Around Captain McVay's raft, one particular shark passed so close that the boys tried knocking the pilot fish leading it with a paddle, in hopes of capturing and eating it. When they realized they couldn't kill the pilot fish, they swung at the shark itself— an enormous twelve-footer—hoping to drive it away. Instead, the shark circled the raft in ever-tightening rings, at times bumping the raft's bottom with its dorsal fin.

And then, just as quickly as they began, the attacks stopped, the ghostly shapes dropping back into the gloom beneath. The sea was a bloody mess of bits of clothes and drowning men with arms and legs sheared off.

This pattern of attacks in low-light conditions, particularly at twilight and in the dawn hours, soon established itself as the rhythm of the men's days: the sharks would attack in the morning, then cruise through the wounded and the dying all day, feeding again at night on the living.

BY midmorning Tuesday, the boys were deeply bewildered and distraught. Their thinking now wasn't so much about being rescued. They just wanted to survive the sharks.

In the nearly thirty-six hours since the sinking, the Haynes group had drifted ahead of the middle of the pack by about one mile. Close behind, about four miles to the north, were McCoy and his group of four rafts. About four miles east, Captain McVay and his four rafts, one net, and nine men floated.* Trailing McVay by about one mile was the largest group of rafters and survivors perched atop floater nets, led by Twible and Redmayne. All the while, the teardrop formation of survivors was widening and it now covered about twelve miles from its northern end to its southern boundary and thirteen miles from its eastern edge to its expanding western leading edge. The groups were drifting farther and farther apart.

As the sharks rampaged through Haynes's group, many of whom had blindfolded themselves as protection against the harsh storm of morning light and photophobia, the rough tails

---

* On Tuesday, McVay picked up a ninth and final boy adrift on a raft. It took the captain and his crew nearly five hours to paddle the 1,500 yards to his rescue.

ripped abrasions in the boys' dangling legs. Dehydrated, their raw skin leached of its protective oils by immersion, their bodies were turning rubbery. Ed Brown's legs and arms bloomed with hideous bruises that arose at the slightest touch. The bleeding attracted smaller tropical fish that began to nip at the exposed pieces of flesh, while at the same time, barracudas began flashing about. It seemed to the boys that everything around them wanted them dead. Even the thick, humid air of the afternoon choked those suffering from the onset of pneumonia.

Dr. Haynes paddled up to find one man—and soon there would be others—staring longingly into his trembling hands, at the winking jewel of water cupped within.

The boy looked up. "Whaddya say, Doc? Just a little sip?"

"No!" Haynes warned. "You can't drink it!"

"C'mon, it can't hurt," whispered the boy.

"It's certain death—do you understand?"

The boy smiled, an inscrutable smirk, and it unnerved Haynes, but he stood his ground. Finally the boy poured the water out and swam away. Haynes, however, was horrified. He knew that if they began drinking the seawater, they'd start dying in droves.

At this latitude, the Pacific was a steady 85 degrees, warm by most ocean standards. But it was still more than 10 degrees cooler than core body temperature, and since the sinking the boys had been turning hypothermic. This condition affected each survivor differently, depending on his percentage of body fat and the amount of clothing he was wearing (the more the better in terms of heat retention). But on average, the boys were losing about 1 degree Fahrenheit for every hour of exposure in the water during the nighttime hours, when the air temperature dropped to the mid-80s. During the nights, which felt brutally cold in comparison to the days' nearly 100-degree heat, the boys' body temperatures dropped as much as 10 degrees.

As soon as the sun set, as it did with guillotine-like speed this close to the equator, the boys started shivering uncontrollably. This was the body's way of generating heat, but it quadrupled the rate of oxygen consumed. Hypothermia depresses the central nervous system as the body slows to conserve energy, and at a core temperature of 93 degrees (nearly 5 degrees below normal), speech becomes difficult, apathy develops, and amnesia typically scts in. At around 85 degrees, the kidneys stop filtering the body's waste—urination stops—and hypoxia, or poisoning, commences. Breathing becomes labored, the heart beats raggedly, and consciousness dims. The afflicted fall into an inattentive stupor.

By Tuesday at dawn, Dr. Haynes estimated the core body temperatures of the *Indy*'s boys were probably hovering right around 92 degrees. Later, after the shark attack, as the sun rose and baked them, their temperatures began to rise a degree or two, perhaps as many as five. In essence, the boys had fallen into a pattern of abrupt energy drain and renewal. But increasingly, they were building a deficit that eventually even the heat of day wouldn't be able to erase. With their body temperatures dipping low, the boys were wobbling off into the land of fatal judgment.

BACK on land, some three hundred miles across the Philippine Sea, the port director's office on Leyte was a busy place this sunny Tuesday morning. In the harbor, warships from Nimitz's and MacArthur's fleets were moored, awaiting food servicing and other resupply.

Carved from jungle scrub by invading U.S. forces, the island's installation was a grid of gravel roads, Quonset huts, and command posts.* Military jeeps roared through scorching heat and dust, delivering progress reports of the invasion's plans.

On Leyte there were two central posts of command, one subordinate to the other. In the village of Tolosa stood the Philippine Sea Frontier, under the acting command of Commodore Norman Gillette (who had purportedly recalled the tugboats dispatched after the *Indy*'s SOS). Twelve miles down the island's shore, in the village of Tacloban, was the Leyte Gulf Naval Operating Base, under the command of Commodore Jacob Jacobson. It was Jacobson who, in the post-midnight hours of July 30, was awakened in his hut by Clair Young bearing the news that the USS *Indianapolis* had just been sunk. Reporting to Jacobson were two officers, Lieutenant Commander Jules Sancho, the port director of the naval base, and Sancho's operations officer, Lieutenant Stewart Gibson. Both Sancho and Gibson were new, inexperienced officers; it was their job to oversee the routes of incoming and outgoing shipping traffic into San Pedro Bay. The pace was hectic in the port director's office—in the last month, Gibson had routed more than 1,500 ships, mostly merchant vessels in the business of supplying warships for the invasion of Japan.

At Tolosa, Gillette was also new to his post, having taken the place of the previous commander thirty days earlier; his was a temporary command in a complex military operation. Reporting to him was an operations officer, Alfred Granum, who maintained what was called a plotting board. For the past few days, Granum had been using it for the massive job of rerouting ships from typhoon-struck areas in the north, near Okinawa.

* Its beaches had been stormed by some 200,000 Allied troops on October 20, 1944.

This morning, sometime after 11 a.m., the *Indy*'s scheduled ETA, Granum moved the ship's marker into the "arrived" slot on the board. He assumed her voyage had been uneventful; at least he had heard nothing to the contrary. Combatant vessels were always assumed to have arrived at their destinations, unless contradictory news was announced.

On this same day, 1,300 miles away on Guam in the Marianas Sea Frontier headquarters, the HQ from which the *Indy* had sailed, a similar marker for the ship was removed from a plotting board in that office. Now both commands, the one at the *Indy*'s point of departure, the other at her port of call, were certain she had completed her voyage. The minutes began piling into hours, and no one noticed that the ship had not docked in the harbor.

No one, that is, except Lieutenant Gibson.

This was because the naval base at Tacloban made its own list, the Leyte Gulf Ships Present List, which noted new arrivals in the harbor. This information was gathered by a boat moored in San Pedro Bay whose job it was to identify each ship as it entered the harbor. But the *Indianapolis* was not among the seventeen ships listed as having shown up on Tuesday.

Lieutenant Gibson saw this list, and at that point, he might have done two things: he might have informed his superior officer, Lieutenant Commander Sancho, or Captain Granum at the Philippine Sea Frontier that the *Indy* had not arrived. But Gibson did neither. Instead, he marked the *Indy* as "overdue" and placed her on an "Expected Arrivals and Departures" list for Wednesday, August 1. Gibson did this because combatant ships like the *Indianapolis* were not under the jurisdiction of port directors such as Sancho, but of higher commands. He assumed the *Indianapolis* had been diverted by new orders to another destination.

As to why he didn't run this assumption by Sancho or Granum, the answer lies in a seemingly benign naval directive called 10CL-45. Initiated by chief of naval operations Admiral Ernest King six months earlier, in order to reduce daily mountains of shipping dispatches as well as in hopes of tightening security around the movements of ships, the directive instructed that henceforth the "arrival of combatant ships shall not be reported."

What was implied—but not intended—was that the *nonarrival* of combatants would also remain unreported. And this was how Lieutenant Gibson had interpreted the directive when it was discovered the USS *Indianapolis* hadn't arrived that morning.

Out at sea, Vice Admiral Oldendorf, commander of Task Force 95, to whom the *Indy* was to eventually report, also had no reason to be concerned. Oldendorf knew the *Indy* was due to report to him, but assumed details about her ETA were forthcoming.

Likewise, Rear Admiral McCormick, to whom the *Indy* was to report that day in preparation for joining Oldendorf, was unfazed. Steaming on his battleship *Idaho* from Leyte to the nearby island of Samar, McCormick assumed the *Indianapolis* had simply changed her course. He knew that combatant ships—and especially a flagship like the *Indianapolis*, which was at the beck and call of Admiral Spruance—were regularly diverted from their original orders.

It would have been a two-hour plane trip from one of Leyte's airstrips—or a day's cruise by rescue boat from her harbor—to reach the boys, but no one was leaving.

BY late afternoon, life for the boys had mutated from horrific to unbearable.

Those with broken arms and legs and backs had gone into shock and died; others had succumbed to massive bleeding or head wounds that suspended them in a netherworld. Still others simply drowned because they were too exhausted to keep swimming.

They'd been afloat now without food, water, shelter, or sleep for over forty hours. Of the 1,196 sailors who'd set sail from Guam three days earlier, probably no more than 600 were still alive. In the previous twenty-four hours alone, at least 200 had likely slipped beneath the waves or been victims of shark attack.

Since the sinking, each boy had been floating through the hours asking himself the same hard question: *Will I live, or do I quit?* And, as Tuesday unfolded, some of the starved, bleeding, and delirious men began to form their answers. For those who gave up, death now seemed a matter of destiny. They started committing suicide.

Those still lucid enough looked on in disbelief as their former shipmates calmly untied their life vests, took a single stroke forward, and sank without a word. Others suddenly turned from the group and started swimming, waiting for a shark to hit, and then looked up in terrified satisfaction when it did. Others simply fell face-forward and refused to rise. A boy would swim over to his buddy, lift his head by the hair from the water, and begin screaming for him to come to his senses. Often, he refused, and continued to quietly drown himself.

McCoy woke with a start to find one less boy in his cluster of rafts. The original head count of seventeen had by now dwindled to about twelve. Ed Payne and Willis Gray hovered in and out of consciousness, while Felton Outland and Bob Brundige remained alert. The beating of the rafts together in the swells had enlarged the hole in the floor of McCoy's, and the exposed balsa, its canvas ripped away, was shredding. There was talk of cutting the rafts loose to put an end to the constant collisions, but the idea frightened the boys, who found comfort in one another's presence. McCoy didn't know what to do.

Things were becoming increasingly surreal. Nearby, in Mike Kuryla's raft, one sailor in the group had opened his wallet, given away the few dollars inside, and said, "I'll see you, good buddies." Kuryla had picked up the bills and yelled out, "I'm going to spend this and have a drink on you guys." But the desperate boy ignored his weary attempt at humor and swam away. He was never seen again.

McCoy, drained and hollow-eyed, couldn't take his eyes off the life vest belonging to the boy who'd slipped away from the group during the night. The empty vest spooked McCoy. All its straps were still tightly tied—it looked like some trick that Houdini might've played. Then McCoy peered into the water and got another shock: the boy was floating below him, spread-eagled, about fifteen feet below the surface. He lay motionless until a current caught him; then it was as if he were flying in the depths. *Jesus,* McCoy thought, *Mother of God.* He started saying the rosary over and over. McCoy had never been overly religious; his mom was the spiritual one in the family. But now he began the process of what he'd later call his purification; he started asking God to forgive him for his sins. He was resolved to live but he was getting ready to die.

MEANWHILE, some of the other boys were reaching a similar point of acceptance. Even though they were scattered widely and separated by miles of water, it was as if they could sense one another's determination, as if tapping into a collective dream of survival.

In Dr. Haynes's group, Stanley Lipski had somehow managed to hang on until late the previous night. "Lew, I'm dying," Lipski had finally whispered in Haynes's ear. "Please tell my wife I love her. Tell her I want her to marry again." Haynes had felt a shocking sense of relief. He cradled his moaning friend in his arms, staring into the sightless black scabs that had been his eyes, and said good-bye.

Around him, marine captain Parke moved from man to man, giving his life vest to a boy without one, slapping those who looked to be thinking of drowning themselves. The hard-charging marine was spending an enormous amount of time looking for replacement vests, both for others and for himself. Dr. Haynes was worried about him, and about Father Conway—the priest also never stopped swimming among the boys, hearing their confessions and administering last rites.

As he floated in his life vest, Ed Brown cursed himself for making such an effort to get back to the *Indy* on the morning she sailed from Hunters Point. If only he had lingered a little longer with the girl he had met the night before. . . . If only he had missed the gangway. . . . Around him, he could hear the other boys mumbling to themselves. He watched one put his head down, drift to sleep, and drown. Another sailor paddled up to Brown and croaked, "I've had enough of this. I'm going."

Brown hated the fact that they were giving up. He might die, but he would not choose to give up. His father had told him that no one should ever quit.

CAPTAIN McVay was no quitter, but his spirits were threatening to wilt and slip past despair. The realization had sunk in that his absence from this morning's 6 a.m. meeting with the tractor planes hadn't triggered a rescue effort. Still, considering the adequate rations, he attempted to remain optimistic about their survival. "Something's happened," he told the boys. "I don't know what, but they're going to miss us sooner or later." He tried fishing for the bonito and mackerel he saw schooling below the raft, but after an enormous shark ripped at his fishing lines and stole his baited hooks, he gave up in disgust. He surveyed what was left of his weary and nauseated crew, perched precariously on the rafts' rails and staring at the burning sky. They were still looking for planes, for any signs of rescue.

"Don't give up, men!" McVay told them constantly. His mind was beginning to cloud with misgivings about his life to come if he ever stepped back ashore. For the boys, rescue would be the end of the ordeal. For him, if it came, it would only be the start of another hell—one that would be his alone to bear. He tried to match the strength of the boys, who were bleeding and suffering without bitterness or complaint. And yet at the same time, he watched them with an increasing sense of guilt, wondering if they held him responsible for what had happened.

At nightfall, he gathered the group together and recited the Lord's Prayer as the rafts headed into another silent, freezing night, their third since the sinking.

HAYNES was desolate, drifting into uncharted territories of pain. Like marine captain Parke and Father Conway, he had been paddling for nearly two full days, trying to do his best to encourage the boys and sustain their dwindling hopes. By day's end, though, Father Conway was in terrible shape, and Captain Parke was beginning to show signs of total collapse.

Haynes himself was slipping in and out of consciousness, experiencing alternating moments of clarity and confusion. *You have patients to take care of,* he kept reminding himself. He thought of home, of his wife and sons 10,000 miles away. What would they do if he died? The question made survival seem even more essential. But when he snapped back to reality, he slumped deeper into misery and disbelief.

Overhead, more planes—bombers and transports—passed without pause, and Haynes prayed. He prayed that in a few hours they would be discovered, steeling himself against any other thoughts, any other possibilities.

BY nightfall, the situation at sea took one more precipitous turn. The dehydrated boys, their tongues swelling, their throats squeezing shut, and their minds unhinging, began drinking salt water. After hours of resisting the temptation, they drank furtively at first, as if ashamed. Then they began to gorge themselves, murmuring in pleasure as they sipped through bleeding lips from the cool mirror of the sea.

Dr. Haynes looked on in horror, his worst fear realized: soon these boys would all be dead. He swam among them, screaming and punching at their faces. But his pleas to stop were ignored. The boys lifted their dripping chins, regarded him coolly with glazed eyes, then lowered their jaws back to the waiting sea. Finally, the exasperated doctor realized he could do nothing but float and watch, and steel himself for the coming physiological apocalypse.

As they drank, the boys were setting off a complex series of chemical reactions, all of them volatile. The sea contains twice the salinity that the human body can safely ingest, and as the boys drank, their cells were shrinking, expanding, and exploding as they sacrificed what's called their "free water." This was the cells' attempt to lower the sodium deluging the bloodstream, and it was futile.

The boys' kidneys were scrubbing their blood before dumping it back into the circulatory system, but they were unable to keep ahead of the sodium tidal wave. Haynes knew the boys were shorting out on salt, succumbing to what in medical terms is known as hypernatremia. He watched some of them foam at the nose; a root beer–colored substance dripped down their chins as their eyes rolled back in their heads. He watched their lips turn blue, heard their breathing grow ragged. In their brains, neurons were misfiring or not firing at all. Electrical activity was disrupted in much the way a car's battery would cease to work properly if the composition of its power cells was altered. It was a continuous loop of self-destruction, and Haynes knew the only remedy was massive rehydration.

Some of the boys now asked him if they could evaporate the salt from the seawater by cupping it in their hands and holding it up to the sun. He gently shook his head, told them, "No, son," and begged the boys to be patient. He began keeping a close eye on those he knew weren't married or who were without close ties on shore. Those with families, he discovered, were fighting the temptation to drink from the sea.

Those who succumbed fell into violent fits and, finally, comas.

At first, they whooped and hollered and spun circles in the water, arms flailing, until finally a kind of explosion took place and they went limp. More than one boy came to rest in a ring of circling sharks. The dead and near-dead floated motionless, facing the sky, bodies jerking, eyes blinking in terror. Some of the poor boys clawed the air in thirst or panic. Their throats were too dry to scream.

It was dark now, and Haynes could feel the anxiety swirling around him. The life vests, the boys' last line to hope, were growing waterlogged. Some were riding as much as six inches lower in the sea, making it even more difficult not to swallow salt water. The vests possessed an estimated buoyancy limit of forty-eight hours, and they were approaching that limit. After this, the boys would be floating on borrowed time. And they knew it.

As Haynes grew feverish and started to shake, he felt his power of reasoning slipping away. The night was rent by screams rising up all across the water, the awful music of the savaging as the sharks attacked around the edges of the group. Haynes had yet to see a shark attack close up, but this was almost worse. It was torture; too much was left to his imagination.

He instructed the boys to tie their vests together and form a protective mass. They obeyed, huddling in moaning clusters as the temperature plummeted. Soon all were shivering uncontrollably. One boy chewed completely through a rope he'd placed between his chattering teeth. It was so cold they began announcing when they had to pee so others could gather around them.

It was as if everything that had come before had completely slipped away.

CHAPTER EIGHT

Genocide

At first you get in a situation where you abhor it.
You can't stand it. It's terrible. But you can't get away from it.
So you stick with it. And then you get so that you tolerate it.
You tolerate it long enough, you embrace it.
It becomes your way of life.

—LEWIS HAYNES,
LCDR, Medical Corps, USS *Indianapolis*

DAY THREE
WEDNESDAY, AUGUST 1, 1945

———

WHERE does a man go when there are no more corners to turn, when he's running out of hope, out of luck, out of time?

In the very early hours of Wednesday, August 1, the men started killing one another. Haynes had spent the night listening to the sounds of shivering and chattering teeth. Then, from somewhere not far off he heard a shout: "There's an enemy here! He's trying to kill me. Get him!"

This was followed by piercing screams, but Haynes had no idea what was causing them. He could see, but barely, boys fumbling with the knots holding their vests together. Then, suddenly, the circle of boys blew apart, as if parted by an invisible wind. They scattered in all directions.

Haynes, swimming into the pandemonium, saw boys with knives blindly stabbing at buddies who were still tied to them. Those unable to punch or stab rose up and tried to drown the closest breathing thing they could find. One sailor gouged out another's eyes with his fingers.

Haynes watched as one sailor tried stabbing another, who, in turn, was rescued by two nearby boys. They jumped atop the sailor with the knife and held him under. As they drowned him, they screamed long, defiant cries of anguish. Then the rescuers turned on each other. Hypothermia, dehydration, hypernatremia, photophobia, the onset of starvation—Haynes knew what was turning the minds of these boys inside out. In a matter of ten minutes, an estimated fifty boys were killed. The melee had the intensity of a flash fire.

Haynes tried paddling away from the bursts of violence around him, but wherever he went, another fight was raging. Then he was jumped by two gibbering figures carrying knives. As they shoved him deep underwater and held him down, he knew he was drowning. Kicking and punching at his attackers' arms, the doctor managed to break free, shooting to the surface with a wrench. Swimming away as fast as possible, he kept his eyes trained on his attackers until he reached the fringe of the chaos. He was heartsick; the boys had become a pack of fighting dogs.

Sharks, he realized, were still circling, and he was certain they were pursuing him. But if he returned to the group, he was sure he would be drowned. So he floated, trying to catch his breath, and attempted to remain perfectly still. His mouth was just inches from the surface of the water, which he knew was poison to him. His vest was so waterlogged he wondered how much longer it would hold him up. Even the slightest movement of his hands was a monumental effort—he was that tired. Convinced that he would soon slip beneath the waves, he cried out for help.

Suddenly he heard a voice in his ear: "Easy, Doc," it said, "I've got you."

It was the pharmacist's mate, John Schmueck, with whom he had stood aboard the *Indy* watching their helpless patients slide into the sea. Schmueck shoved his arms through Haynes's life vest and hoisted the gasping doctor onto his hip. "Nothing's gonna happen to you now, Doc," the voice said. But Haynes was out cold.

PRIVATE McCoy had cut himself and his four raftmates free of the other rafts in their group sometime before sunset the previous day. They were now adrift, bucking and gliding through the dawn. *Well?* he wondered. *What now, dumb shit?*

The trouble with the boys on the other rafts in his group had begun late the previous day. An argument had broken out, and somebody on one of the rafts finally pulled a pistol. The fight had centered on whether or not breaking up the group would increase their chances of survival. Somebody had suggested they should strike out separately in the hopes that one of the rafts might sail into a shipping lane.

Mike Kuryla, on the raft next to McCoy, had thought the idea was plain dumb. After the gun appeared, though, he shut up.

McCoy had been in favor of the idea; he was sick of waiting. The water around him had become a floating morgue. Bodies and pieces of bodies—arms, legs, half-eaten torsos—were floating by, and McCoy had been willing to do almost anything to get away. His raft had been nearly destroyed by the constant pounding of the other rafts as the waves pitched them together. Of the ten feet of raft, only about seven were still usable—the thing couldn't even be called a raft anymore. He had known that striking out for a shipping lane was a cockeyed idea, but it was better than watching the other boys kill each other.

His raftmates Payne and Willis didn't have much of an opinion. They were asleep. Felton Outland was also fading, into unconsciousness, his face and arms blistered with welts, which McCoy guessed were caused by the stinging tentacles of a jellyfish. Somehow, McCoy and the rest had missed getting stung as their raft drifted over the nearly invisible predator.

As for Bob Brundige, he had rallied but he was still speaking very little. It annoyed McCoy, who enjoyed shooting the breeze to pass the time. He was about to say something about this when

Ed Payne woke and started acting crazy. Payne was shouting in a high-pitched wail: "I don't wanna die. I don't wanna die." It was bad enough for McCoy when the boys were asleep. Now the raft was turning into a floating mental ward.

"Shut up," McCoy told him sharply. "We ain't gonna die."

A plane flew over at what looked to McCoy to be about 5,000 feet. He pulled out his pistol and this time the gun fired. He knew it wouldn't work, but he had to try. Nothing. The plane just kept on flying.

One of the boys, maybe Payne, said, "Give me some of your water."

McCoy was shocked. "I don't have no water," he said. "Hell, you know that."

"You *do* have water. You're keeping it from us!" Now the boy pulled a knife.

"Shit," said McCoy, "is that what it's coming to? You wanna start killing each other, huh? Fine, but let's use our bare hands." He was in no mood for this looney-tunes horseshit. "See?" he said, grabbing the knife away from the boy and tossing it over the raft's side. Then he pitched his pistol as far as he could and said, "All right now, come on. Let's do it."

Nobody moved. What passed for normalcy returned to the raft.

Across the water, in other groups, boys were making deals with God, promising to read the Bible, to write their parents more, to never steal or cheat, so help them, if only they could survive this day.

In the raft group commanded by Ensign Twible, chief engineer

Redmayne was losing it. He had started sipping salt water some-time late Tuesday night, and he now informed Twible that he was going to swim belowdecks and start the *Indy*'s engines. Twible was beside himself. Of the original group of 325 boys, about 200 were still alive, and this disorganized mass was operating under the strictest rules of survival of the fittest. Boys who couldn't mus-cle onto a raft were doomed to spend every minute floating in their life vests, more fully exposed to the sharks.

And now there was Redmayne to contend with. Twible feared that in his delirium, the wounded officer would drown. For sev-eral hours, Twible had been struggling to keep him afloat. He finally jabbed him with a morphine syrette. Redmayne barked, "Whadya do that for!" and then he slumped over.

The young ensign tied the straps of Redmayne's vest to his own. He would tow the 200-pound officer behind him, like a fish on a stringer.

IN the early-morning light, Dr. Haynes came to in the arms of his friend and slowly craned his head around. Everywhere there were more mutilated bodies, limbs swaying silently on the morn-ing tide.

Haynes looked out as far as he could see. But he saw only ocean and more ocean, rolling in ominous green humps over the horizon. No planes, no ships, not one goddamned thing that promised life or offered even a shred of hope. He saw boys buck naked or wearing tattered shreds of underwear. Some had tied hats or socks around their necks, fashioning makeshift protective scarves. They stared at the morning sky with sunken eyes.

Who's there? the eyes seemed to beg as they studied the clouds.

No one, pal, came the answer in their shipmates' hollow faces. *No one but you.*

As the merciless sun rocketed into the sky Wednesday morning, it revealed a new day without faith. And yet many of the survivors found themselves reaching even deeper inside and summoning a grim refusal to die. No one believed that help was coming, but they tried to convince one another to hang on, as if for the hell of it. They had been afloat fifty-five hours. At this point slightly more than half of the 900 or so who had left the ship were still alive. Boys had been dying at an average rate of one every ten minutes for the past three days. And it looked like the cycle would only accelerate.

The seawater was eating Dr. Haynes's boys alive. Their sunburned, waterlogged arms and legs were stamped with painful red sores, called saltwater ulcers, some as small as cigarette burns, others as big as basketballs. The salt water was even dissolving hair from some of their bodies. After another cold night in the water, the men's body temperatures hovered around 88 degrees, precariously within the coma zone. Their kidneys were shutting down, their hearts were racing, and they were gasping for air.

And then they began hallucinating en masse. The visions came whirling over the horizon through the bright morning sun— whole islands, grocery stores, old girlfriends, wives, automobiles, and mountains of ice cream materialized on the water around the boys, who looked on overjoyed and amazed.

It was the beginning of the final act.

THE rafts of marine private McCoy and Captain McVay drifted ahead of what remained of the other groups. McCoy and McVay were about eight miles apart, and each was about seven miles from Haynes.

Amazingly, Captain McVay's crew was nearly untouched by madness. The other good news was the relative smoothness of the sea, which had replaced Tuesday's swells. Assessing his collection of rafts, McVay knew the boys were teetering on the brink of exhaustion. In a low voice that, given his parched mouth and throat, was a huge effort, McVay pleaded with the boys to stay still and expend as little energy as possible. Quietly, he begged them to keep looking out for planes.

The tension was nearly unbearable. At one point, as many as nine sharks were circling the rafts. The crew had spent hours fishing and they'd had little luck, although John Spinelli had been able to catch one fish. He'd cut it into strips and arranged them on the raft's edge to dry in the sun. But McVay had been afraid to let the boy eat the small, black triangular fish, fearing it might be poisonous. Spinelli obeyed and tossed it overboard. The sight of this was torture for the others, who'd been sucking sullenly on milk tablets or nibbling at their meager rations of salty Spam and crackers.

McVay's four rafts were spread out over seventy-five feet of ocean. He was trying to create as large a visual target as possible for passing aircraft. At 5 a.m., after spotting a plane's red and green running lights, McVay had shot two star shells—illuminating rounds—from a pistol he'd scavenged from his raft's emergency box. Later, he spotted what he thought was a B-24 or B-29 bomber flying in a westerly direction. It had to have taken off from Tinian and was almost certainly on its way to Leyte.

But as had been the case time and again, with so many planes that had offered a moment or two of hope, the diligent boys' signal mirrors had failed to attract notice. McVay knew that his sense of self-discipline was the only thread holding his boys to sanity.

John Spinelli didn't like the terrible quiet on the raft, but he was more troubled by what he saw in his captain's eyes. Spinelli knew what McVay must be feeling, but could do nothing. Turning his glance toward another of his raftmates, Spinelli noticed the increasingly odd look in the boy's eyes and told himself to watch this one carefully. All morning, the guy had been gazing at the enormous shark trailing their rafts. The fish had bumped the rafts, nuzzled them, even lifted the rafts' corners as if testing its power. The guy never took his eyes off the fish. It was like he was hypnotized.

Suddenly, as the shark passed again, the boy slashed out with a tiny, two-inch penknife. Spinelli couldn't believe it—the crazy bastard had actually managed to stab the shark between the eyes! Cannonballs of water landed around the group of rafts as the shark thrashed, thumping the tiny craft with long, leathery strokes of its tail. It seemed all the rafts would tip and break apart.

Spinelli was pissed off, confused, and a little amazed. He thought of his baby daughter, now three weeks old. He had laid eyes on her for a total of two days before being ordered back to the *Indy*. He figured that was all he was going to get in this life—two lousy days.

McVay raised his voice: "We are going to be all right! We are going to be all right!"

Like a lid clapped on a box, his firm voice silenced the boys. They looked at one another, grumbling, and settled back into their corners. Spinelli and some others grabbed their mate and pinned him to the side of the raft. Someone yanked the knife from his hand and threw it overboard.

McVay knew he had to do something quick if he was to get anyone back to shore. If they didn't kill themselves, they'd starve. He reminded them that rescue had to be on the way. Then he doled out each man's daily ration of one sliver of Spam and a malted milk tablet before announcing that, thenceforth, he would be cutting the rations in half. This would double their survival time, he figured, to twenty days.

As he and his boys chewed and stared into a blinding horizon, peace—or something approximating it—gradually returned to the rafts. To while away the long afternoon, McVay started questioning the boys about their personal lives. He wanted to know about their wives and girlfriends. He himself fell into a reverie about his comfortable life in D.C. with his wife, Louise.

Spinelli, who had served under the *Indy's* previous captain, the hard-nosed Johnny "General Quarters" Johnson, knew that few captains would ever get this personal with their crew, not even when everything was FUBAR—"Fucked-up Beyond All Recognition," like things were now. He admired McVay's soft-spoken calm. The old man, in his opinion, had been getting the job done— hey, at least they hadn't died yet. Spinelli realized he was learning something essential, something he couldn't yet put into words. He and the boys listened raptly as the stoic, gray-haired captain confessed, "I'm going to have some explaining to do." McVay didn't know what he might tell the families of the dead—if he survived. He knew there was little he could say that would help.

On board the *Indy,* McVay had sometimes talked of becoming an admiral. But now he said, "I should have gone down with the ship." The boys on the raft disagreed.

It was as if, in his candor, McVay was discovering what it meant to be a captain and a leader. He had commanded ships, but until now, relying on the barest of resources—some crackers, pieces of fishing line—he'd never felt the pull of the lives he held in his hands, or the full measure of what it meant to be placed in harm's way. He assured the boys they would be rescued by the next day. And they believed him.

IN McCoy's raft, Ed Payne had taken to drinking his urine. He was kneeling—or trying to—on the edge of the raft, his hand cupped at his zipper while he peed into a ration tin. And then he brought his hand to his mouth. McCoy was amazed Payne even had anything left. The boy was becoming a real problem, but McCoy didn't blame him. As the afternoon sun pressed down, McCoy was so thirsty he was thinking of taking a pee himself. But he couldn't bring himself to do it, figuring it might make him even crazier. He reached over the raft and cradled a cool palmful of water. He burned for a sip.

Who am I? Where am I? he wondered.

I'm Giles McCoy from St. Louis, Missourah, and I'm one tough sonofabitch.

Brundige was hanging tight, actually calm. "You look funny," he said out of the blue.

McCoy looked up. "What do you mean?"

"You look like hell."

"Well, you oughta see yourself. You're not so pretty." Brundige wasn't. His face was blackened by oil; around his eyes was a faint white stripe where he'd tried wiping it away. His tongue protruded slightly from his mouth.

McCoy's own tongue felt hard and dry, like a root. His skin was cracked and sore, bleeding in places. If he looked like Brundige, he was sure glad he couldn't see himself. He thought about his mother and her laugh when she beat him at Ping-Pong. He thought of his father, about the night he knocked him across the front yard, and the way he'd cried at the train station.

After McCoy made it onto the *Indianapolis*, he had sat down and written a letter to his father apologizing for disobeying him the night he went to his good-bye party. He was no longer a boy, and yet not a man—he knew that. But, hell, he was going to war— he was going to kill people. He thought he deserved a send-off.

His whole life, McCoy had hated bullies, but he'd loved to fight. The Marine Corps had taught him how to lie in a stream for hours breathing through a straw, how to shoot to kill, how to *survive*. He'd always had the firm conviction of his own toughness.

Now he realized he hadn't even known what strength was.

İN Dr. Haynes's group, the hallucinations were reaching full boil. One boy got in his car and was ready to drive home, but then lost his keys. Another saw an island overflowing with ice-cold coconut milk and dancing girls. One delirious sailor was seen starting an imaginary outboard motor with furious yanks at a rope and then puttering away.

By midafternoon, passenger trains were pounding along imaginary rails ringing the horizon, and hotels were springing up on city blocks floating atop the water. Some of the boys checked into the hotels and drowned, while others started swimming to catch the trains and vanished beneath the waves.

At one point, even Dr. Haynes succumbed. Spotting a shark, a five-footer—his first time seeing one at close range—he was seized with the desire to kill it with his bare hands and drink its blood. But no matter how hard he splashed at the creature, no matter how loudly he swore at it, it would not attack. It seemed to be mocking his rage. He couldn't believe it. The shark didn't want to eat him! Chuckling, the doctor paddled away, somehow feeling better.

He then came upon a group of boys. They looked odd—something was wrong with the picture. They were floating in single file, dog-paddling in place. Haynes asked one of them, "What's up, son?"

"Shhh, Doc," one guy said. "There's a small hotel on the is-land there, and they got one room and you can get fifteen minutes' sleep. You get in line—you'll get a turn."

Haynes craned his head and, for a moment, dammit, he be-lieved he could see the hotel wavering atop the water. Nearby, other odd things were going on. Another twenty-five boys had queued up, as if preparing to set out on a journey. They told Haynes matter of factly that they were going to swim to Leyte, and that they figured it would take them about two days. They said their good-byes, promising to meet up again on land. Then they kicked out over the glass of the sea. They made it only 200 or 300 yards before sinking.

What struck Haynes as the grandest hallucination of all, how-ever, was the moment, about midday, when the *Indianapolis* her-self ghosted over the horizon and sailed back into the boys' lives. At times, they yelled that the ship was steaming toward them. At others, it was drifting peacefully below them in the clear, green water, all her flags flying smartly, her portholes relit and gleam-ing. Some of the boys dove down to the ship and began swimming through her long passageways, back to their bunks, to the mess halls, and to the water fountains, where they drank deeply. "I found it," they screamed in heartbreaking relief, breaking back to the surface. "There's fresh water aboard! Come on fellas, let's go! She ain't sunk!"

More boys took deep breaths and dove to the ship, and in the aqua light of their dreams they sat at tables eating ice cream and drinking tall glasses of water. "Don't drink! *Don't do it!*" Haynes shouted, his throat raw, his voice breaking, as he watched their dreams turn to nightmares.

B<small>Y</small> late afternoon, the men on McCoy's raft were trying to kill him. At least, he thought they were. Ed Payne swore he was going to jump off the raft. McCoy was certain he wanted to commit suicide. Gray looked like he wanted to jump, too.

Everybody, thought McCoy, was going crazy. Everybody, that is, except Brundige. He was glad Brundige wasn't losing his grip. He just wished he'd say something.

"Goddammit," McCoy told Payne and Gray, "you've got families, relatives—you've got things to live for."

One of them—Willis Gray—looked up and said, "Live for? Shit."

"We're going through this day after day," said Payne, "and nobody is looking for us. To hell with it! It's easier to die than to live." Payne looked like he really was going to jump.

McCoy felt that he and Brundige were in a kind of unspoken contest, each trying to prove who was the tougher sonofabitch. It would be a last hurrah before the lights went out, before McCoy slumped over and drowned and the sharks started eating him.

"Don't you worry, guys," he announced, speaking particularly to Payne. "I'll take care of you. I'll make sure the sharks don't get you."

Payne began moaning, and then he jumped and began to swim. McCoy studied the water; it was so clear, like a glass floor he might walk across. As usual, he could see sharks down there, circling. He dove and started swimming.

He swam about fifty feet and caught the sailor, grabbed hold of his vest, and dragged the blubbering kid back to the raft. He yelled up to Brundige, "Come on, give me a damn hand here!" And Brundige, tall and strong, reached down and lifted Payne into the raft. McCoy swam up through the hole in the busted bow. He pulled himself onto the suspended lattice floor. And then Payne got up on the side of the raft, looked around, and jumped over again.

McCoy looked at Brundige, thinking, *I saved his ass once, do I gotta do it again?* He looked at the sharks and jumped. He swam out over them and stroked up behind Payne, jerked him hard, and brought him back to the raft. Now McCoy was mad—and dead tired. It was as if all the blood had drained from his arms and legs. He was so thirsty it was a struggle not to sip some salt water as he splashed back aboard. He slammed Payne against the rail of the raft. Payne was crying, and McCoy looked at him and whacked him on the face, screaming, "Now, dammit, cut that out, cuz you're going to kill yourself!"

Payne's eyes widened, and his head rolled back and forth on the rail. "Why'd you hit me?" he asked. "Don't hit me no more!" He was crying, but no tears were coming; Payne was too dehydrated for tears.

McCoy turned around, and there was Willis Gray on the raft's edge, jumping. The sonofabitch. He'd walked off the raft like he was stepping off a street corner. This time, McCoy just sat there and watched. He thought Gray was dumb for jumping. He said it out loud: "You know, you are a real turd."

"Hell, we just can't leave him out there," announced Brundige. McCoy looked at him. "I just don't have no more fire." Then Brundige hit the water. Batting and kicking at the sharks, he towed the boy back to the raft, and McCoy started lecturing: "What in hell do you think you're doing, son? Tell me, what's going on?" But there was no answer—Gray didn't understand. His eyes were blank spots on an empty map. Looking at him, McCoy felt suddenly certain that his own death was out there waiting, too.

"You know what?" he said. "They're not comin'. Nobody's going to rescue us." He turned to the rest of them: "We are going to die," he said. "We are all going to die."

It felt good to say it. His stomach felt queasy, as if he had butterflies. In fact, all day he'd felt nauseated. And it wasn't from swallowing fuel oil. It was a sickness that came from lying to himself.

"We are going to die," he said again. He was feeling better by the minute.

THE sun was like a hammer in the sky. As the day wore on, the bodies piled on the surface of the sea in ragged heaps that swirled as the sharks tugged them from below. Carrying on with the grim ritual he'd been dutifully executing the past three days, Dr. Haynes set out to bury the newly dead. He was no longer a doctor, it seemed; he was now a coroner. So be it. The realization wrenched him back to reality, but this was a blessing he had mixed feelings about.

As he paddled by, some of the boys stirred, lifting their oil-caked heads to stare bleary-eyed at the sun. "Hey, Doc, take a look at this guy, will ya!" a few of the more lucid called out. "Hey, Doc, is this guy alive?"

Stroking up to one boy, Haynes gently lifted him by the hair and peered into his eyes. "Are you alive, son?" he asked.

"Yes, Doctor, I'm alive," the man croaked.

"Good. That's real good." He moved on to the next candidate.

"Son?" He lifted the head. "Are you with us?" There was no reply. "Son?" Haynes tapped on the cold, opened eyeball. When he found a reflex, he felt an immense sense of relief.

Then he moved quickly to the next boy. He tapped again; this eye was bloodshot and swollen—a sign, Haynes knew, of edema caused by the ingestion of salt water. There was no reflex. It was like touching the blank and glassy eye of a stuffed animal. Haynes had to declare the boy dead.

"This man is dead," he said aloud. It was strange, but saying it made it seem more real. It made him feel like he wasn't alone. At the sound of Haynes's voice, several boys turned to watch. More than a few of them didn't have life vests. They were half dog-paddling and half drowning, heroically supported by comrades who themselves were close to giving up. The boys supporting these swimmers had enormous sores on their hips from the chafing of their heavy loads. Yet none of them wanted to let go of their charges. They were clinging to them as if saving themselves. The boys without vests had either untied them in their delirium or had voluntarily taken them off because they were losing buoyancy. Either way, they needed relief.

Time was critical—Haynes needed the dead boy's life vest—and he moved quickly. It was not easy work because his burned hands were badly swollen, practically unusable. He tried not to look into the boy's eyes as he struggled to loosen the knotted straps. They were soaked with fuel oil, which made them impossibly tight. Untying them was painful, methodical work.

When he was done, he removed the boy's dog tags. He wrapped them around his own arm, where they clinked tinnily. Haynes then paddled behind the body, placed one hand on the vest's collar, and gave a gentle pull, easing out first the shoulders and then the arms. It looked very much like someone removing a coat from a sleeping child. Finally, the corpse slid free from the vest. Haynes quickly tossed the vest aside and then snatched the body before it could sink. The bodies of the bigger boys required more strength than those of the smaller ones, and strength was something Haynes hadn't much of. Still, he was determined not to let any corpse sink without praying over it.

He drew the cold, wet body close, grabbed it tight in a bear hug, and paused. Aboard a ship, the chaplain would do this duty, but Father Conway was close to death himself. Haynes groped for a way to say good-bye to these boys, many of whom he knew only in passing. But he always said something. With his cheek pressed to the dead boy's cheek, he could smell the salt and sweat, and he began: *Our Father, who art in heaven, hallowed be thy name . . . . Thy kingdom come, thy will be done . . .*

Sometimes he made it to the end of the Lord's Prayer, and sometimes he didn't. After several hours of burying the dead, he was often so spent that he could do nothing more than hold the dead boy and pray in silence, feeling, in his addled state, that he'd been an utter failure as a doctor.

HE opened his arms and watched the body fall. It dropped for a long time, twirling feet first, like a man falling down a crystalline elevator shaft, getting smaller and smaller, no bigger than a doll when it finally disappeared.

Why, oh why, Haynes wondered, *can't I do anything to save these boys?*

NOW that he was going to die, McCoy decided he wanted to die clean. It made no sense, he knew, but nothing did now. Dying suddenly seemed like play. He untied his vest, tossed it in the raft, and slipped over the side of the raft for a last bath.

Brundige boomed, "What the hell you doing, marine?"

McCoy ignored him. The water was cool, the air hot, the shock instant. McCoy stroked around the raft. To his surprise, he was having fun. Looking down, he could see thirty or forty feet below, and he wondered what the water felt like down there where the sharks circled in glassy coils. He didn't care about them anymore, didn't give a damn. He dove. He felt like he was flying, as his head poked through a cool band of water. Half his body was warm, the other cold. He looked up and to his surprise he saw that he was only about six feet deep.

He prayed that his mother would understand why he had not been able to make it home; he prayed that she would know he'd tried his hardest to get there. And then he asked God to forgive him his sins.

He broke the surface, paddled over to the raft, and hoisted himself up. And then he began scrubbing himself with his T-shirt, rubbing at the smeared oil on his chest and arms. He wanted to be clean because he wanted to be identified if anybody found his body. He realized he'd probably be chewed up by sharks, but he hoped they'd at least leave his face. He wanted somebody to be able to recognize him.

Brundige told him, "You still got oil all over you, you know. You stupid thing." He said it again: "You stupid thing."

McCoy liked that—*You stupid thing*. It made him laugh. He *was* a stupid thing. Sitting in this ocean, he felt like nothing more than a speck. All his life, he had thought he was tough. Now he felt like a speck, and he felt relieved to know the truth. He looked at Payne, Outland, and Gray, who were now passed out, sitting in the water up to their chins. McCoy decided he had better tie them together for safekeeping. He asked Brundige to help, and they drew the boys so close that their foreheads were touching. McCoy and Brundige cinched up all the straps on the vests to prevent their heads from falling into the water. They floated like that inside the raft, their feet dangling. McCoy and Brundige were each in a corner, hanging on the rails.

Sometime before nightfall, they started betting each other about who was going to die first. "I'm sure as shit gonna stay alive longer than you," McCoy said.

"Like hell," Brundige shot back. "I'm a Tennessee farmer, and I'm pretty damn tough."

"Well, I'm a marine from Missourah, and I'm a lot tougher."

"You go to hell." After a while, they fell silent and drifted. Around them, Payne, Outland, and Gray started moaning. The sharks were circling the raft again.

"Well," said Brundige, "I guess nobody's gonna miss me but my mom and dad."

"My mother's gonna miss me," said McCoy. "And I'm sure my dad will, too. And I also know I'm gonna outlive you."

"We'll see."

"You know," McCoy said finally, "if some damn shark gets me, I hope the sonofabitch gets indigestion." He laughed. "I really hope he has a hard time *digesting* me."

They fell asleep with their heads resting on each other's shoulders.

BY nightfall, Haynes was burying Father Conway and Captain Parke. The big marine went first. His selfless lending of life vests to struggling swimmers had finally taken its toll. Parke, an astonishingly strong and disciplined man, had died in mid-hallucination; he suddenly broke away from the group and started swimming for the horizon. His death shocked those still lucid enough to understand it.

Conway was next. The deteriorating condition of the priest crushed Haynes. He remembered the day Conway had come to his cabin on the *Indy* with the money for leave. It was the most generous thing anyone had ever done for the doctor.

For the past three days, Conway had kept drowning men afloat, praying with them as they died, refusing to quit even when it must have felt impossible to swim another inch. A few hours ago, however, he had finally succumbed to delirium, keening in Latin and babbling prayers, a soaring, incoherent litany. As Conway sang, Haynes had cradled the naked priest in his arms, smoothing his balding, sunburned head with a gentle hand. As Conway's condition worsened, his keening grew in intensity. Soon he was blessing Haynes, hitting him repeatedly in the face as he delivered absolution. Haynes did nothing to stop the crazed priest. He watched and waited for him to die.

When Conway fell limp, the silence was deafening. Haynes heard only the water gurgle and swish around him. When it was clear that Conway was dead, Haynes removed his vest and set his friend's body sailing into the deep.

HAYNES was left holding the dog tags he'd collected from the boys he'd personally buried over the past three days. There were well over 100, their silver chains wrapped tightly around his fist. Suddenly they felt so heavy he could hardly believe it. He was so exhausted he could barely lift them up anymore.

"Oh, shit," he said. And then he sadly tossed them away.

BACK on Leyte, the port director's office noted once again that the *Indianapolis* had failed to arrive. Once again, she was dutifully marked as overdue. The thinking in the office was that she would reach the harbor the next day, Thursday, August 2.

On the island of Tinian, B-29s were taking off continually, loaded with thousands of pounds of bombs. During the raids, a new plane lifted off every few seconds. The sky over Japan was raining bombs.

In an air-conditioned bunker on Tinian, a team of weapons specialists had gathered, and among them was Captain James Nolan. He and the other experts were huddled in the specially built bunker to assemble the pieces of Little Boy. Around this same time, the flight crews of the 509th Composite Group, led by Lieutenant Colonel Paul Tibbets, were practicing secret dummy bombing runs over Japan. Tibbets would eventually drop Little Boy from his B-29 *Enola Gay* on Hiroshima.

Nobody thought to miss McVay and his boys.

PART THREE

Rescue

CHAPTER NINE
Dead Drift

Captain McVay was like a father to our group. He kept us calm.
He kept saying, "We are going to be rescued." And we just figured,
"Well, somebody's gonna find us one of these days!"

—JOHN SPINELLI,
ship's cook, second-class, USS *Indianapolis*

Days Four and Five
Thursday, August 2–Friday, August 3, 1945

SOMETHING had gone wrong with the sock again. Lieutenant Chuck Gwinn wondered if he should land the bomber and fix it before getting airborne again. Or should he push ahead on his patrol sector, hoping for the best as he navigated by the seat of his pants, by dead reckoning? Gwinn decided to land. Better safe than sorry.

He banked the bomber back over the jungle scrub of Peleliu and brought the big plane down. A rancher's son from San Martin, California, Gwinn was in his third year of service in the navy. With him this morning was a crew of four naval aviators: copilot Lieutenant Warren Colwell; chief radioman William Hartman; and two bombardiers, Herbert Hickman and Joseph Johnson. Gwinn, twenty-four, had logged over 1,000 flight hours as a navy test pilot. Normally, he and his crew flew a plane affectionately called the *Miss Deal*; this morning, they were out of luck—the *Miss Deal* was undergoing repairs. Instead they were flying a plane with the inelegant moniker PV-1 49-538, call-named *Gambler 17*.

No problem. This flight was supposed to be routine. Piece of cake.

The plane, like the *Miss Deal*, was a Lockheed PV-1 Ventura bomber, with a split rear tail, two engines, and a range of 950 miles. On board, she carried two forward-firing .50 caliber machine guns and six .30 caliber guns on flex mounts; her bomb bay could hold 2,500 pounds of bombs. Her job was searching out and bombing Japanese submarines, but Gwinn, the lowest-ranked

211

pilot in his unit, had yet to be tested. Although he had patrolled miles and miles of the Pacific between Peleliu Island and the Japanese homeland, he and his flyboys still had not seen any action. Nothing.

Life on Peleliu was hell on earth. The island was a no-man's-land, 500 miles from the coast of the Philippines, and 500 miles north of New Guinea. Daily temperatures reached 120 degrees, and stayed there. The humidity was drenching. The island, scene of one of the last major battles before the U.S. Marines' decisive victories at Iwo Jima and then Okinawa, had come at a great cost: about 10,000 marine casualties. But the entire garrison of 10,500 entrenched Japanese soldiers had been wiped out. A bloodbath.

On the morning of August 2, this hotly contested piece of real estate was home to the Peleliu unit of the search and reconnaissance command, which fell under the supervision of Vice Admiral George Murray, commander of Marianas naval operations back in Guam. This was the same command from which the *Indy* had sailed six days earlier, the command that had given McVay his sailing orders. Reporting to Vice Admiral Murray was Captain Oliver Naquin, the surface operations officer who had neglected to tell McVay about Japanese subs along the Peddie route, part of which Gwinn would soon be patrolling.

At this morning's flight briefing, Gwinn had learned that he might see American convoys passing in his patrol sector, which ran north from Peleliu for 500 miles. Other than that, the coast should be clear. He was to keep his eyes peeled for enemy subs cruising, and to sink any he spotted with a dive-bombing run. His other task was to test out a new antenna used in loran navigation, an innovation that had made the bombing of Japan an easier task. The long whip antenna was attached to the rear flank of the plane and steadied with the weighted sock, which kept it from slipping around. The problem was, the sock wouldn't stay on.

By 9 a.m., Gwinn had a new one secured, and forty-five minutes after his original departure, he taxied down the runway and roared the bomber north, over the Philippine Sea.

At about the same time, 700 miles to the west of Gwinn, on the island of Leyte, Lieutenant William A. Green received a report of the nonarrival of the USS *Indianapolis* from the naval operating base. Green's job in the Tolosa office of the Philippine Sea Frontier was to monitor incoming dispatches regarding shipping traffic, and in the case of emergency, take up the matter with his superior, Captain Alfred Granum, the operations officer who maintained the office's plotting board, and who had registered the *Indianapolis* as "arrived" in Leyte two days earlier.

This was the second nonarrival report Green had received; a similar report had come in on Wednesday. Now he requested permission from the Plotting Section to remove the ship entirely from the plotting board in Tolosa. Once more, it was simply assumed that the *Indy* had been diverted to other action.

Gwinn leveled the PV-1 off at 3,000 feet, the prescribed altitude for patrol and recon. The sea below him blinked like shattered stained glass. Scanning the horizon, he saw nothing.

And then, the new sock on the whip antenna fell off. This time, Gwinn kept flying. He would make do, although his radioman informed him that long-range communications would be rendered inoperative. Dead reckoning was a tricky navigational procedure way out here, and Gwinn didn't want to run out of fuel; he would be forced to ditch. And there were sharks in these waters.

The antenna was whipping back and forth against the aluminum side of the plane. At 11 a.m., Gwinn decided to try and fix it by jerry-rigging some kind of new weight. He didn't know exactly what he was doing; he was making this up as he went along. Bombardier Joe Johnson stood aft, looking out a window, trying to figure out what they could do to keep the antenna from beating the plane up any further. Inching out of his pilot's seat in the cramped cockpit, Gwinn made his way down the narrow passage of the plane toward the rear, ready to give Johnson a hand. He lay down on the plane's floor to fix the loose antenna, gazing through the window in the plane's belly at the endless sea below.

And then he spotted something. It looked like an oil slick, and it probably meant one thing: there was a Japanese submarine nearby, perhaps disabled by an earlier attack. If an American ship had been downed, Gwinn reasoned, he would have read about it in a report.

Could it be true? Would they see action? He jumped up and hurried back to the cockpit. It sure as hell looked like the slick of a leaking sub. Gwinn was ecstatic.

He changed the course of the plane and followed the slick to the north, beginning preparations for a bombing run. The bomb bay doors opened and he ordered the bombs, snug in racks and hanging ready to be "pickled," or dropped. He next ordered the depth charges readied. The charges looked like fifty-five-gallon drums and were loaded with the explosive Torpex. They could be preset to detonate at different depths and then dropped out the bomb bay doors.

At 11:20, Gwinn lowered the PV-1 and started cruising at 200 miles per hour up the oil slick. Over the intercom, he told his bombardier to get ready. After flying about five miles, cruising at 900 feet, he spotted something in the water.

But what the hell was it? Gwinn was confused. As it came into focus, he realized it was a group of figures, and they seemed to be waving—it looked like they were slapping at the water, as if trying to attract attention. Enemy? Friendly? He had to think fast.

He yelled over the intercom to abort the bombing run and banked for another pass.

Gwinn took the plane down to 300 feet and roared up the slick. He quickly counted about thirty heads. He took a dead reckoning fix because the loran antenna was inoperable—he needed some kind of navigational point to report what he was finding.

A patrol plane, Gwinn's PV-1 was loaded with emergency life rafts, beakers of water, life vests, and other lifesaving gear. As the plane passed low, Gwinn's crew dropped a raft, vests, and a sonobuoy out the rear side hatch. Aiming the falling equipment was tricky—he feared hitting the floating bodies. The blackened shapes were now waving frantically as he passed over. He couldn't see their faces clearly—it looked like they were covered with . . . oil? As he flew, he saw others who were clinging to life rafts.

The sonobuoy was a one-way floating microphone used in anti-submarine warfare. Gwinn hoped that whoever it was he'd spotted would swim over to it and yell out a name, an identity—anything. So far, no sound was coming back.

In an instant, his mission had flipped from search and destroy to search and rescue. At 11:25, he radioed a message to the search and reconnaissance headquarters on Peleliu; it read: SIGHTED 30 SURVIVORS 011-30 NORTH 133-30 EAST—the numbers indicating the latitude and longitude of the sighting.

This was the first report of the USS *Indianapolis* disaster.

But who were these people in the water? The idea that they were U.S. boys seemed out of the question; Gwinn was certain that he would have been briefed if an American ship had been sunk. He counted close to seventy more heads, and then after another minute spotted at least fifty more. The numbers indicated that these weren't survivors from a sub, which carried crews of 100 or less. These boys had to have come from a major ship.

Gwinn wagged his wings—*I see you*—and skimmed low overhead, now looking down at bodies so closely crowded around the rafts that it was hard to estimate their number. He could make out lone swimmers only if they kicked the water and raised a splash. When they stopped kicking, they melted into the blue of the sea, as if swallowed by it. The pilot, whose vision was somewhat occluded, could ultimately make out four loosely scattered groups: the first contained about thirty people and was approximately six miles from the second group of about forty; the third group, two miles from the second, looked like about fifty-five to seventy-five people. There was also, Gwinn now saw, a fourth group, which numbered around twenty-five to thirty-five.

Gwinn, in fact, had just spotted parts of both Dr. Haynes's group of swimmers and the large raft group under the command of Ensign Harlan Twible, who was still towing the unconscious officer Richard Redmayne by his life vest straps. Over the course of the night, both groups had been slowly breaking up into scattered clusters. Gwinn just missed Captain McVay and his small band of nine men and four rafts. Nor did he see McCoy and his gang of four. These two groups had drifted about eight miles ahead of the Haynes and Twible groups.

In the last fourteen hours, McCoy had drifted some twenty-three miles, for an astonishing total of about one hundred and five miles since the sinking three days earlier. McVay had drifted another sixteen miles in the same period for a total of one hundred and three. Haynes and Twible had each covered about seventeen miles and drifted roughly ninety-seven and eighty-seven miles, respectively, in all. As Gwinn circled, they continued their swift momentum, driven by the current and the wind.

DR. Haynes had drifted into another world, far from the realization of what was happening. When he looked up to find life vests tumbling out of the sky, it seemed to him the heavens were raining gear. When he saw them crash about 100 feet away, he felt too weak to swim to them. But, with painfully slow strokes, his neck bleeding as his own waterlogged vest chafed against it, he somehow managed to cover the distance. He grabbed a few vests, hugged them tight, and then steeled himself for the return trip to his boys.

Minute by minute, he felt his mind clearing as the glinting plane circled. He counted about 100 boys left in his scattered group, which had numbered at least 400 three days earlier. At this point, because of the failing vests, each boy was sunk up to his chin, treading furiously just to keep his nose above the water. Even as the PV-1 circled overhead, some boys gave up and drowned.

Bob Gause waved his hat as if it were a signal flag. Never much of a churchgoer, he'd nonetheless spent the last twenty-four hours praying with all his heart, praying harder than he ever imagined possible. It seemed it had paid off. All around him, boys started singing out of tune, while others became so excited they started flapping their arms, often drowning themselves in the process.

Jack Cassidy, covered with saltwater ulcers, was wearing three life vests but he was still sinking into the heaving sea. His eyes were so matted with fuel oil that he had to pry them open with bleeding fingers to look up and see the plane, and the dye bombs that were now being released from its belly.

As the orange dye spread around them and marked the boys' positions, some of them began to sing even louder, shouting that the plane was an angel. They truly believed saviors were visiting from heaven.* Haynes, however, noticed with alarm that, in the commotion, his dwindling group was continuing to drift apart. Operating on nothing but a vapor of adrenaline, he tore open the pockets of the new life vests, looking for the precious cans of water he guessed would be stored there. But every one of the cans had exploded on impact when they hit the ocean. The survivors, Haynes knew, might live only a few more hours without water. He watched anxiously as some of the boys made their way to the rubber life raft that the plane had dropped. Soon the raft was crammed with as many as twenty men, with another twenty or so clinging desperately to the lifelines.

Meanwhile, Gwinn was trying to get a loran fix, which would offer a more accurate position than the dead reckoning fix had given. He struggled to the back of the plane, grabbed hold of the

---

* In the years following their rescue, the survivors of the *Indianapolis* missed no opportunity to call Chuck Gwinn their "angel." They mobbed him whenever he showed up at their biannual reunions and made him an honorary member of their survivors' organization. Gwinn, who died in July of 1993, was often moved to tears by this display of affection.

antenna wire, and reeled it in. Then he fitted it with a piece of rubber hose, hoping that its weight would be enough to prevent the antenna from tearing loose.

The radioman announced that he had, in fact, just gotten a reading. Now Gwinn had a position to report. He was in business. He then sent a second message. More urgent than the first he had sent an hour and twenty minutes earlier, it read: SEND RESCUE SHIP 11–54 N 133–47 E 150 SURVIVORS IN LIFEBOAT AND JACKETS.

With this new message, the otherwise normal day back at the Peleliu search and recon command suddenly unraveled. The chaos quickly spread throughout the Philippine Sea Frontier, and finally to the Marianas command in Guam.

The search and recon unit had already responded to the first message, thanks to the quick thinking of one of its officers, Lieutenant Commander George Atteberry, Gwinn's superior officer. At 12:05 p.m., when Atteberry had received Gwinn's message, he thought his pilot had stumbled upon the survivors of a plane wreck. He knew he had to act quickly. Worried for Gwinn's safety, Atteberry quickly calculated that the pilot had enough fuel for another four hours of flight before he would be forced to turn around and head back to Peleliu. Atteberry wanted to make sure, therefore, that the survivors were covered by some kind of air support after Gwinn's departure.

And so he decisively took matters into his own hands. From his Quonset hut office he called across the island to the duty station handling the dispatch and command of a squadron of amphibious planes called PBY-5As, or Catalinas. These planes were designed with floats to land on water, and their crews specialized in locating survivors of ship and air disasters. Atteberry informed the duty officer that he wanted a Catalina to leave immediately in order to relieve Gwinn by 3:30 p.m. But the duty officer wanted official confirmation of the spotting of survivors. Unfortunately, there was none; no commanding officers above Atteberry's rank of lieutenant commander knew about the accident yet. Events had unfolded so quickly that Atteberry had not had time to transmit a message to Vice Admiral Murray, commander of the Marianas, in Guam, whose jurisdiction included the area in which the survivors were drifting.

Frustrated, Atteberry hung up and decided to drive over to the duty station and hash it out in person. Once there, however, he realized that the duty officer would never be able to get a Catalina rescue plane up in time to meet Gwinn's turnaround time. He quickly drove back to his office and ordered up a Ventura bomber from his own squadron. The plane was fueled, and Atteberry and a crew of four lifted off the island.

The time was 12:44.

A minute later, Gwinn's second, more urgent message requesting that a rescue ship be dispatched to his search area arrived at Atteberry's command on Peleliu. Because he was in the air, Atteberry did not intercept this transmission, but he would be arriving at the rescue scene in an hour and a half in any case.

Two important people did receive it, however, and it immediately swung the effort into hyperdrive. One of the largest sea rescues in the history of the U. S. Navy was under way.*

First to receive the message was the surface operations officer for the Philippine Sea Frontier, Captain Alfred Granum. He was surprised to hear news of so many downed soldiers or sailors. He

---

* There is debate about which sea rescue of World War II constitutes the largest. The *Indy*'s, which involved a total of eleven aircraft and eleven ships over a six-day period (including post-rescue recovery of bodies), certainly ranks among the most significant.

had no idea to what command they belonged—he had no knowledge of any ship under the Philippine Sea Frontier jurisdiction that was overdue. It was his superior officer, Commodore Norman Gillette, the acting commander of the Philippine Sea Frontier, who three days earlier had received notice of an SOS from the *Indy* and then had ostensibly recalled the tugboats dispatched to the sinking site.

Curious, and more than a little concerned, Granum called down to Lieutenant Stewart Gibson, the port director operations officer at Tacloban. (Gibson, two days earlier, acting per the navy directive 10CL-45, had ignored the *Indy*'s nonarrival in Leyte.) Granum then contacted Lieutenant William A. Green, the officer in the Philippine Sea Frontier command at Tolosa, who that morning had requested permission from Granum's office to remove the *Indy* from the Tolosa plotting board. Granum instructed Green to leave it exactly where it stood on the board; they had received reports that there were men in the water.

The second crucial person to receive Gwinn's second message was Vice Admiral Murray on Guam. Less than fifteen minutes later, he sent a dispatch to the command on the western Carolines—the island chain to which Peleliu belonged—that read: ORDER 2 DESTROYERS AT BEST SPEED . . . RESCUE 150 SURVIVORS IN LIFEBOATS. Murray, under whose jurisdiction the chilling prospect of rescue rested, was taking no chances. He had heeded Gwinn's message and done what the lone pilot had requested. Two ships would soon be rushing to the boys in the water.

As the rescue effort heated up on Guam, a navy PBM-5, an amphibious transport plane, was flying patrol from Saipan to Samar when, through a break in the cloud cover, the crew noticed a brilliant flash, as if reflected off a large bronze mirror. Looking down, they saw a large oil slick glinting below them. Radar reported another plane in the area, which they determined was friendly. It was, in fact, Gwinn and his crew.

The PBM-5 emerged from the clouds, and the crew began dropping all of their survival gear, including their own life jackets and rafts. They reported large and small groups with sharks all around the perimeter. When they had nothing left to drop, they regained altitude and radioed Saipan and Leyte requesting permission to put down and pick up survivors. The request was denied.

LIEUTENANT Commander George Atteberry, in his Ventura bomber, call-named *Gambler Leader*, arrived at the wreckage site at 2:15 p.m., quickly joining Gwinn, who was glad for the company. He led Atteberry on a half-hour tour of the area, about a twenty-mile-wide stretch of ocean. Now they had to wait for a ship to pick up the boys, trying to reassure them in the meantime by continuing to circle overhead. By this point, Gwinn was definitely running out of fuel; Atteberry was forced to send him back to Peleliu. Gwinn, who had spent an emotional four hours circling the frantic boys in the water, was shaky and worried as he headed back to his base.

Atteberry had patrolled the area alone for a half hour when, to his surprise, the call numbers of another plane came over the radio. The plane belonged to Lieutenant Adrian Marks, a tall, slim, twenty-eight-year-old lawyer from Indiana who had been a navy flier and instructor for three years. Marks was part of the Catalina squadron that Atteberry had tried to raise two hours earlier back in Peleliu. Marks had been hunkered down in a sweltering Quonset hut, trying to decipher what appeared to be a garbled radio message. It read, in part: "Am circling life rafts." It was from Gwinn, and upon reading it, Marks had jumped into action. He thought maybe a carrier pilot had been forced to ditch in the open sea.

Marks went immediately to the Catalinas' HQ. He had just missed Atteberry but found out that he had been looking for a plane. Marks knew that the standby plane was already out on a mission. If he left, there would be no planes available to be dispatched in case of an emergency. He weighed the decision, decided this *was* an emergency, and fueled up his plane, the *Playmate 2*. He and his crew of nine aviators, including one co-pilot, two radiomen, and two bombardiers, loaded the mammoth plane with life rafts, parachute flares, dye markers, and shipwreck kits containing water and rations. Bigger than Atteberry's Ventura bomber, the PBY-5A Catalina, known as a "Dumbo," was a two-engine, high-wing plane built for hunting subs and landing in smooth water to pick up downed pilots. Landing in the rolling open ocean would be dicey, to say the least.

At 12:42, Marks had taken off from Peleliu, following the coordinates Gwinn had radioed from the wreckage site. During the three-hour, 280-mile flight, a call came over his radio from one of the ships, a destroyer escort named the USS *Cecil J. Doyle* on patrol north of the Palau Islands. Its captain, Graham Claytor, asked after Marks's mission. Upon discovering that Claytor had received no dispatch about the men in the ocean, Marks gave him the news.

As luck would have it, Claytor, about 200 miles from the *Indy*'s crew, decided to turn his ship around. He began steaming south at twenty-two and a half knots. Claytor did this without first radioing his command at Peleliu or asking for orders, a strict violation of his duties as a captain. He was, however, a confident man, with a distinguished record. A lawyer in civilian life, he had been president of the *Harvard Law Review* and clerk to Supreme Court justice Louis Brandeis before entering the navy in 1942. He was a man used to thinking for himself. At 2:35 p.m., he made contact with Atteberry. He informed him that he would be traveling at the best possible speed, but put his ETA at no earlier than sometime after midnight.

Meanwhile, CINCPAC, the naval command in Manila, began radioing all ships: BREAK RADIO SILENCE X REPORT YOUR POSITION. The purpose of this dispatch was to determine which ships were at large in the Philippine Sea. As the responses began flooding into HQ, the *Indy*'s was noticeably absent.

Then, in the midafternoon, the Philippine Sea Frontier, under Commodore Gillette's command, finally got into the act. Having discovered that there were not just one but three ships overdue at Leyte, it sent this feeler out over the airwaves to the Marianas command at Guam: INDIANAPOLIS (CA 35) HAS NOT ARRIVED LEYTE X ADVISE.

Guam responded: INDIANAPOLIS (CA 35) DEPARTED GUAM 2300Z 27 JULY IN ACCORDANCE OUR 280032Z OF JULY XXX.*

This was unwelcome news for the Frontier. Captain Granum, the operations officer, aware that the *Indy* had been scheduled to meet Admiral McCormick at Leyte for gunnery practice, sent an urgent cable: HAS THE INDIANAPOLIS REPORTED TO YOU?

---

* When adjusted for differing military time zones, this dispatch confirms that the *Indianapolis* left Guam on July 28, 1945, at 9 a.m.

Rear Admiral McCormick had just returned to his anchorage in San Pedro Bay after finishing the training tour off the Leyte coast—maneuvers in which the *Indy* should have participated. When asked by Granum if the *Indy* had reported to him, McCormick cabled back a chilling one-word reply: NEGATIVE.

LIEUTENANT Adrian Marks reached the scene of the survivors at 3:20 p.m., and what he found astounded him. Lieutenant Atteberry informed Marks that there were a great many people scattered over a wide area. He said not to drop any lifesaving equipment until he had made a full tour, which Marks quickly did. Both pilots then decided (as had Gwinn earlier) to steer away from the people clinging to rafts and to concentrate on those held up solely by vests. Thirty minutes after he arrived, Marks began bombing the boys with his provisions.

At about the same time, the destroyers *Ralph Talbot* (DD 390) and *Madison* (DD 425) received orders to cut short their patrols near the island of Ulithi and head directly to the rescue site. Their ETA: twelve hours from the present; sometime early Friday morning.

Marks knew the situation was dire. From his recon altitude of a mere 25 feet, he had a clear view to the deep green sea and the hundreds of sharks circling the men. Night, which he knew was the sharks' normal feeding period, was approaching.* One of

---

* The sharks had, in fact, remained a constant presence throughout the men's ordeal, even during the daylight hours. Not long after Gwinn showed up, a massive shark attack—involving an estimated thirty fish—had, in about fifteen minutes, taken some sixty boys perched on a floater net.

Marks's crewmen watched as a shark attacked one of the men and dragged him under. As Marks himself witnessed more attacks, his anxiety grew. It looked to him as if the survivors were so weak they couldn't even begin to fight back.

Speed was clearly of the essence. Marks skipped the usual communication protocol, sending an uncoded message back to Peleliu: BETWEEN 100 AND 200 SURVIVORS AT POSITION REPORTED X NEED ALL SURVIVAL EQUIPMENT AVAILABLE WHILE DAYLIGHT HOLDS X SURVIVORS MANY WITHOUT RAFTS . . . .

In the same message, Marks announced a bold decision: WILL ATTEMPT OPEN SEA LANDING. He had never tried to land in the open sea before; all previous attempts by members of his squadron had ended in disaster. In fact, his squadron was now under standing orders that prohibited making them.

A few minutes later, he yelled into his crew's headsets, checking to make sure they agreed with his decision to attempt a landing. They gave him the thumbs-up. The team was going in. He cut the throttle, dramatically lifting the nose of the lumbering Catalina and setting her down in a power stall. Hitting the top of one wave, the *Playmate 2* was knocked back skyward fifteen feet. Then it came down even harder. At any moment, the plane could blow apart. On the third huge blow she settled down like a hen over an egg, her seams and rivets popping and seawater streaming in. Marks's crew shoved cotton and pencils into the holes in the metal skin of the plane. The radio compartment, located midplane, was taking on water, and the radioman began bailing immediately, starting a pace that would keep all the crew busy at a rate of ten to twelve buckets an hour. The propellers were still spinning, and it was essential that they didn't dig into the sea, or they would flip the plane.

Marks's copilot, Ensign Irving Lefkovitz, moved to the side hatch and began preparing for rescue. Marks himself had no idea where to steer the plane; the whole craft pitched up and down as if on a carnival ride surrounded by rising and falling walls of water. Circling above, Atteberry became Marks's eyes in the fading twilight. The race was on to collect as many of the survivors as possible before total darkness consumed them all.

Marks had landed among the group led by Dr. Haynes. Their numbers had dwindled from the previous day's 110 to about 95, the group having lost at least 5 more boys this afternoon. All of them were yelling at the plane, beckoning the pilot to come closer. Marks gunned the twin engines throbbing atop the high wings and powered the Dumbo through the seas, searching out those near death. It was tricky. The normal taxiing speed of the *Playmate 2* was thirty-five miles per hour, too fast to pick up any men. Marks hit upon a solution: as he gunned the motors, another crew member raised and lowered the landing gear, using them as brakes. It worked.

EARLIER in the day, upon learning of Gwinn's position coordinates, Captain Granum, back in Tolosa, had kicked the rescue effort into high gear. He had confirmed the *Indy*'s departure from Guam and concluded that the latitude and longitude reading corresponded to ones she had probably passed over on her trip to Leyte. That she was almost certainly the missing ship in question was becoming clearer by the minute. With the approval of Commodore Gillette, Granum issued urgent orders dispatching several patrol vessels and planes to the rescue area. He was now coordinating the rescue operation with the efforts of the Peleliu search and recon command, from which Gwinn, Atteberry, and Marks had flown.

At the same time, the commander of the nearby western Carolines, under the jurisdiction of Vice Admiral Murray on Guam, ordered all ships and planes in the vicinity to come to the rescuers' aid.

Shortly before Marks landed in the late afternoon, two B-17 Flying Fortresses from the Third Emergency Rescue Squadron of the Army Air Forces in Peleliu had arrived at the rescue site. The crew aboard these long-range bombers, who had heard Gwinn's earlier messages, unloaded seventeen life rafts, two twenty-six-foot wooden lifeboats, numerous life vests, and three dozen five-man rubber life rafts to clusters of boys in Haynes's group.

Around 7:15 p.m. another PBY, the *Playmate 1,* also landed. This plane was piloted by Lieutenant Richard Alcorn of the U.S. Army Air Forces. He set down two miles north of Marks and immediately began cruising through the surf, passing dead bodies and floating debris, the ship's detritus that had been borne along with the boys. To aid his search in the dusk, Alcorn turned on his plane's light. Mistaking it for survival flares, other planes arriving on-scene began dropping supplies on him. Despite the mishap, Alcorn was actually able to pick up one survivor before he realized that he could do no good in the dark; he had landed too far afield from most of the survivors anyway.* Alcorn quickly realized, however, that he could be of use by operating his plane's lights as beacons to guide circling aircraft and rescue ships to the scene. He would spend a total of more than fifty-one hours in the area, returning to Peleliu only to refuel.

---

* There is no record of the survivor's identity.

HAYNES, exasperated that his boys were still dying with rescue so imminent, knew he had to do something. After Marks had dropped his rafts, Haynes paddled over to one of them, but found himself too weak to pull the toggle that would self-inflate the craft. In the end, it had taken three boys to release the cord. They elected Haynes to be the first to board the safe, dry refuge, an honor he at first refused, but they were insistent. After agreeing, he had to remove his bulky life vest, a torturous process. Free from the thing for the first time in nearly four days, his shoulders rubbed raw and bleeding, he was hoisted up by the boys and flopped over the rail. Immediately, he started looking for water on board—he had to find water. But he found none.

He managed to help lift ten more boys into the raft, and a remaining twenty had to hang on to the lifelines around it. Soon, however, the afternoon heat grew unbearable and the boys in the raft jumped back into the cooler sea. Their core body temperatures were now dipping below eighty-five degrees, at which point most major motor functions stumble and cease. That they were functioning at all was a miracle, but looking at them, Haynes thought they all looked like cadavers. The condition of the men was so acute, he knew that they couldn't wait much longer for water.

His suffering now seemed natural. He felt close to God, as if he were about to be lifted up, pinched between two massive, invisible fingers reaching down from the sky. With great mental strain, he tried to operate a desalinating pump stored in the raft but found he had trouble even reading the directions. Yet he didn't give up. For several long hours he pumped what he thought was potable water, only to discover that each batch was poisoned with the tang of the sea. He cursed his increasing stupidity until, in a fit of despair that had been steadily building, he pitched the pump overboard. For the first time since the sinking, he fell to pieces.

He started weeping. He wept angrily over his failure to find water for his boys, over his inability to keep so many from dying. He felt ashamed that he couldn't do more for them, but he knew he was doing the best he could. And that was all he could ask of himself anymore.

CIRCLING overhead, Lieutenant Commander Atteberry began directing Marks toward microgroups of hard-struggling survivors. The two planes were in constant radio contact as Marks taxied the plane through the swells. Often all he could see were walls of water and then a glimpse of the next wave.

The *Playmate 2*'s side hatch was open, and a Jacob's ladder (a series of steps strung on rope) hung from its lip. A crewman stood on the rungs as Marks handled the plane.

"Okay, Dumbo, come right," radioed Atteberry. "Steady as you go . . . left, a little bit."

"Okay, we see him!" Marks radioed back. Fearing he might run over a survivor, Marks cut the engines. The crewman on the ladder reached down and grabbed hold of a boy who was floating face down, gripping his arms and yanking. What he pulled from the sea nauseated him: it was only the upper half of a body. They repeated the taxing process; often, when the crewmen grabbed hold of the swimmer, they found the boy was too weak to hang on.

Adrian Marks was asking who these men were. He pulled aboard one boy, a petty officer, who told him they were from the *Indianapolis.*

Marks now had the information that for the past five hours had eluded the command back in Peleliu and Guam. But he was too busy to code a message communicating the ship's identity to the outside world. He aimed the plane toward the next cluster of men. The world could wait for the news; he had work to do.

As Marks's plane floated past, picking up survivors, Haynes decided to make a try for it. Dr. Haynes didn't really swim as much as claw his way over the water about sixty feet. By the time he reached the rope ladder hanging from Marks's hatch, he was nearly dead.

But he didn't get on the plane. Looking up through blurry eyes, he called out for a beaker of water and a life vest. He pulled the vest on, loosely tying it. Then, pushing the beaker ahead of him as he paddled, he finally made it back to the raft. After downing a small cup, he poured out an allotment and then pointed to a boy. "This is for him," he croaked, his throat parched, before handing the glass down the line of waiting hands. When the glass came back, Haynes refilled it. And repeated the process, choosing a new boy to drink. The sight of the water trembling in the glass was excruciating for Haynes; it was all he could do to prevent himself from gulping it all down himself. And by the looks of the sunken, vacant eyes of the rest of the boys, he knew that they were all exercising incredible restraint. As he continued serving them, he felt a blooming sense of pride—not one of these sailors was cheating by drinking out of turn. Haynes would forever marvel over this moment.

Lifting the boys aboard the *Playmate 2*, Marks discovered that many had swollen, broken legs and arms; boarding was a hideously painful process. At times, as Marks and his crew gave a heave-ho, the flesh of the latest retrieval remained in their hands. The seawater had eaten away all the body hair from some, who came aboard whimpering, pale, and smooth-skinned as newts. Marks and his crew were horrified.

Soon Marks had picked up some thirty boys and watched as they were carefully arranged on the deck of the Catalina. They thrashed uncontrollably in their delirium, kicking holes in the fuselage. Within a matter of a few hours, the entire water supply would be exhausted. Each boy was forced to wait several minutes between refilling his cup in order not to upset his shrunken stomach. After two drinks, which totaled just one cup of water, the boys fell into a deep sleep, broken only by requests for more fluid.

Ed Brown and Bob Gause were hauled aboard, sandwiched between several dozen other boys. Brown had spent the day floating and staring at the oblivion of the sky, hypnotized by what he saw there. It was a Western Union telegram that stretched from horizon to horizon, and it read: DEAR MRS. BROWN, WE REGRET TO INFORM YOU THAT YOUR SON IS MISSING IN ACTION. Now he lay on the plane's deck, overjoyed, even as his rescuers stepped and walked over him.

In his exhaustion, Bob Gause was sitting in several inches of water, remarking that it must really be raining like hell for the inside of the plane to be this wet.

"What do you mean, rain?" said a boy sitting next to him. "It's not raining." Then the two realized the plane was taking on water; it appeared to be sinking. (The water, in fact, was entering the plane at the seams split during Marks's rough landing.) A number of the boys started bailing like crazy, fearful they were going to start their ordeal all over again.

Some of the hallucinating sailors had reacted violently to the idea of rescue. Soon the *Catalina*'s deck was stacked tight with boys kicking senselessly at phantoms. The odor of vomit and excrement filled the plane. Having run out of room inside the plane, Marks stacked more boys on the wings, where they were wrapped mummy-style in parachutes and bound with rope to prevent them from rolling off. By nightfall, he had rescued 56 survivors. Approximately 300 still waited, but darkness, total now, made further rescue efforts impossible. Marks could do no more until daylight; he resolved to wait until the rescue ships arrived.

His job was done. The *Playmate 2* drifted through the dark, echoing with the howls of the boys stored inside.

CAPTAIN Graham Claytor and the *Cecil J. Doyle* steamed into the field of debris and bodies at 11:45 p.m. Claytor wasted little time getting involved. Lowering a motorized whaleboat, he began off-loading survivors from Marks's Catalina into the *Doyle*'s sick bay. At 12:52 a.m., Friday, August 3, the high-speed transport *Bassett* (APD 73) arrived, and within four hours the destroyers *Ralph Talbot* and *Madison* and the destroyer escort *Dufilho* (DE 423) were also in the area. Although more than twelve hours had passed since Gwinn sighted the survivors, not one of the rescue vessels, except for Marks's, had yet learned the name of the boys' ship.

During the predawn hours, the *Bassett* would pick up 152 survivors, the single largest group to be plucked from the sea, before being ordered to return to Leyte. These boys were primarily from the Twible group of rafters, who were drifting about fifteen miles to the northeast of Haynes's swimmers. Between these two floated Captain McVay and his group of nine. Alone, and leading the drift about seven miles to the northwest of Haynes, were McCoy and his four raftmates.

Many, to the amazement of the *Bassett* crewmen, didn't want to be rescued. When the *Bassett* lowered its Higgins boats, the boys swimming in the searchlights became convinced that their rescuers were Japanese sailors. (Higgins boats, also called LCVPs, are high-sided, flat-bottomed craft often used by marines for beach landings.) Likewise, the rescue crews, who still didn't know the identity of their catch, weren't so sure a trick wasn't being played on them. All they could see were oil-blackened faces and the whites of deeply sunken eyes staring back at them. Drawing his pistol, one rescuer yelled out, "Hey! What city do the Dodgers play in?"

"Brooklyn!" came the reply. The crew gunned its boat ahead to the rescue.

To get the boys aboard required some imaginative thinking. One rescuer convinced the survivors he was taking them to a dance and made them form a conga line leading to the Higgins boat. Others were told they were heading out for a night of liberty on the town. Twenty-year-old *Bassett* rescuer William Van Wilpe was uncommonly brave, jumping into the sea from his boat after three survivors had fallen out. They sank immediately, dead weight. Van Wilpe emerged on the surface carrying all three in his arms, a Herculean effort. Later, when he dislocated his shoulder, he popped it back into place himself and quickly resumed his duty.

Jack Miner tried feverishly to swim away from the approach of an LCVP, but was too weak. He was lifted over the rail of the craft, kicking and struggling. Lifted up by a burly, bearded sailor, Miner believed he was in the arms of the angel Gabriel. He stopped struggling when a slice of orange was shoved in his mouth. To Miner the fruit tasted like heaven, and when he finished it, he sucked greedily on the rind.

AT 4 a.m., the searchlight of the *Cecil J. Doyle* found Dr. Haynes's raft in its sharp beam.

Sitting next to the doctor was one of his boys who had lost his marbles. "Hey," the kid yelled up to the *Doyle*. "Have you got any water on board?"

The eager answer came back, "We got a lot of water on board!"

The kid was silent. After a moment, he said, "'Cause if you ain't got any water, go away and leave us alone!"

A cargo net was rolled down the metal hull of the *Doyle,* and Haynes was hauled from the sea with a rope tied around his waist. He was naked, burned, and half out of his mind. But he pushed away the men holding him up, announcing: "I can stand on my own!"

"Who are you?" Claytor asked him.

"This is all that's left of the *Indianapolis,*" Dr. Haynes rasped. "We have been in the water four days."

The crew of the PV-1 Ventura bomber who accidentally discovered the crew of the *Indianapolis* during a routine patrol on August 2, 1945. As pilot Wilbur "Chuck" Gwinn circled, he could see crew members drowning in sodden life vests. Front row, left to right: Lt. Wilbur Gwinn and Lt. Warren Colwell; back row, left to right: Herbert Hickman, William Hartman, and Joseph Johnson. *Courtesy of the collection of Robert Krauss*

Pilot Adrian Marks (front row, second from right), who landed the plane in dangerous ocean swells and picked up fifty-six survivors, and his crew of the PBY Catalina. *Courtesy of the collection of Giles McCoy*

Two survivors (William R. Mulvey on left) aboard a raft pull themselves toward the rescue ship *Register*, after four and a half days afloat, sunburned, dehydrated, and severely malnourished. Most survivors also suffered massive skin ulcers. *National Archives*

Mike Kuryla (left), Bob McGuiggan (center), and an unidentified sailor in the hospital on Peleliu. High school friends from Chicago, Kuryla and McGuiggan each thought the other had died before being reunited. *Courtesy of the collections of Bob McGuiggan and Mike Kuryla*

Exhausted survivors (William R. Mulvey on right), awaiting transfer to the hospital ship USS *Tranquility*, rest on a barge at Peleliu. *Courtesy of the collection of Giles McCoy*

Welcomed by sailors and nurses on Guam, the survivors are transferred from the USS *Tranquility* to ambulances destined for local hospitals. *Naval History and Heritage Command*

August 1945: Admiral Raymond Spruance, visiting the survivors at Base 18 Hospital in Guam, awards them Purple Hearts. *National Archives*

WESTERN UNION

Received at FAIRFIELD TAXI SERVICE 1853 Post Road, Fairfield, Conn.

WU9 108 GOVT 3 EXTRA WASHINGTON DV VIA MANISTEE MICH 13

MRS ELIZABETH DODGE HAYNES=

&7 FAIRFIELD BEACH FAIRFIELD CON=

A REPORT JUST RECEIVED SHOWS YOUR HUSBAND LIEUTENANT COMMANDER
LEWIS LEAVITT HAYNES USN HAS BEEN WOUNDED IN ACTION 30 JULY
1945 DIAGNOSIS EXHAUSTION FROM OVEREXPOSURE PROGNOSIS GOOD
YOUR ANXIETY IS APPRECIATED AND YOU WILL BE FURNISHED DETAILS
WHEN RECEIVED. YOU ARE ASSURED THAT HE IS RECEIVING THE BEST
POSSIBLE MEDICAL CARE AND I JOIN IN THE WISH FOR HIS SPEEDY
RECOVERY COMMUNICATIONS MAY BE ADDRESSED TO HIM CARE US BASE
HOSPITAL #18 NAVY #926 FPO SANFRANCISCO CALIFORNIA TO PREVENT

The telegrams Elizabeth Haynes received from Washington and from her husband, Lew, apprising her of his condition. *Courtesy of the collection of Lewis Haynes*

WESTERN UNION
1211P

Received at FAIRFIELD TAXI SERVICE 1853 Post Road, Fairfield, Conn.

POSSIBLE AID TO OUR ENEMIES PLEASE DO NOT DIVULGE THE NAME OF
HIS SHIP OR STATION UNLESS THE GENERAL CIRCUMSTANCES ARE MADE
PUBLIC IN NEWS STORIES=

VICE ADMIRAL RANDALL JACOBS THE CHIEF OF NAVAL PERSONNEL.

WESTERN UNION

Received at FAIRFIELD TAXI SERVICE 1853 Post Road, Fairfield, Conn.

WU2 INTL=USNAV VIA COMPACIFIC 161 321 31 EFM

MRS LEWIS L HAYNES=

72 FAIRFIELD BEACH FAIRFIELDCONN=

INJURY IS NOT SERIOUS AM GETTING ALONG ALL RIGHT. ALL MY LOVE
LEW.

Marine privates first class Paul Uffelman (left), Giles McCoy (center), and Mel Jacob (right), sailing for the United States aboard the USS *Hollandia*, after their convalescence on Guam. Of the thirty-nine-man marine detachment aboard the *Indianapolis*, only nine survived the disaster. *Courtesy of the collections of Bill Van Daalen and Giles McCoy*

JAPAN SURRENDERS, END OF WAR!
EMPEROR ACCEPTS ALLIED RULE;
M'ARTHUR SUPREME COMMANDER;
OUR MANPOWER CURBS VOIDED

HIRING MADE LOCAL

Communities, Labor and Management Will Unite Efforts

6,000,000 AFFECTED

Draft Quotas Cut, Services to Drop 5,500,000 in 18 Months

By LEWIS WOOD

SECRETS OF RADAR GIVEN TO WORLD

Its Role in War and Uses for Peacetimes Revisited in Washington and London

By WILLIAM S. WHITE

Hirohito on Radio; Minister Ends Life

The Japanese Cabinet agreed to...

Third Fleet Fells 5 Planes Since End

Two-Day Holiday Is Proclaimed; Stores, Banks Close Here Today

ALL CITY 'LETS GO'

Hundreds of Thousands Roar Joy After Victory Flash Is Received

TIMES SQ. IS JAMMED

Police Estimate Crowd in Area at 2,000,000 — Din Overwhelming

By ALEXANDER FEINBERG

PETAIN CONVICTED, SENTENCED TO DIE

Jurors Recommend Clemency Because of His Age — Long Indictment Spoke

By G. H. ARCHAMBAULT

World News Summarized

WEDNESDAY, AUGUST 15, 1945

PRESIDENT ANNOUNCING SURRENDER OF JAPAN

Terms Will Reduce Japan To Kingdom Perry Visited

WASHINGTON, Aug. 14 —

By JAMES B. RESTON

TREATY WITH CHINA SIGNED IN MOSCOW

Complete Agreement Reached With Chungking on All Points at Issue, Russians Say

Cruiser Sunk, 1,196 Casualties; Took Atom Bomb Cargo to Guam

WASHINGTON, Aug. 14 —

MacArthur Begins Orders to Hirohito

YIELDING UNQUALIFIED, TRUMAN SAYS

Japan Is Told to Order End of Hostilities, Notify Allied Supreme Commander and Send Emissaries to Him

MACARTHUR TO RECEIVE SURRENDER

Formal Proclamation of V-J Day Awaits Signing of Those Articles — Cease-Fire Order Given to the Allied Forces

By ARTHUR KROCK

WASHINGTON, Aug. 14 —

Orders Given to the Japanese

The announcement of the sinking in the *New York Times*, which appeared August 15, 1945, was overshadowed by the day's bigger headline news.

The survivors of the USS *Indianapolis* sail home aboard the USS *Hollandia. Courtesy of the collection of Giles McCoy*

Captain McVay, testifying at the Washington Navy Yard, December 1945. McVay was the first captain in the history of the U.S. Navy to be court-martialed subsequent to losing his ship in an act of war. *Courtesy of the collection of Giles McCoy*

Testifying at the court-martial on December 5, 1945, Dr. Haynes told the court that "under McVay's command the *Indianapolis* was a very efficient, trim fighting ship, and I would be honored and pleased to serve under him again." *AP/Wide World Photos*

Commander Mochitsura Hashimoto, of the Japanese submarine *I-58*, arrives in Washington, D.C., on December 10, 1945. The highly unusual prosecution's move of calling a former military enemy to testify raised protests in Congress and in newspapers across the country. *AP/Wide World Photos*

Former marine private Giles McCoy greets Rear Admiral Charles McVay at the Indianapolis airport during the first survivors' reunion in July 1960. The two men had not seen each other since the court-martial. *Courtesy of the collection of Giles McCoy*

Fifteen years after the sinking, Giles McCoy, David P. Kemp Jr., Felton Outland, and Ed Payne (left to right) are reunited in Indianapolis. McCoy and his raftmates were the last survivors to be pulled from the water. *Courtesy of the collection of Giles McCoy*

CHAPTER TEN

Final Hours

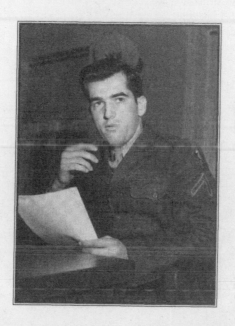

The worst part was giving up my life, accepting that I was
going to die—it wasn't the sharks, and it wasn't seeing your
buddies die. It was when you realize you're going to die.
And we were young men, healthy men. All of a sudden, there's
no chance, we can't make it. They've forgotten us.
We can't last out here forever—we're gonna die.

—GILES McCOY,
private first-class, USMC , USS *Indianapolis*

Day Five and After
August 3–4, 1945

CAPTAIN Claytor was astounded by the news that he was rescuing the men of the USS *Indianapolis*. As fate would have it, he now realized, he had actually been searching for one of his own relatives: Captain McVay was married to Claytor's cousin, the former Louise Claytor.

The previous evening, before arriving on the scene, Claytor had received a bulletin from the Philippine Sea Frontier: 1ST VESSEL ON SCENE ADVISE IDENTITY OF SHIP SURVIVORS AND CAUSE OF SINKING. Now, in the early hours of Friday, August 3, nearly thirteen hours after the boys had originally been spotted, Claytor was finally able to spread the word. At 12:30 a.m., he radioed the commander of the western Carolines: HAVE ARRIVED AREA X AM PICKING UP SURVIVORS FROM THE USS INDIANAPOLIS (CA 35), TORPEODOED [*sic*] AND SUNK LAST SUNDAY NIGHT.

The news was a stunning blow, and it quickly rippled all the way back to Pearl Harbor and to Admiral Ernest King, chief of naval operations, in Washington, D.C. Both King and Admiral Nimitz, in particular, were concerned about the impact of the tragedy on the impending plans to bomb Japan. They feared a controversy in the midst of what could be the war's—and the navy's—finest hour.

On the same day that the remainder of the *Indy*'s men were being rescued, President Truman was bound from London to the States aboard the cruiser *Augusta*. He was returning from the Potsdam conference, the meeting that united Great Britain, Russia, and the United States in the final fight against Japan. On board the ship, gathering a few reporters around him, Truman announced that America had a new kind of weapon that could end the war.

By this time, the last components of Little Boy had arrived on Tinian for final assembly, as well as an order designating Hiroshima as its target. But off Guam and Tinian, the weather was worsening. Heavy seas limited B-29 strikes on Japan and complicated scheduling an actual bombing date. The crew of the *Enola Gay*—the B-29 that was to drop the bomb—was forced to wait for clear skies.

B ACK in the waters of the South Pacific, the search continued at full speed. With the aid of powerful spotlights, as many as seven rescue planes circled over the site in coordinated patterns, directing the ships' efforts below. Using Higgins boats, motor launches, and Stokes stretchers (wire baskets) lowered by the ships' cranes, the boys were retrieved, one by painful one. The crew of the *Bassett* was awestruck by what it found. Some of the boys pulled aboard were so hideously disfigured that their rescuers, most of whom were about the same age as the survivors, broke down and wept as they hauled the living corpses aboard.

At 4:30 a.m. on August 3, the destroyer USS *Madison* became command central, taking over from the debilitated *Playmate 2*. At 6:30 a.m., their survivors all off-loaded, the crew of the *Playmate 2* removed the salvage gear from their craft, took one last look around, and boarded a motor launch, which took them to a waiting rescue ship, the *Cecil J. Doyle*. They were leaving the plane behind. The Catalina was covered with scars and slits in her metal skin from the pounding of the waves she'd endured on landing.

She was leaking oil out her belly, and her wings were dented and punctured; she would never fly again. To keep her from falling into the hands of the Japanese, she had to be destroyed. On board the *Doyle,* Marks watched as the ship's anti-aircraft guns—the deck-mounted 40 mms—opened up and riddled the plane. Then he bade the *Playmate 2* good-bye as she sank.

THE rescue ships were a mess: a slippery film of seawater and fuel oil coated the decks, and dead bodies were laid in rows on the sterns. After being fed fruit and water, the survivors were treated for exhaustion, dehydration, shark bites, saltwater ulcers, shock, burns, and malnutrition. (A healthy nineteen-year-old boy usually carries about 20 percent body fat; many of the survivors had lost an estimated 14 percent of theirs. Over the course of the four days, one sailor had lost more than thirty-five pounds.) While the skin of some boys had turned extremely pliable in the salt water and tore easily, the skin of others was so toughened that doctors aboard the *Bassett* were forced to hunt relentlessly and painfully for a usable vein while administering IVs. The survivors, many moaning incoherently, were led to showers, where they were set on stools and doused with diesel fuel to remove the oil that clung stubbornly to their bodies. Many of the boys only began to realize they had been rescued when the freshwater rushed over them. They laughed with joy, then fell into fits of weeping.

The crew of the *Doyle* moved out of its bunks. They gave the survivors fresh underwear and T-shirts and waited on them hand and foot throughout the night, bringing coffee, soup, ice cream, and fruit. In the wardroom, Adrian Marks found himself alone with Dr. Haynes, who chattered fast and furiously in a hoarse whisper about the past days' events. He seemed compelled to get his story out as quickly as possible. "Doctor," Marks asked, trying to offer comfort, "why don't you rest? Your voice is almost gone. You can tell it tomorrow."

But Haynes, who couldn't stop crying, continued talking, questions flooding out of him. "Why didn't they know we were missing?" he kept asking. "Why weren't they looking for us? Why! Why! Why!"

After being led to the shower, Haynes, finally silent, sat back on the stool and opened his mouth before the water hit. Desperately, he tried to lick the freshwater right out of the air. In spite of the excruciating pain of the scrubbing, he started to giggle hysterically, like a child.

BY midafternoon on August 3, the aftershocks of the disaster were rippling through the naval command. The following order was relayed to all ships: UNTIL FURTHER ORDERS ALL SHIPS WITH 500 OR MORE TOTAL PERSONNEL ON BOARD SHALL BE PROVIDED WITH AN ESCORT BETWEEN ULITHI AND LEYTE REGARDLESS OF SPEED.

The Philippine Sea Frontier at Leyte, to which the *Indy* had been headed, also issued this directive: ALL COMBATANT SHIPS 5 HOURS OVERDUE SAHLL [*sic*] BE REPORTED TO ORIGINATOR.

Fine rules, but too late for the boys of the *Indianapolis*.

BY the early morning of August 3, Captain McVay still had not been found.

It had been a sleepless night for the captain and his crew. John

Spinelli was lying listlessly in the raft, dreaming of the candied Bing cherries his mother had sent from New Mexico, and which had gone down with the ship in his locker. He reached out, picked one from the jar, and savored its heady kick. "Dear Lord," he prayed, "thank you for getting me this far."

McVay wondered just how much longer they could hold on. At about midnight the night before, his spirits had lifted when he spotted the faint searchlight of the *Doyle* ten miles away and understood without a doubt that a search-and-rescue effort was under way. The earlier planes had not been a fluke—they were actually looking for him and his men. Others had made it off the *Indy;* he was overjoyed.

But who could say if his group would be found? With so much ocean, it would be hard, he knew. They were constantly drifting to the south and east. Since about 12:30 a.m., Monday, July 30, McVay and his flotilla had drifted a total of about 116 miles.

This morning there were planes executing what looked like a box pattern; that is, they were cruising in regular opposing lines overhead, scrutinizing every mile beneath them. McVay fired a flare—he was down to a precious remaining few. But none of the planes noticed. He and the boys looked on as the search continued in the distance. They were frantic.

Suddenly one of the boys croaked, "Fellows?" Nobody turned—all eyes were on the planes. "Fellows," he repeated. "Do I see a ship, or am I hallucinating?"

McVay looked up in surprise. There was a ship bearing down on them, its bow throwing a crisp white wake. McVay stood and started waving wildly, shouting, "Here! Over here!"

It was close to 10:00 a.m. The ship was the high-speed transport *Ringness* (APD 100), which had picked up a blip on its radar screen at over 4,000 yards—about 2.25 miles—and steadily tracked it. It was a stroke of unimaginable luck for McVay and the boys. The blip had been triggered by the ammunition can that the captain had used earlier to make a failed smudge pot. Into the can, he had piled shredded kapok torn from a life vest, and then ignited the fiber with a shot from his flare gun. Although not in the way he intended, the smudge pot had saved them.[*]

After more than four days afloat, with no more than slivers of Spam and some malted milk tablets to eat, Captain McVay of the USS *Indianapolis* managed to climb up the Jacob's ladder over the side of the *Ringness* under his own power.

Once on deck, he and the exhausted crew were whisked to the ship's sick bay, where a pharmacist's mate checked their blood pressure and heart rates. All of the group had fared remarkably well. The boys were showered and given fresh dungarees; a clean uniform was found for McVay. John Spinelli was amazed that even the *Ringness*'s officers were helping scrub down the dirty survivors. He had never been more grateful. But he found the news of the scope of the disaster unsettling; as he tried to get some rest in a bunk, each crashing wave against the ship's hull brought back vivid, unwelcome flashbacks to the torpedoing.

McVay was placed in a private cabin. When Captain Meyer entered, he found him lying on the bed; McVay did not get up. Meyer sat in a chair, and, after a moment, McVay volunteered that he wanted to talk about what had happened. Meyer had prepared a dispatch describing the *Indy*'s torpedoing to be radioed to

---

[*] The former captain of the *Ringness*, William C. Meyer, did not recall an ammo can appearing on his radar and claims that circling search planes guided the *Ringness* to McVay. But John Spinelli recalled being told that this was how the group had been located.

CINCPAC at Pearl Harbor, and he read it aloud. It included the words *not zigzagging,* and, upon hearing them, McVay requested they be omitted. Meyer was understanding yet persuasive in his argument to let the words stand. Seeing that McVay was trauma-tized, Meyer reminded him that the truth of what had happened would come to light at a court inquiry, which the two captains knew was imminent.

McVay agreed. It was as if he'd forgotten himself—he did want the words in the message; it was the right thing to do.* After Meyer left the cabin, McVay was alone with his thoughts. And fears: the prospect of life after the disaster. What a captain dreads most had happened. With his ship gone, he could sense that his career might soon disappear as well.

SHORTLY thereafter, the *Madison, Ralph Talbot,* and *Dufilho* formed a 3.5-mile-long scouting line and combed the area, con-tinuing the search through the night. The *Register* (APD 92) and *Ringness* (also in a search line) steamed for Peleliu and the make-shift hospital there (the *Doyle* had departed for the island earlier). By the end of the day, Admiral Nimitz would order the hospi-tal ship *Tranquility,* presently anchored off Ulithi, to Peleliu in preparation for transporting the survivors to the more substantial Base 18 Hospital on Guam.

By 2:30 p.m., the *Ringness* and *Register* had discovered thirty-eight more survivors drifting in the far northern tip of what had been the teardrop shape of the mass. When the search planes

* Previous accountings have described McVay as a willing participant in composing the dispatch, while portraying Meyer as reluctant to include the details about the zigzag-ging. Meyer, however, while supportive of the captain, stands by this second version.

didn't turn up any other survivors in the immediate area, the captain of the *Madison* decided to return to the southeast area for one more look. The search, which had been in progress for over twenty-four hours, was nearing a close.

MCCOY was certain that he had died long ago, maybe yesterday, maybe the previous night. It was hard to tell. His throat was on fire; he regretted every ounce of water he'd ever wasted. He and Brundige drifted in their raft, sunk up to their chins.

The entire previous day, they'd watched the planes circle, knowing that a rescue effort was under way. After the sun had gone down, they had spotted what they thought was a ship's wobbly searchlight. All night long, they had stared at the light in silence. It rose straight from the sea, pencil-thin, and flattened against the ceiling of clouds. Payne, Outland, and Gray were still unconscious. But McCoy and Brundige didn't let the light out of their sight; they could practically reach out and touch it. They hoped and prayed it meant rescue, but rescue never came.

Now, on the morning of August 3, Brundige, spotting planes on the horizon, again roused himself. "Look, they came back, just like you'd said," he told McCoy. "But they're not coming our way."

"They will," said McCoy. "They will. They gotta work their way around to us."

As the day wore on, the planes got smaller and smaller in the sky. And then they disappeared. Gone. No one was coming. No one.

McCoy and Brundige assumed their burial position and then started to weep. They pressed close to the tied-together mass that was Payne, Outland, and Gray, and added their vests' straps to the cluster. Now all five were floating inside the raft as one, foreheads touching. "We're gonna go out of our gourds," said McCoy. "We're gonna die. But at least this way we won't fall over and drown in our vests." It was taking longer to die than McCoy expected.

And then, near dusk, he heard a noise. It was a plane. *Not another one,* he thought. *Not another goddamned plane that won't see us.* But not only had it seen them, it was coming right at them; fifty feet off the water, a Catalina seaplane passed over so close that McCoy could even see the guy inside its clear bubble blister. He was yelling something and pointing down at them. The plane banked sharply and circled. Then, on its second pass, a dye bomb was tossed out the hatch. It sent a chartreuse plume spreading around their raft.

And then the plane flew away. McCoy knew they had been spotted, but were they actually going to be picked up? He trusted nothing, and no one. Still, he felt lighter, alive. He knew he was coming back from the dead, and it was a wonderful feeling.

Out of nowhere a ship appeared. One moment, the sea was empty, twilight crawling across it; the next, there stood the massive gray hull of what looked like a transport ship. A guy on deck spun a line overhead and tossed it far out. On the end of it was a monkey fist, a lead weight wrapped with twine. It was an excellent shot; the fist landed directly at McCoy's side. He grabbed it and squeezed, crying out, "You found us! I can't believe you found us!"

After an unsuccessful attempt to reel in the raft, two of the ship's crew members jumped into the water and started swimming. They didn't get far, though; once they spotted the sharks circling the raft, they turned around and scrambled up the net on the ship's side. McCoy couldn't believe it. These guys were going to let a few sharks scare them off? Shit. He'd seen *sharks*.

He watched in grateful amazement as two more jumped overboard without hesitation and stroked up to them, knives in their hands. As they began cutting at the vests' straps and separating the five boys, McCoy, dazed, kept repeating, "I just can't believe you found us! You found us! *You found us!*"

His crew of four were covered in oil and burned, their faces swollen beyond recognition. McCoy himself was severely dehydrated, and the outlines of his ribs and cheekbones were visible through his skin. His tongue, sunburned, protruded from his mouth. He shaded it like a man cupping a flame from the wind.

The two crewmen towed them to the waiting rescue ship, where a boatswain's chair (resembling a child's swing) was lowered down by crane and they were lifted aboard. All except Mc-Coy. He insisted on climbing up the net ladder. When he reached the top, he was so weak he fell to the deck; kissing it, he burst into tears. He tried rising again but found he couldn't. He was unable to stop crying.

He was carried by stretcher to a shower, where the *Ringness* crew began the long, painful bath. He was then led to a bunk in the crew's quarters and fed water from a spoon for an hour. Never in his life had anything tasted so sweet. He lay there savoring the small sips. Finally he fell asleep, tumbling into a deep and soundless chasm of peace, where he lay for twenty hours.

McCoy and his raftmates were the last crew members of the USS *Indianapolis* to be rescued. They had spent about 112 hours—or more than four and a half days—adrift without food, water, or shelter from the sun.* His group of five had drifted the farthest of any of the survivors, an astounding 124 miles. As they slept in their bunks aboard the USS *Ringness,* they resembled sunburned skeletons more than the young men they were.

BY the following day, Saturday, August 4, the armada of rescue boats and planes had combed hundreds of square miles of ocean. During the afternoon, rescue crews received a good scare when the *Dufilho* reported solid underwater sonar contact with a Japanese submarine. The destroyer performed a depth charge attack, but it was without result, and the rescue effort was resumed. No other survivors were discovered, however, and by 5 p.m. the search seemed to be concluded.

In all, the *Cecil J. Doyle* collected 93 men, including the 56 men Marks had hauled aboard the *Playmate 2.* The high-speed transports USS *Register* and USS *Ringness* picked up a total of 51 survivors, among them Mike Kuryla, who'd been in one of the three rafts cut free from McCoy's and set adrift. The USS *Bassett* posted a whopping 152, including the Twible rafters group. The destroyer escort USS *Dufilho* and the destroyer USS *Ralph Talbot* picked up 25 survivors between them.

The casualties were astounding, and the death toll rattled the battled-hardened crews of the rescue ships. Of the 1,195 crew members and passenger Captain Edwin Crouch who had sailed from Guam, only 320 had survived the torpedoing and long ordeal at sea.

---

* It has previously been reported that Captain McVay and his group were the last to be rescued; according to former *Ringness* captain William C. Meyer, these prior accounts are erroneous.

In less than a week, four more would die in military hospitals, reducing the total number of survivors to 316. Of the nearly 900 men who died, it's probable that 200 were victims of shark attack, an average of 50 men a day. In all, 880 men were lost.

Adrian Marks would be haunted by the sight of the sharks and the conditions of the rescue for the rest of his days. "I will never forget how dark were the early hours of that night," he later remarked. "There was no moon and the starlight was obscured by clouds. And even though we were near the equator, the wind whipped up and it was cold. We had long since dispensed the last drop of water, and scores of badly injured men, stacked three deep in the fuselage and ranged far out on both wings, were softly crying with thirst and with pain."

As for McCoy, he would always wonder about those boys who might've been left behind. "They were basically all done looking when they found us," he would say. "I wonder how many were left out there and just watched those ships and planes finally disappear from sight.

"We couldn't have lasted another day."

CHAPTER ELEVEN
Aftermath

I went to church, and then I went to a gin mill.
I had some of the money [that guys had given me in the water]
it was all brown and stained with salt. And I had a drink.
And then I came home on a train, and that was it.
I was home.

—MICHAEL KURYLA,
coxswain, USS *Indianapolis*

AUGUST TO DECEMBER 1945

ON Saturday, August 4, reconnaissance ships started the work of retrieving and identifying dead bodies.* The normally routine logbooks of the four principal ships involved—the destroyer escorts *French* (DE 367) and *Alvin C. Cockrell* (DE 366) and the destroyers *Helm* (DD 388) and *Aylwin* (DD 355)—read like something from a horror movie. The *Helm* carried the following report for its August 4–5 patrol:

"All bodies were in extremely bad condition and had been dead for an estimated 4 or 5 days. Some had life jackets and life belts, most had nothing. Most of the bodies were completely naked, and the others had just shirts on. Bodies were horribly bloated and decomposed—recognition of faces would have been impossible. About half of the bodies were shark-bitten, some to such a degree that they more nearly resembled skeletons. From one to four sharks were attacking a body not more than fifty yards from the ship, and continued to do so until driven off by rifle fire.

"For the most part it was impossible to get finger prints from the bodies as the skin had come off the hands or the hands were lacerated by sharks. Skin was removed from the hands of bodies containing no identification, when possible, and the Medical Officer will dehydrate the skin and attempt to make legible prints.

"All personal effects [were] removed from the bodies for purposes of identification. After examination, all bodies were sunk,

---

* Arriving on the scene on August 5 was the unescorted transport ship USS *General R. L. Howze* (AP 134), carrying 4,000 troops to Manila. In apparent contradiction to the naval directive of August 3, unescorted ships were still being routed through the Peddie area in which the *Indy* was sunk. The USS *Cecil J. Doyle* ordered the *Howze* from the area.

using two-inch line and a weight of three 5"/38 cal. projectiles. There were still more bodies in the area when darkness brought a close to the gruesome operations for the day. In all, twenty-eight bodies were examined and sunk."

A total of about ninety-one bodies would be retrieved by the ships and buried at sea, with identification made whenever possible. Not until August 9, after searching hundreds of miles of ocean, would the last ship leave the area.

THE unfolding disaster of the *Indianapolis* now turned inland, to Peleliu, where Captain McVay and the majority of the crew had been taken by their respective rescue ships for medical treatment.

As the USS *Ringness* had made its way through the night of August 3 across the Philippine Sea, Captain McVay, watching the lights on Peleliu draw near, must have sensed that he was turning to a new fight for survival, this time with the navy. Minutes before the ship docked, he had stood on the bridge and with a shaking voice told his rescuers, on behalf of all the *Indianapolis* crew, how grateful he was. Captain Meyer thought he had never seen such humility and compassion in an officer.

On Peleliu, a news blackout was ordered: no information about the sinking would leak from the island. Marine guards blocked access to the wooden hospital barracks where the boys were convalescing. No word would leak to the outside world that 1,196 U.S. sailors had been lost and forgotten at sea for nearly five days.

On Sunday, August 5, dressed in khaki and looking more like a man recovering from the flu than from a disaster at sea, McVay held a press conference. But everything he said—as well as any news stories written by correspondents on the island—was subject to the scrutiny of military censors. The United States was still officially at war, and regular wartime news protocols still very much applied. Whatever views and personal feelings McVay expressed at the conference would be held by censors for publication until after the war's end.

"What would be the normal time before you would be reported overdue?" a reporter asked the captain.

"That is a question I would like to ask someone," McVay shot back. "A ship that size practically runs on a train schedule. I should think by noon [on Tuesday], they would have started to call by radio to find out where we were, or if something was wrong. This is something I want to ask somebody myself—why didn't this get out sooner?"

This was as close to a public condemnation of the navy as the captain would ever allow himself to make.

THE following day, Monday, August 6, 1945, the *Enola Gay* took off from the airstrip at Tinian Island. At 8:15 a.m. the plane dropped Little Boy on Hiroshima. A member of its assembly team had written on its side: "This one is for the Boys of the *Indianapolis.*" More than 118,000 Japanese of the city's estimated population of 350,000 were killed by the world's first atomic bomb. (A total of 140,000 would be dead as a result of its aftereffects by the end of the year.) Temperatures at the epicenter of the explosion exceeded 1 million degrees, and winds of up to 500 miles per hour were whipped up by the blast.

By Wednesday, August 8, McVay, Haynes, McCoy, and all the other survivors had been reunited at the Base 18 Hospital in

Guam.* Still under marine guard, they were not allowed to talk with any unauthorized personnel about their ordeal. McVay, who didn't need direct medical attention and was billeted in a nearby Quonset hut that served as officers' quarters, visited with the boys in the enlisted men's hospital barracks. They were overjoyed to see him, profoundly glad that he had survived the ordeal. Their captain, looking fit and rested, betrayed no emotion about the trouble brewing.

Many of the boys recovered at a rapid rate and soon were playing basketball and baseball on the base. Others were not so lucky; the saltwater ulcers covering their broken arms and legs had eaten the muscle to the bone. One boy's ears had been fried to the texture of corn flakes by the sun. Dr. Haynes would require a month of convalescence before walking again; his feet, burned by the flash fires of the torpedoing, were painfully tender, as were the third-degree burns on his hands and face. Private McCoy, nourished by a diet of ice water and raw eggs, his head shaved to remove his oil-matted hair, was undergoing a daily, painful treatment that involved a nurse cracking open the burned, dried skin on his face and peeling it away with tweezers to apply an antiseptic ointment. Fortunately, the nurse would peel off just one side of his face each day.

When Admiral Spruance paid a visit to the hospital, the boys lined up and he pinned Purple Hearts on their hospital pajamas. They hadn't seen him since his departure from the *Indy* after the kamikaze attack at Okinawa on March 31, more than four months earlier. They were profoundly moved as he went from bed to

---

* Those rescued by the *Bassett* and taken first to Samar had traveled by airplane to Base 18. The majority of the survivors traveled from their initial hospital lodgings on Peleliu via the hospital ship *Tranquility*, a journey of two days.

bed shaking hands, offering congratulations. The admiral even stopped to play a few hands of Hearts with some of the boys. On Guam, the purpose of the *Indy*'s record-breaking voyage across the Pacific was finally revealed to the officers of the ship. Dr. Haynes was lying in his hospital bed when an army medical officer approached and asked if he could have a word. "I know who you are!" said Haynes, recognizing the man. He was James Nolan. Haynes had last seen him posing as an artillery officer aboard the *Indy* during the trip from San Francisco to Tinian. Nolan explained that he was actually an army medical officer specializing in radiation medicine. Then he informed Haynes that the *Indy* had carried the bomb dropped on Hiroshima. Haynes said little; in fact, he found he had no reaction at all. Like many of the crew, he simply would be glad when the war was over.

On Thursday, August 9, a second atomic bomb, this one named Fat Man, was dropped on Nagasaki. The blast of Fat Man killed 40,000 Japanese and wounded another 60,000. On the following day, August 10, Japan sued for peace.

On August 9, Admiral Nimitz, from his office in Guam, had called for a court of inquiry concerning the sinking of the ship; Nimitz had asked that this proceeding start in less than a week.

With the whole of the Pacific command thrown full throttle into preparations for the invasion of Japan, Nimitz and the chief of naval operations, Admiral King, were eager to sort out the matter and return to the pressing business of war. The inquiry would investigate the cause of the disaster, the reason for the rescue delay, and determine what culpability, if any, existed among the players. This was pro forma in the aftermath of any possible violation of military law. But amazingly, one of the judges sitting at the inquiry would be Vice Admiral Murray, commander of the Marianas in Guam. It was under Murray's command that Captain Oliver Naquin had given McVay the incomplete intelligence report concerning enemy submarine activity along the Peddie route.

At 8 p.m. on the evening of August 14, President Truman stepped into the Rose Garden and triumphantly declared the end of World War II into a bouquet of microphones. After nearly four years of fighting, it was finally over.

Some of the *Indy*'s boys sat up in bed and cheered at the news as it was announced over the hospital's loudspeakers. It had been twelve days since the first men were rescued; the sinking was still a secret. No one, except U.S. military brass and some hospital workers on the islands of Samar and Peleliu, knew of the disaster. This was about to change.

Minutes before Truman's announcement, the White House released this terse bulletin: "The USS *Indianapolis* has been lost in the Philippine Sea as the result of enemy action. The next of kin of casualties have been notified."

Some families first learned the dreaded news as they were gathered around radios listening to Truman's speech. McCoy's mother was met at her home in St. Louis, Missouri, by a marine bearing word that her son was missing in action. (A number of the survivors' families first received telegrams that their sons were MIA, and these mistakes were corrected by follow-up telegrams.) She told the marine, "No, sir, I know my son's all right," and then she slammed the door.

This was a terrible confirmation of an already profound suspicion. On the night of the *Indy*'s sinking, Mrs. McCoy had sat straight up in bed, convinced that something terrible was happening to her son. "Giles," she said, shaking her husband awake. "Giles Jr. is in trouble, I know it."*

In Fairfield, Connecticut, Dr. Haynes's wife received a telegram that read: A REPORT JUST RECEIVED SHOWS YOUR HUSBAND HAS BEEN WOUNDED IN ACTION 30 JULY 1945. DIAGNOSIS: EXHAUSTION FROM OVER-EXPOSURE . . . . YOUR ANXIETY IS APPRECIATED. Shortly, she received a second telegram, this one from her husband, who was unhappily convalescing in a wheelchair on Guam. INJURY IS NOT SERIOUS, Haynes wrote. AM GETTING ALONG ALL RIGHT. ALL MY LOVE, LEW.

O N August 15, military censorship of the war's news was lifted, and the newspapers were subsequently filled with stories about the *Indy.* The *New York Times* called the sinking "one of the darkest pages of our naval history." Newspapers across the country soon echoed the sentiment. The public was saddened and bewildered. How could such a calamity occur so close to the end of the war? they wondered.

These news stories were soon buried, however, by larger headlines recounting America's victory. On V-J Day, celebrations consumed the country; New York City was showered with ticker tape parades. Whether the navy's timing of its announcement of the *Indy*'s sinking was by design or happenstance, the effect was the same: the public quickly forgot the disaster. But the families of the boys who died in the sinking started demanding explanations. The navy, as of yet, had few answers—but it was looking for them.

* McCoy and his mother later figured out that at about the time she'd awakened, McCoy was making his way to the raft that held Payne, Outland, Gray, and Brundige.

On August 13, the court of inquiry's proceedings opened at the headquarters of the commander on Guam. McVay rode there with McCoy, who was now his personal driver. He had visited the young marine in the hospital and offered him the job because he was aware of McCoy's loyal service as an "orderly," or messenger, aboard the *Indianapolis* for Admiral Spruance.

As their jeep climbed up the steep CINCPAC hill, McVay asked McCoy how he'd fared in the water.

"Fine, sir. I got along just fine."

"Well, we were damn lucky to survive." He paused. "You know what? I think they're going to put it to me."

McCoy asked what he was suggesting.

McVay replied that he suspected that the navy was going to pin blame for the sinking on him, using his failure to zigzag as an excuse.

On August 20, after hearing the testimony of forty-three witnesses, the inquiry ended. The court had pored over the minutiae of the case, including the question of the incomplete intelligence reports McVay received at Guam before sailing. On the witness stand, Captain Oliver Naquin testified that he had felt the danger of an enemy sub attack was "practically negligible." And the court believed him.

Also under consideration was the failure of the port director at Leyte to report the *Indy*'s nonarrival at her scheduled ETA. It found this circumstance regrettable, but understandable due to the ambiguous nature of the navy directive 10CL-45, which the port director had interpreted to extend to the nonarrival of combatant ships. The court primarily blamed the sinking and ensuing deaths of the crew on two things: McVay's failure to zigzag in conditions that it considered "good with intermittent moonlight"; and his failure to send out a distress message.

McVay himself testified that he doubted a message had left the ship during the short time it took to sink. The testimony of radio technician Jack Miner, who witnessed the SOS message leaving the transmitter during the sinking, was apparently disregarded. The court believed McVay. Also found to be at fault were Rear Admiral McCormick's staff for their incorrect decoding of the message notifying him of the *Indy*'s impending arrival in Leyte, and Lieutenant Stewart Gibson, for failing to report that the *Indy* had not met her ETA. The court recommended disciplinary action for McCormick's staff and a letter of admonition for Gibson.

For McVay, it recommended court-martial.

The matter was now in the hands of the secretary of the navy, James Forrestal, who would decide if legal action should proceed.

IN early September, after nearly a month of convalescence on Guam, the survivors boarded the carrier escort *Hollandia* and set sail for the United States.

On September 26 they were met in San Diego by a meager homecoming parade sponsored by the local Salvation Army, which handed out miniature bottles of milk to the boys as they walked off the ship. Most of them had no interest in taking part in the festivities. Generally speaking, they did not share the postwar jubilation that swept up most of the 5 million soldiers returning home; the sinking and disaster had tainted their experience.

McCoy went home on a two-week leave to his mother, father, and three sisters in Missouri. He tried to put the war as far in his past as possible but remained on active duty, with another two years to serve. He did not relish this prospect.

Dr. Haynes had no intention of quitting. But he did return to

Connecticut for a thirty-day leave with his wife. At home, he met his newborn son for the first time.

Captain McVay had flown to Washington, D.C., in early September. He tried hard to convey his sense of grief and loss in letters he wrote to the bereaved families, which he composed in a temporary office in the navy yard while the investigation into the *Indy*'s loss continued. He was consumed with guilt over the deaths of so many young men. His punishment, he felt, would be a long life.

On November 29, close to four months after his rescue, he learned that he was to be court-martialed. The trial would begin in five days, on Monday, December 3, 1945.

Admiral Nimitz and Admiral Spruance had disagreed with the inquiry's initial recommendation and suggested a letter of reprimand. However, the chief of naval operations, Admiral King, a stern and "by-the-book" navy man, pressed for the trial, and Secretary Forrestal agreed.

Unbelievably, the navy had not yet finalized the charges. In fact, the navy's judge advocate general (JAG) sent Forrestal a memo explaining that only one of the inquiry's contemplated charges could be proved. Because McVay had already admitted during the inquiry that he wasn't zigzagging before the torpedoing, a trial was not actually necessary to convict him on this charge. Nevertheless, they called it Charge I.

Consulting with Forrestal, the JAG omitted the inquiry's charge that McVay failed to send a distress signal. In its place they agreed to charge him with "failure to abandon ship in a timely manner." They called this Charge II. Making this charge stick, however, was problematic. Since the ship had gone down so quickly, it could be difficult to prove the difference between a "timely" and "untimely" abandonment.

In reality, they had little choice. Without a second, halfway viable charge, they had no trial; sentencing of McVay on Charge I could have taken place immediately.

"It is, therefore, respectfully submitted," the JAG explained to Forrestal, "that Charge II (failure to abandon ship in a timely manner) should not be omitted, despite the fact the evidence may be held insufficient. Full justification for ordering the trial on Charge II springs from the fact this case is of vital interest not only to the families of those who lost their lives, but also to the public at large."

McVay had less than a week to prepare his defense. King, eager to hurry the proceedings, had refused McVay his first choice of counsel when his preferred lawyer proved not immediately available. McVay ended up with an inexperienced lawyer.

Before the trial, McVay was asked by a news reporter what he thought the outcome might be. "I was in command of the ship," he replied, "and I am responsible for its fate. I hope they make their decisions soon, and do what they want with me."

As it turned out, then, the question as to why hundreds of U.S. sailors were left to float for as many as five days in a hostile ocean would not be considered by the court. That is, the conduct of the navy would not be on trial. This legal sleight of hand had been achieved by the navy's careful selection of charges. By law, all questions to the court had to pertain only to the two it had drawn—"failure to order abandon ship in a timely manner" and "hazarding his ship by failing to zigzag." There was no possibility of the establishment of navy culpability.

Still, by and large, the American public sensed that McVay was getting a raw deal. *Time* magazine suggested that the tragedy of the sinking represented a "colossal blunder" by the navy.

On December 3, 1945, Charles Butler McVay's court-martial convened in a converted classroom at the Washington Navy Yard. Such trials were usually semiprivate affairs executed swiftly out of public view. On the morning of McVay's trial, the courtroom was filled with reporters, photographers, and citizens curious to get a glimpse of the first captain in U.S. history to be court-martialed for losing his ship as the result of an act of war.*

The proceedings were well orchestrated and got swiftly under way. McVay sat stiffly in his chair in a spotless uniform, nervously fiddling with a pencil, sensing the walls closing in on his career.

Called to testify, Dr. Haynes found McVay a forlorn version of his former self. On the stand, the JAG lawyer wouldn't allow Haynes to talk about the boys' time in the water but asked instead about visibility the night of the sinking. The good doctor told the prosecutor that, yes, visibility on the night of the sinking was poor; in fact, all the survivors called to the witness stand provided testimony to this effect. In rebuttal, the prosecution argued that conditions were clear enough for the *Indy* to be sunk; therefore, visibility at some point was at least partially clear. The trial was not going well for McVay—the prosecution was driving home Charge I.

---

* A month earlier, Congress had begun hearings concerning the attack at Pearl Harbor. A post-attack court of inquiry had found Rear Admiral Husband Kimmel and Major General Walter Short guilty of "derelictions of duty" and "errors of judgement." A July 1946 congressional report would strike the first charge but retain the second.

What McVay didn't know was that his counsel was missing the one piece of evidence that might have acquitted him. McVay and his lawyer were unaware of the ULTRA intelligence that had been withheld from McVay during his meeting with Captain Oliver Naquin. In fact, a report labeled "secret" and sent to Admiral King by the navy inspector general had blamed the navy for failure to make full use of this intelligence. It had also explained that it would be necessary for the prosecution to return to Guam in order to fully explore the situation. King, in his haste to get the trial under way, chose to disregard the report. From the navy's point of view, the ULTRA intelligence wasn't entered into testimony because it was so top secret that, in essence, it didn't exist.*

DURING the trial's second week, it seemed that McVay's fortunes might change.

The navy made the surreal prosecutorial decision to fly Mochitsura Hashimoto from Japan to Washington to testify against the captain. His presence in the courtroom raised an uproar among politicians and citizens, and in newspapers across the country. *Newsweek* carried an editorial from the *Army and Navy Bulletin* declaring that "responsibility for the debacle . . . must be fixed several echelons higher than a lone commanding officer." On the floor of the House of Representatives, Massachusetts congressperson Edith Rogers called Hashimoto's presence

---

* It is unlikely that even the court's seven judges possessed sufficient security clearance to allow them knowledge of ULTRA's existence. The details of the program would remain classified until the early 1990s. The court of inquiry and Navy Inspector General documents detailing the charges against McVay, and the navy's thinking in arriving at them, were not declassified until 1959.

an "outrage against justice" and demanded his testimony be stricken.

Nevertheless, the prosecution explained that Hashimoto's testimony about "what he saw, what he did, and how he did it" on the night of the sinking was relevant to the charge that the captain endangered his ship by failing to zigzag. The assembled panel of seven navy admirals agreed, and Hashimoto was allowed to proceed. Dressed in an ill-fitting blue suit, the visibly uncomfortable commander made his way to the witness stand, where he quickly proceeded to embarrass the navy by explaining that zigzagging would have made "no change in [the] method in firing the torpedoes." He would have sunk the *Indianapolis* no matter what course she was on.

A few days later, the prosecution was dealt an apparent second blow by the testimony of the highly decorated American submarine commander Glynn Donaho. Asked to describe the usefulness of zigzagging as a defensive maneuver, the respected commander explained that the move was of negligible value.

Nonetheless, after two weeks of testimony, on December 19, Charles Butler McVay was convicted of "hazarding his ship by failing to zigzag." As the navy JAG had suspected, he was acquitted of the charge of "failing to sound abandon ship in a timely manner." He was demoted 100 points in permanent rank and another 100 in temporary rank, which meant he would never become an admiral. In view of his outstanding service, however, Admiral King and Admiral Nimitz recommended his sentence be remitted, or, in effect, suspended. (Technically, McVay could have been fined or dismissed from service.)

Four other officers were also punished. Lieutenant Stewart

Gibson received a letter of reprimand, while his superior officer, Leyte port director Jules Sancho, received a milder letter of admonition. Captain Alfred Granum and his ranking officer, Commodore Norman Gillette, acting commander of the Philippines Sea Frontier, also received letters of reprimand.*

McVay had received the announcement of his sentence standing ramrod straight without a hint of emotion. He was a navy man, and he would live and die by its rules; it was as natural to him as breathing. And yet, his naval career was over. He would never command another ship. He left the courtroom on Louise's arm, looking stonily composed.

Back at home, through the Christmas season, he began receiving the hate mail—"Merry Christmas! Our family's holiday would be a lot merrier if you hadn't killed my son"—he would continue to receive for the rest of his life. Louise made it a point to patrol the day's mail pile and remove the bitter correspondence. If she didn't, McVay would bundle the letters with rubber bands and tuck them in his dresser drawer, as if forever wanting to remind himself of his guilt.

Three months after the court-martial, he left Washington.

---

* All of these letters, however, would eventually be withdrawn by Secretary Forrestal. The military records of the four men would emerge unblemished by the sinking of the *Indy*.

CHAPTER TWELVE

Back in the World

We returned to our loved ones [afterward], but we were never the
same again. Most were markedly changed. Young boys had
become mature older men, aged beyond their years.
All because of those days in the sea.

—HARLAN TWIBLE,
ensign, USS *Indianapolis*

IN the aftermath of Captain McVay's court-martial, some of the survivors returned to military service, while others drifted back into civilian life and disappeared inside whiskey bottles. Many got lucky, put the disaster behind them, and joined the postwar American boom. John Spinelli, who'd floated under the captain's watchful eye, moved back to New Mexico with his wife and new daughter, became a butcher, then worked for thirty-seven years reading utility meters.

Others became nightclub owners, bricklayers, or electricians. Jack Miner took over his father's paper company. Mike Kuryla worked for a construction company in Chicago, and Ed Brown became a traveling salesman in California for the auto industry. Harlan Twible became CEO of a global manufacturing company. Jack Cassidy worked as a state policeman in Massachusetts. Bob Gause returned to Florida as a commercial fisherman. (His sideline exploits as a shark hunter are said by some to have served as inspiration for the Captain Quint character in *Jaws*.) Whatever had happened to them on the water was in the past. They moved into the stream of America, and they *worked*.

Dr. Haynes went on to a successful career in military medicine, even serving in Vietnam, before leaving the service in 1965. Today Haynes, eighty-nine, lives near the seventeenth fairway of a golf course outside Boston. He plays every week with his second wife, Margaret. However, he is still troubled by nightmares of the sinking and finds it difficult to attend church.

"Every church I go to recites the Lord's Prayer," he explains. "And every time I say the prayer, I still cry."

PRIVATE McCoy became a chiropractor in Missouri, earned a doctor of osteopathy degree, and devoted his life to helping other people.

One day in 1958, he heard a knock at the front door of his home in Boonville, Missouri. On the porch he found one of his raftmates whose lives he and Bob Brundige had tried so hard to save. Since the sinking, Felton Outland had been thinking of the man who had helped keep him alive. On impulse, Felton had just driven the 900 miles from his family's farm in Sunbury, North Carolina, to thank Private McCoy for his life.

The two men stared at each other. Then they embraced and began weeping on the porch. They ended up talking for two days, a flood of memories pouring forth between them.

After Felton left, McCoy found himself moved by Outland's gratitude. Armed with the survivor's list published in Richard Newcombe's *Abandon Ship!*, he began writing letters across the country trying to locate his former shipmates. He decided he wanted to organize a reunion of the men of the USS *Indianapolis*.

Many of the survivors wrote McCoy back, angry that he was dredging up memories long buried. McCoy himself was troubled by nightmares. But encouraged by a psychiatrist he had approached for advice about organizing the reunion, McCoy managed to find 220 of the original 316 survivors. In July 1960, they met for the first time in fifteen years at a hotel in downtown Indianapolis. The reunion turned out to be a scorching experience.

The survivors unloaded years of repressed fear and anger, the shame of bad deeds, the smoldering guilt of having been unable to keep someone alive. For many of the men, their survival at sea still felt like a miracle rather than a triumph of will over insurmountable odds and death. In the aftermath of the sinking, many of the men said, they felt like they had been resurrected.

They talked for hours, arranged in assigned seats that re-created the groups they had floated with fifteen years earlier across the Philippine Sea. They emerged from the reunion gray-faced and drained, but liberated. McCoy felt a bond with these men that he knew he would never experience with anyone else.

AFTER the court-martial, McVay had been reassigned to the naval air station outside New Orleans, far from the glamour of life on the high seas. He was given a navy desk job. Still, he worked hard at tilting his life back toward some shade of its former hap-piness. He and Louise lived in a comfortable house on Fourth Street, and the two were regular guests at parties that often ended with the captain standing at a piano singing, followed by the light-hearted retelling of stories about life in the navy. On weekends, they camped in a tidy shack on Bayou Liberty, north of New Or-leans, and spent hours fishing for speckled trout. In 1949, after thirty years of military service, McVay retired and began selling insurance. For the first time in his adult life, he was a civilian.

McVay attended the first survivors' reunion in 1960. On the plane ride to Indianapolis he was filled with worry and doubts; he'd spent the last fifteen years wondering if his former crew held him responsible for the disaster. He was shocked to tears when he stepped from the plane with Louise and found the survivors lining the airport's runway, all of them saluting, tears streaming down their own faces.

McCoy hadn't seen the captain since those moments back in the navy yard courtroom when he had testified on his behalf. In court, when McCoy had finished speaking, McVay had simply raised a finger and winked: *Thanks*. Now, over drinks in McCoy's hotel room, McCoy told him, "Captain, you got a raw deal. And I want to do something about it. I'd like to see if we can get your name cleared."

The captain mulled this over and then his face darkened.

"No, that's all right, McCoy," he said. "I got what the regulations called for—I got what I deserved."

When the reunion was over, the men gathered on the hotel roof and cheered and saluted the captain as his car pulled away for the airport. It was the last time they ever saw him.

BACK at home, McVay began a slow spiral into despair. Louise was diagnosed with cancer and died suddenly in 1961. After years of self-restraint, he began to fall apart.

Within a year, he impulsively married Vivian Smith, an old flame from his youth, and moved to Winvian Farm in Litchfield, Connecticut. There were happy times: they went to Egypt; they attended the Metropolitan Opera in New York; they threw grand parties at the farm. But then in 1965, he received what must have been a final blow: his grandson, in whom he had taken a special interest, died from a sudden illness.

He took to spending his days quietly, often alone, puttering in a workshop building furniture, or playing bridge, or rowing a blue boat around a small pond he'd dug on the property. One morning his stepson, Winthrop Smith Jr. (from Vivian's previous marriage), paused before the bathroom door in the Litchfield farmhouse and heard the captain weeping.

When he opened the door, he saw McVay, dressed in his khaki, clutching a letter—more hate mail from the families of dead sailors. He told the young boy, "*I can't take this.*"

Which leads us to this story's beginning, to that cold morning in November 1968, when Captain Charles Butler McVay III stepped out onto his front steps with a gun and consigned himself to history.

After the cremation, a memorial service was held in Arlington National Cemetery, complete with a twenty-one-gun salute. His remains were flown to Louisiana, where he'd spent the happiest times of his life.

If you'd been standing on the beach at Bayou Liberty that winter in 1968, you might have seen a plane pass by overhead; you might have seen the door open and a small box tipped to the wind. The contents went scattering, like a twisting scarf of smoke.

A man's bones and skin can be burned away into powder and ash, but what's left is without form. Courage, duty, and honor have no permanent home.

What was left of Charles Butler McVay melted on the water and was gone.

Epilogue

Eternal father strong to save
whose arm does rule the restless wave . . .
Oh hear us when we pray to thee
for those in peril on the sea.

—U.S. NAVY HYMN,
Reverend William Whiting (1825–1878)

TWENTY-EIGHT years after Captain McVay's death, in response to a 1996 request for a new investigation by the survivors of the USS *Indianapolis*, the U.S. Navy's judge advocate general delivered this pronouncement: "The conclusion reached is that Captain McVay's court-martial was legally sound; no injustice has been done, and remedial action is not warranted."

Over the years, conspiracy theories waxed and waned among some survivors as they tried to explain why Captain McVay was court-martialed. Some believed Admiral King was seeking revenge for a personal insult allegedly inflicted years earlier by McVay's father. Still others believed the politically powerful father of one dead crew member successfully lobbied President Truman himself to press ahead with the trial. Ultimately, though, these theories added up to little. The court-martial's effect was the ruin of McVay's career, and what remains today is the question of whether this was just.

The answer, explained Captain Bill Toti, a former U.S. Navy submarine commander, is negative. In a careful but biting critique of the navy's treatment of the captain (published in October 1999 in *Proceedings*, a Naval Institute publication), Toti pointed out: "Here was a man who, because of the unique and absolute nature of the responsibility of command, was culpable for the misfortune that befell his ship—the captain's own statements point to the fact that he understood this truth well.

"Despite that, there was nothing he could've done to prevent that misfortune, and he should never have been prosecuted in the first place. The lesson here is that a decision can be legally correct and still be unjust."

In the years since the sinking, many of the survivors of the disaster worked tirelessly to clear their captain's name. "The *Indianapolis*

was a trim, fighting ship," said Dr. Haynes, "and I would be proud
to serve aboard her once again." Or, as Bob Brundige, McCoy's
former raftmate, once said before his death in 1994, "We would've
rode to hell with Captain McVay."*

At a September 1999 hearing before the Senate Armed Services Committee, former marine private Giles McCoy defiantly
told the panel of assembled navy admirals, "Captain McVay's
honor has been violated. You're sitting here telling me Captain
McVay hazarded our ship by failing to zigzag? I want to tell you,
our ship was hazarded long before Captain McVay [left port]."

Later, said McCoy, one of the admirals "came up, grabbed my
hand, and said, 'I want to tell you, McCoy, you're right.'

"But then he said, 'Good luck,' and walked away.

"I think we won the battle," admitted McCoy, "but we haven't
won the war."

On October 12, 2000, that war began drawing to a close when
Congress passed a resolution exonerating Rear Admiral Charles
Butler McVay III. It also recommended a Unit Citation for the
final crew of the USS *Indianapolis*, fifty-five years after they came
home from their solitary victory parade in San Diego.†

The resolution reads:

"(1) In light of the remission by the Secretary of the Navy of the
sentence of the court-martial and the restoration of Captain Mc-

* The survivors' efforts to clear McVay's name were diligently aided by a Ransom Middle School student from Cantonment, Florida, named Hunter Scott, who took up
the cause in 1997 as part of a history project. Where the gray-haired, senior citizen
survivors of the *Indy* hadn't succeeded, Scott was able to bend the ear of Washington's
politicians.

† Former *I-58* captain Mochitsura Hashimoto, who supported the survivors' exoneration efforts, was pleased to hear this news. A Shinto priest, he died at age ninety-one
on October 25, 2000, in Kyoto.

Vay to active duty by the Chief of Naval Operations, Fleet Admiral Chester Nimitz, that the American people should now recognize Captain McVay's lack of culpability for the tragic loss of the USS Indianapolis and the lives of the men who died as a result of the sinking of that vessel; and

"(2) in light of the fact that certain exculpatory information was not available to the court-martial board and that Captain McVay's conviction resulted therefrom, that Captain McVay's military record should now reflect that he is exonerated for the loss of the USS Indianapolis and so many of her crew."*

What the congressional resolution didn't do, however, was void the court-martial conviction from the captain's record, which, in a manner of speaking, would finally set their captain free.

---

* In response, the navy said once again that "internal and external reviews have supported the fairness and legality of the court-martial proceedings and appellate action" regarding McVay's court-martial.

Afterword: 2001

AS it turned out, justice in the case of Captain Charles Butler McVay arrived far more swiftly than the survivors of the USS *Indianapolis* had expected. On July 13, 2001—fifty-six years after the sinking of the ship, and forty-one years after Giles McCoy and many others first began the effort to clear McVay's name—the Department of the Navy, in step with the congressional resolution, made public its decision to likewise exonerate the court-martialed captain.

The secretary of the navy, Gordon R. England, instructed that the following declaration be appended to McVay's military service record: "The American people should now recognize Captain McVay's lack of culpability for the tragic loss of the USS *Indianapolis* and the lives of the men who died as a result of the sinking of that vessel. Captain McVay's military record should now reflect that he is exonerated for the loss of the USS *Indianapolis* and so many of her crew."

In this reversal of its long-held refusal to review McVay's case, the navy echoed wording chosen by the United States Congress in its October 2000 resolution declaring McVay's "lack of culpability for the tragic loss of the USS *Indianapolis* and the lives of the men who died."

In a subsequent letter to England, McCoy typically didn't mince words: "Thank you, sir, for getting the Navy Department Admirals off their butts in exonerating our late captain."

The announcement of the navy's decision attracted immediate national attention. In a July 14, 2001, *New York Times* story (citing an Associated Press report), an elated McCoy explained that Captain McVay had not been guilty "of anything except the fortune or misfortune of war."

I was taking a quick vacation during the book's publicity tour when I learned of the exoneration. The tour's readings had been emotional—in every city or town I visited, there was usually someone in the audience who was either a survivor of the disaster or related to one. These events had come to serve as a sort of meeting place of the generations: old, young, men, and women.

The proprietor of the lakeside cabin where I was staying handed me the news: Call your publisher. Something has happened concerning Captain McVay.

There was no phone at the resort, so I drove to a gas station and from a pay phone got the details. I had been about to go swimming with my kids, so standing there in T-shirt and shorts, it was a surprising experience to be instead discussing the exoneration with CNN, swept up in the excitement. When I checked in with survivor Ed Brown in California, he told me he'd broken into tears upon hearing the news.

Other survivors echoed similar feelings of relief and joy. For while the navy's exoneration did not go so far as to erase McVay's conviction from his record, McCoy feels—as do many of his shipmates—that in the court of public opinion his captain's name finally has been cleared, the cloud under which the legacy of the USS *Indianapolis* had lingered these many years removed.

"I think it's the best we can ever get," McCoy told me afterward, from his home in Florida. "I imagine Captain McVay is looking down and smiling on all this."

The crew was also awarded a Unit Citation for its role in the delivery of the components of the bomb Little Boy to Tinian island. These men—now in their seventies and eighties—have at last been recognized by the U.S. Navy for their service to their country.

What, after all these years, prompted the navy to reverse its decision fifty-six years after the court-martial?

In short, it was the result of dogged optimism and persistence on the part of hundreds of individuals.

But key people should be singled out. England acted in part as a result of the invaluable urging of Senator Bob Smith (R-NH), who had been alerted to McVay's case originally by Florida school student Hunter Scott's own lobbying in Congress. The exoneration effort had also received critical support from Mike Monroney, a tireless volunteer advocate of the cause in Washington, D.C., and Captain McVay's son, Kimo McVay, who passed away just before the announcement, on June 29, 2001. Captain Bill Toti, Special Assistant to the Vice-Chief of Naval Operations; Rep. Julia Carson (D-IN); Rep. Joe Scarborough (R-FL); and Sen. John Warner (R-VA) also provided important assistance along the way. In particular, Captain Toti's constant study and advocacy for this outcome were essential.

SADLY, news of the exoneration arrived too late for Dr. Lewis Haynes, who passed away at his winter home in Florida on March 13, 2001, at the age of eighty-nine.

Even at the end of his life, Dr. Haynes, still haunted by the ship's sinking, had spent many a troubled night dog-paddling in his sleep, tossing and turning, adrift in the Philippine Sea.

I learned this at Lew's funeral, at which I was honored to speak at the request of his wife, Margaret. *In Harm's Way* had not yet been published, but the doctor's friends and relatives were aware of his excitement about the book, and many expressed curiosity as to why I'd chosen to write it. I thought I knew the answer, but at Lew's funeral I found myself fumbling for a way to convey what I'd felt most deeply about all the heroic and yet humble men of the USS *Indianapolis*. To my own surprise, I realized I didn't truly understand it myself. Why *did* this particular story exert such a pull on me?

My hope had been to make readers care enough about the survivors' ordeal that they would care even more today about the case of Captain McVay and his court-martial. I'd written the story as I'd heard it, which was as a kind of legend told around a kitchen table late at night. And readers had found inspiration in the survivors' struggle. "Your book is changing *ME*," one man had written, in the same way that "you describe meeting the men and telling their stories has changed you. I also have sought adventure, from [being in] the Navy, to rock and mountain climbing, even some business adventures. I have had great stresses and also great fortunes. The story of the *Indianapolis* needed to be told." Others, already aware of the survivors' ordeal, were surprised by what they hadn't known. "As someone who's read virtually every story written about the disaster," wrote Mike Monroney, "I wasn't prepared for your incredibly vivid narrative. It was frightening. And it was excellently done . . . the book will be an immense help in the effort to have Captain McVay vindicated." Clearly, I was a long way from my first tentative introduction to the survivors and their story.

When I'd attended that first reunion in July 1999, I felt a bit lost, wandering the Westin Hotel in Indianapolis and wondering what or where the "story" was. Research material was scant or out of print; except for local media, there wasn't another reporter around for miles. Not hours after my arrival, I was considering leaving. And then I met the men.

When I returned to the next reunion in August 2001 (five months after *In Harm's Way* had been published), I found myself surrounded by a group of about 600 people, many of whom I now knew by name. The reunion was a happy yet bittersweet affair. In one corner of the hotel lobby, a group of elderly men were joking with one another; in another, other survivors were sharing a painful moment reminiscing about lost shipmates. And all around were bustling families—young kids, teenagers, new mothers—looking on, learning how people face the past, and the future.

Because I had written about the ship, some people assumed I might know how a particular relative had died. Maybe every third person who approached me was in tears. And as had been true throughout the tour, some of the most poignant responses came from teenagers and from women who felt that in reading the book they'd been offered a glimpse into their own father's or grandfather's lives.

During the Q&A part of the reunion's reading, a survivor named Frank Centazzo stood up and approached the microphone. I had never interviewed Frank for the book, a fact about which he good-naturedly reminded me. And then he turned serious: for fifty-six years, he announced, he'd felt ashamed by the behavior of some of the men in the water. Why had some surrendered and died? Why had others acted less than admirably?

It wasn't until he'd read *In Harm's Way*, he said, that he'd understood why. He was referring to passages describing the devastating effects of saltwater ingestion and exposure on the men.

As he stood there, his voice wavering, he thanked me for writing the book.

I remember being speechless. And thinking, Why hadn't anyone ever told this proud man what had happened?

SHORTLY thereafter, the final pieces of the puzzle fell into place. I was finishing an interview with an NPR reporter and as he was leaving my office, he asked, "Anything you want to add?"

And suddenly, I understood what I hadn't grasped before. Of all the dreams I had while writing *In Harm's Way*, the most powerful was one of floating on a burning, inhospitable sea, willing myself to stay alive. During my interviews with survivors, nearly all of them had recalled that, at some point, they had made a vow to themselves: *I am going to live.*

This had always struck me as a startling, existential moment—it had haunted me, and still does. What the men were remembering were those people back on land who had at some point told them—in words or through deeds—"never to give up."

I told the reporter that I wondered if I had ever said anything to my own son, to my daughter, to my wife, to any of my friends—to anybody—that would act as a lifeline if they found themselves in a similar situation.

I said that I didn't know, but that I hoped I had.

When people tell me they like the book I wrote, I tell them that the book wrote me.

> January 17, 2002
> Lake Ann, Michigan

The Final Chapter: 2022

THE story of the USS *Indianapolis*, like the sea into which it disappeared on July 30, 1945, continues to offer up discoveries.*

On August 19, 2017, an expedition financed by explorer and philanthropist Paul Allen, and led by expedition director Robert Kraft, discovered the USS *Indianapolis* lying on the bottom of the Pacific Ocean, in 18,044 feet of water. The crystalline pictures and video sent back by the expedition's remote cameras revealed a ship practically preserved in time after seventy-two years of resting in cold darkness.†

Until its discovery, the ship had often sailed through the crew's daily thoughts, its final destination unknown—in a way, the ship was still at sea, far beyond human reach. The crew's last glimpse of it had been as it tipped on its bow and flew into the deep, and into history.

Today, the ship's exact location remains confidential and is considered a gravesite. But its remarkable discovery allows the crew and families, of those who'd survived and those who were lost at sea, to know that its final destination was no longer a mirage.

While taking part in a 2019 PBS documentary about the ship's discovery, *USS* Indianapolis: *The Final Chapter*, I sat

---

* In 2018, crew and casualty numbers were adjusted to account for a longtime error in the ship's sailing list, making the final tally of survivors 316 men. See "Setting the Record Straight: Loss of the USS *Indianapolis* and the Question of Clarence Donnor," by Richard Hulver and Sara Vladic, *Proceedings,* March 2018.

† Correspondence/interview with Robert Kraft, November 2020.

in a hotel conference room as survivor Richard "Dick" Thelen looked into the camera and recounted his relief and elation about the discovery, feelings shared by many of the remaining crew and families. Earlier in life, Dick had kept secret his service aboard the *Indy*.

For the first seven years of his first marriage as a young man, he did not tell his wife that he'd been aboard the ship when it sunk. The experience was too painful. I originally met him in 1999, at an annual reunion of survivors, and over the years I watched with a sense of awe as his public speaking and outreach extended to civic groups and schools.

It was Dick who first told me that he'd "heard a voice," an experience that I'd discovered and reported on that was shared by many of the crew, voices of loved ones or acquaintances—it didn't seem to matter—that drew them back to the world of the living just when they felt in peril of giving up hope of rescue and resigning themselves to death. In Dick's case, the voice was his father's, urging him not to give up. He kept dog-paddling.

"*Never give up*, that's what I tell school students now," Dick once told me.

On September 13, 2021, Richard Thelen passed away, at age ninety-four. As of this writing, there are two survivors remaining.

THIS brings us to the heartbeat of the *Indianapolis* story: the recognition of our personal experience, of our story, can make us whole again.

To *tell* one's story, and to be *heard* doing this—and to make sense of what doesn't make sense—is part of the journey of being alive.* At the same time, not to be allowed to tell one's story is to be denied one's humanity.

The dramatic journey of the crew's survival, experienced vicariously by us as readers, is what often draws us to the story of the *Indianapolis* and its crew. *Will they make it? How did they make it? What gold, if any, did they haul back from the cauldron of this experience?* These *existential* questions can be so overpowering as to distract us from the ship's and crew's valorous *military service* during World War II, which sometimes receives less attention than it deserves.

The situation was rectified in July 2020 when the crew was presented with the Congressional Gold Medal, Congress's highest honor. Here was a public proclamation of the highest order of not only the crew's humble heroism but of its hard and critical battle service.

More recognition of the crew followed when, on January 8, 2021, then secretary of the navy Kenneth Braithwaite posthumously honored Father Thomas Conway, the ship's chaplain, with the Navy Cross.

The ceremony capped a yearslong effort begun, in some respect, by Dr. Lewis Haynes after his rescue, to memorialize the selfless sacrifice of his friend who perished tending to shipmates. For three days, Conway had guided stragglers to their comrades, led sailors in prayer, and administered last rites. In 2013, retired navy chaplain Father John Bevins read *In Harm's Way* and was inspired to launch an advocacy campaign for the award.

During the 2020 reunion, the story's aperture opened on a

---

* Further reading is found in the encyclopedic *Only 316 Survived!*, a book I urged survivors to publish with some initial seed money, as they reached their seventies and eighties, in order to create a collective oral history.

tragically untold history, and brought to light for the first time the service of twenty-eight African Americans who served aboard the *Indianapolis*, and who did not survive the ordeal. A new page in the ship's history had begun to be written.

This moment was the brainchild of the USS *Indianapolis* CA-35 Legacy Organization and descendants of the ship's African American crew members. The organization exists "to promote and perpetuate the memory of all who served" aboard the ship, says Jane Goodall, a daughter of rescue pilot Chuck Gwinn. The research team included Dr. Jeanette Pitts, niece of Albert Rice; Jacqueline Dugan and Ernestine Peete, nieces of Magellan Williams; and Janice Alston and Arlene Taylor, great-niece and niece of Henry Jackson. They resolved to record the histories of African American crew members in a book entitled *Heroes in the Shadows: World War II's Untold Story of African American Sailors on the Final Sailing Crew of USS* Indianapolis *CA-35*.

Among the twenty-eight sailors was Magellan Williams, steward's mate, 1C, from Downsville, Louisiana, who was twenty-one when he went down with the ship. Clarence Sims, aged twenty-two, cook, 2C, from Henning, Tennessee, served as Captain McVay's valet and had come aboard two months before Pearl Harbor and spent nearly all four years of the war on the ship, when he was lost at sea. Henry L. Jackson, steward's mate, 1C, was thirty-eight years old, from Beaverdam, Virginia, and had been aboard a little over a year. He, too, did not survive the sinking. Also aboard was Albert Rice, aged twenty, steward's mate, 1C, of Kansas City, Kansas.

Dr. Jeanette Pitts recalls that after the death of his mother when Albert was twelve, he became a mentor, along with his twin sister, of their younger siblings in a close, extended family. An artist and athlete, Albert Rice was proud his family had served in World War I (his nephews would later fight in Vietnam). And he was proud to be aboard the USS *Indianapolis*.

Rice was a young man who liked to teach and lead. "The last time Albert came home—his last furlough—before the ship went down," says Dr. Jeanette Pitts, "he slept there in the bed with his younger brother—my dad—and talked with him [about his life and experiences]." Albert's death was devastating to the family, and later in life Dr. Lee Roy Pitts Sr., Jeanette's father, would nonetheless discover in the tragedy an opportunity to often talk with Jeanette and the entire family about the importance of service and citizenship.

The ship that sailed from California on July 16, 1945, was a mirror of the segregated country it left behind, a floating city where sailors were literally compartmentalized in differing worlds based on rank and race. President Harry Truman would finally desegregate the navy on July 26, 1948 (though desegregation was not immediate), and it would be nearly another sixteen years before the Civil Rights Act of 1964 was signed into law by President Lyndon Johnson.

"Life was hard on all enlisted men in a navy ship in World War II," says Sandra Gall, formerly of the Naval History and Heritage Command. "Living conditions [were] rough, though [it's] not hard to imagine it was tougher for African Americans, who faced racism" from white crew members and officers throughout the entire navy.

"It appears," says Rear Admiral (Retired) Samuel Cox, director of Naval History and Heritage Command, "that how much combat responsibility the messmen/cooks/stewards had, [had] much to do with where the ship's skipper was from." Referencing a 1942 photo taken aboard the *Indy* of twelve African American sailors, who volunteered for additional duty as gunners, and three white officers, including its then captain E. W. Hanson, Cox says it would "suggest that [the] *Indianapolis* was fairly 'progressive,' at least in July 1942."

Cox adds, "It is interesting that although Doris Miller was assigned to *Indianapolis* at the time he is not in the photo of this African American gun crew." Miller had been transferred to the USS *Indianapolis* after his heroic service aboard the USS *West Virginia* during the attack at Pearl Harbor, December 7, 1941. For his decisive action manning a ship's gun, he was awarded the Navy Cross, a historic recognition of an African American's service in the war. He served on the *Indianapolis* until 1943 when he went aboard the USS *Liscome Bay*. He was killed in action on November 20, 1943. At the time the photo was taken, it's likely that Miller, a war hero, was in the United States on a war bonds tour.

THE African American sailors aboard the *Indy* were bunked in a forward area where the torpedoes smashed into the hull. It's impossible to determine how many survived the explosions and made it into the water. Dick Thelen remembered swimming alongside an African American shipmate but losing track of him. It's unlikely, but not impossible, that the two would have known each other aboard the ship.

Because no African American sailors survived the sinking, few of their descendants attended reunions, which began in 1960. When I arrived at my first reunion in 1999, the survivors were several years past their building a memorial to ship and crew in

Indianapolis and were mainly focused on the welfare and histories of those sailors who'd survived.

During several book tours, I continued to meet survivors who had never attended a reunion and continued to decline any invitation. What we now call post-traumatic stress was a nascent idea fifteen years after the war, and even later in life painful memories of survival made it difficult for many survivors to reunite with shipmates.

Likewise, few descendants of the sailors who perished, now called Lost At Sea families by the Legacy Organization, attended any reunions. Their connection to the ship and crew—to the story of what had happened to their loved ones—was fatally interrupted when the ship sank. The surviving crew had dispersed across America, living mostly in silence with their grief and nightmares, as the story of their survival atomized into hundreds of shards of memories. When faced with the grief and questions posed by Lost At Sea families, many survivors didn't know how to respond, as they themselves were plagued by "survivor's guilt." What stood between so many was silence, fueled and stained by this guilt, and in the case of acknowledging the service of the African American crew, a history of racism.

The overall effect was that, over the years, the story of what happened to the men as they struggled to survive was told and retold in a communal act that, by its nature, ended up excluding those who were not present at the reunions.

In 1995, Dr. Lee Roy Pitts Sr. attended a reunion and asked that African Americans and their service aboard the ship be included in its history. "I know going to the reunion, his quest to honor Albert's, his brother's, memory, was its own therapy," says Dr. Jeanette Pitts. He stood on a podium and queried reunion attendees about Albert's life aboard the ship, but this went unanswered. He would leave the reunion disappointed, and he did not attend another.

In 2001, Jacqueline Dugan, niece of Magellan Williams, attended a reunion and similarly came away empty-handed in her search for information or anecdotes about her uncle or his experience. Nonetheless, Dugan, her husband, and son found the reunion an overall positive experience. She does recall that when she asked others if they remembered her uncle, "The look on their face was like, 'I don't want to remember, I don't remember that time.' And that's when I realized I had to stop."

Dugan says, "You could tell, it was harmful to just bring it up," and she retreated to the internet for her research, where she fared little better. "When people tell the story," says Dugan, "they think only of the survivors, and the African Americans who were on the ship are never mentioned. When I tell them that my uncle was [there], it's like, 'Oh, I just thought it was white men on the ship.'"

In discussing how to talk about the ship's history, and about who perished and survived, and about people of color who served aboard the *Indy*, Dr. Jeanette Pitts makes an important point: "I'm looking at *survivorship* as more than just being alive," she says. "Part of this is the *survival* of those who were left behind and how that impacted [them]."

There are sailors who survived the sinking, and then there are the people whose loved ones on the ship did not survive. These people who've been "left behind," in Pitts's words, to mourn are survivors, too, sometimes mourning people about whom they know little. Researching and publishing the lives of African American sailors aboard the ship corrects an injustice in the historical record and may help heal the trauma of loss.

"I don't see it as doing a favor to African Americans or to people of color," she says. "I think it's doing what needs to be done for everyone.

"I want these men's memories to be honored, their sacrifices to be recognized, [for us] to realize that they had the same dreams and hopes that others did—that they had the same, if not more, hardships. They had families they left behind, and there are repercussions through the generations for these families, talents and skills that were lost, children that were unborn."

Fairest Pledger, Magellan Williams's youngest sister, struggles to talk about his death, but less so than her sister Eunice, who refuses to speak about it at all.

"I was only thirteen at the time," says Fairest, when a telegram arrived notifying the family that Magellan was missing in action, and "it just so happened that I got the telegram out of the box." Her parents were away grocery shopping, and she found herself alone with the dreadful knowledge of her brother's death in her hand. How would she tell her parents when they got home? Why had the telegram been left for the family to find as if it were just another piece of news? Couldn't someone in a position of authority have delivered it in person? Hadn't Magellan given his life for his country? These thoughts were with her now, as she stood alone on the country road, as they would be for the rest of her life.

Within a generation, some of the only people left to tell the story of the *Indianapolis* will be the descendants of those who survived and the descendants of those sailors who perished. And because far more did *not* survive, this latter group likely represents a broader spectrum of race and class in mid-century America, and a more complete story of the ship and its crew will continue to be told.

AFRICAN American crew members were not the only group aboard the ship who faced discrimination and whose roles went unacknowledged until recently.

In 2013, Adolfo "Harpo" Celaya explained to the Veterans History Project that he'd seen more than one poster around his hometown of Florence, Arizona, promising that navy men got to see the world.* Harpo was seventeen, too young by law to join without his father's signature. The elder Celaya reluctantly agreed.

When the ship sunk, Harpo, adrift in the sea, discovered that he was not welcome aboard a life raft. "I was going to get on [one] but some of the guys that were on there wouldn't allow me to. I grabbed hold of some rope, and I stayed there.

"My friend Santos Pena said the same thing happened to him. [He] got up to a raft and there were two or three guys on there, they told him to get away."† In 2020, in *Smithsonian* magazine, Celaya explained that after the rescue and during the survivors' return trip to the United States aboard an aircraft carrier, he was tasked to work detail while the white sailors were convalescing. Celaya explained that "any jobs that were not taken by a white person would be given down to anybody that had Hispanic blood."‡

When he complained to an officer, he was thrown in solitary confinement and fed nothing but bread and water for two days.

---

* Adolfo Celaya, video interview with Mike Brian, Southern Arizona Veterans Administration, Veterans History Project, Library of Congress, Florence, Arizona, July 26, 2013.

† Celaya, video interview with Brian.

‡ Meilan Solly, "See 12 Stunning Portraits of World War II Veterans," www .smithsonianmag.com, August 2019.

Celaya told the Veterans History Project, "It was kind of rough for me, I mean, that my country would do that to me."

Celaya reengaged with his shipmates in the early 1970s, at the urging of recue pilot Chuck Gwinn, with whom he'd become close friends. At Gwinn's patient urging, Celaya would finally break a long silence and begin speaking to school students about his navy experience. But the wounds he suffered remained fresh years later, and he didn't attempt to attend another reunion until 2019, an effort, unfortunately, thwarted by illness, but which opened a path of reengagement in 2020 when Celaya, with his shipmates, participated (virtually) in the Congressional Gold Medal award ceremony.* Adolfo Celaya passed away on Thanksgiving Day, November 25, 2021, at the age of ninety-four.

I̶N a story filled with many mysteries, one of the most persistent is the question of whether anyone on shore received a distress message from the *Indianapolis* as it sank. In its detailed and excellent study *A Grave Misfortune*, the Naval History and Heritage Command concludes, as the navy had argued during Captain McVay's 1945 court-martial, that no SOS left the ship and, therefore, none was received onshore.

In the 2001 edition of *In Harm's Way*, I cite several individuals who believe they witnessed receipt of an SOS message from the Indy; two of them testified at a 1999 hearing before the Committee on Armed Services. When I had asked Dick Thelen if he

---

* For further reading about Adolfo Celaya's experience aboard the USS *Indianapolis* and his life after his rescue, see Charles Clemans, *Harpo: War Survivor, Basketball Wizard* (Tucson, AZ: Wheatmark, 2009). On September 16, 2017, the U.S. Post Office building in Florence, Arizona, Celaya's hometown, was dedicated in his name.

believed a message was sent, he said he did. In my interview with radioman Jack Miner, he believed the same. Of course, "believing" doesn't make a fact. What's curious is the persistence, even today, more than seven decades later, of recollections by sailors who insisted they did receive such a message and that it was not acted upon.

For example, in 2020, ninety-four-year-old Alwyn Martinson, of Minnesota, got in touch to tell me that as a twenty-year-old radio operator aboard the USS *Logan* (APA-196) docked in Guam, he received an SOS from the *Indy* as it sank and recorded the Morse code as it arrived at his station.

"They told me, 'You take [the message] up to the skipper,' and somebody sat down at my receiver and took over from me and I took it up to the skipper."

"And what did he do with it?"

"That's a good question."

Martinson says, "Not a day goes by that I don't think about it."

I've included the 2001 account of the "SOS question" in this edition and direct readers to *A Grave Misfortune*, where they may study court-martial documents and consider the conclusion that since no hard copy distress message can be found in official records, no message was received.

I remain agnostic about this logic, neither impeaching nor exonerating, but I do suspect that of the thousands and thousands of messages sent during World War II, many are likely irretrievable. When I posed the question to the National Archives at College Park, Maryland, I received the following answer:

> Ship-to-ship communications and ship-to-command
> communications are *not* [emphasis mine] retained as

permanent records. Some ship-to-ship communications may get retained as permanent records when retained as part of an investigation.

The court-martial of Captain McVay commenced five months after the sinking. It's possible that message traffic of July 30, 1945, received five days before the men were accidentally discovered, was preserved by someone in the immediate aftermath, but no hard-copy evidence has yet emerged in the pentimento of this tale.

Whether or not a message was received "has probably been the most vexing question of the sad saga," says Rear Admiral (Retired) Samuel Cox. "Our historians have given it their best shot, although I am not convinced there will ever be a definitive answer to this question."

Perhaps parts of the *Indy*'s story will remain forever untold.

February 23, 2022
Traverse City, Michigan

About the USS *Indianapolis*/ Gwinn "Angel" Scholarship Endowment

IN June 2002, Doug Stanton, author of *In Harm's Way*, conceived of and funded the *USS* Indianapolis Survivors Fund Scholarship Program to benefit family members of the ship's crew and to help preserve the *Indianapolis*'s historic legacy. The program was generously assisted by USS *Indianapolis* CA-35 Second Watch. In 2008, the fund was permanently endowed by the family of Wilbur C. Gwinn as the USS *Indianapolis*/Gwinn "Angel" Scholarship

Endowment. Gwinn was the pilot who first spotted the survivors and initiated their rescue at sea.

The purpose of the USS *Indianapolis*/Gwinn "Angel" Scholarship Endowment is to preserve the stories of the ship and its crew. Prospective and continuing college students are encouraged to research the story of the USS *Indianapolis* CA-35 and write about their own families.

The scholarship is open to descendants (including stepchildren) of USS *Indianapolis* CA-35 crew members involved in the tragedy—its survivors, sailors lost at sea (LAS), rescue and recovery crew, and those who have merited honorary survivor status by the Survivors Organization. For information, contact the Grand Traverse Regional Community Foundation at https://www.gtrcf.org.

To read more about the African American sailors aboard the USS *Indianapolis*, see https://www.ussindianapolis.org.

Notes

Please note that some of the links referenced throughout this work are no longer active.

PROLOGUE: SAILOR ON A CHAIN

Interviews: Gordon Linke, Jocelyn Linke, Scott Linke, Winthrop Smith Jr., Ed Stevens, Florence Regosia, Michael Monroney, Giles McCoy.

p. 7.   *A pool of blood*: police photographs, November 6, 1968.

p. 8.   *Of the nearly 400 American captains*: Naval History and Heritage Command, www.history.navy.mil; *Proceedings*, October 1999, "The Sinking of the *Indy* & Responsibility of Command," Commander William J. Toti, U.S. Navy; Thomas B. Buell, *Master of the Sea*, p. 328.
         In the early 1990s: Richard A. von Doenhoff, "ULTRA and the Sinking of USS *Indianapolis*," *Eleventh Naval History Symposium*, United States Naval Academy, Annapolis, MD, October 1993.

CHAPTER ONE: ALL ABOARD

Interviews: John Spinelli, Giles McCoy, Mike Kuryla, Dr. Lewis Haynes, Ed Brown, Charlie Sullivan, Bob McGuiggan, Harlan Twible, Grover Carver, Richard Paroubek, Robert Gause, Bill Drayton, Richard Stephens, Gordon Linke.

p. 15.   *He had just come*: Narrative by: Captain Charles B. McVay III, USN, Sinking of USS *Indianapolis*, 27 September 1945; Fletcher Knebel and Charles W. Bailey, *No High Ground*, pp. 101–2; Richard Newcomb, *Abandon Ship!: Death of the USS* Indianapolis, pp. 27–28.
         McVay had a lot on his mind: Katherine D. Moore, *Goodbye Indy Maru*, pp. 122, 132, 141–42; Narrative by: Captain Charles B. McVay.

p. 16.   *Hundreds of telegrams*: Evan McLeod Wylie, "The Last Secret Voyage of the USS *Indianapolis*," *Yankee*, July 1978.
         He'd been told that the earliest the ship: Narrative by: Captain Charles B. McVay.

p. 17.   *One of McVay's boys*: USS *Indianapolis* Deck Logs, March and April 1945.
         Back on land: Moore, *Goodbye Indy Maru*, p. 135.

p. 18.   *The city, still a Wild West town*: "San Francisco History," www.sf5o.com
/qaboard/qaboard.htm.
In the three and a half years: From the weekly reports of the Joint Army
Navy Personnel Shipping Committee.

p. 19.   *Two months earlier*: Hanson W. Baldwin, *Battles Lost and Won: Great
Campaigns of World War II*, p. 280.
But this paled in comparison: Thomas B. Allen and Norman Polmar,
*Code-Name Downfall: The Secret Plan to Invade Japan—and Why Tru-
man Dropped the Bomb*, p. 208.
On the island of Tinian: Walter J. Boyne, *The Clash of the Titans*, p. 281;
Maj. Gen. Charles W. Sweeney with James Antonucci and Marion K.
Antonucci, *War's End: An Eyewitness Account of America's Last Atomic
Mission*, p. 136.

p. 21.   *In July, the Fillmore was showing*: "San Francisco History," www.sf5o
.com/qaboard/qaboard.htm.

p. 22.   *One sailor was arrested*: USS *Indianapolis* Deck Log, June 1945.
Captain McVay was billeted: Moore, *Goodbye Indy Maru*, pp. 126–27.
The more serious business of preparing: USS *Indianapolis* Deck Log,
June 1945.

p. 23.   *Their favorite flavors*: Moore, *Goodbye Indy Maru*, p. 82.
In the military: Paul Fussell, *Wartime Understanding and Behavior in
the Second World War*, pp. 251–67.

p. 25.   *Sailors called marines "gyrenes"*: L. Peter Wren, *Those in Peril on the Sea*,
p. 33.

p. 27.   *During the trip, Roosevelt*: *Life*, November 30, 1936.

p. 28.   *Ever since the seventeenth century*: Steve Ewing, *American Cruisers of
World War II*, p. ix.

p. 29.   *They marched with it*: Letter from James F. Nolan, M.D., to Richard F.
Newcomb, August 12, 1957.

p. 30.   *"going to use biological warfare"*: Letter from Nolan to Newcomb.
A noontime farewell luncheon: Moore, *Goodbye Indy Maru*, p. 141.
What the captain didn't know: Moore, *Goodbye Indy Maru*, p. 138.

p. 31   *One of the ship's major problems*: Moore, *Goodbye Indy Maru*, pp. 132–34,
159; Letter from Richard A. Paroubek to Captain William J. Toti, February 24, 1999.
Of his crew, more than 250: "Facts and Discussion of Facts," unsigned,
undated (NIG report); Moore, *Goodbye Indy Maru*, p. 158.

p. 32   *As the afternoon*: "Record and Proceedings of a General Court Martial
Convened at the Navy Yard, Washington, D.C., by Order of the Secretary
of the Navy: Case of Charles B. McVay, 3rd, Captain, U.S. Navy, December 3, 1945"; Narrative by: Captain Charles B. McVay.
And to make matters worse: Moore, *Goodbye Indy Maru*, p. 142.

p. 35.   *It was an explosion*: Encyclopedia Britannica, www.britannica.com.
         He gathered his officers: Letter from Nolan to Newcomb; Knebel and Bailey, *No High Ground*, p. 101.

p. 36.   *In the canister:* Letter from Nolan to Newcomb; Knebel and Bailey, *No High Ground*, p. 101

p. 37.   *For Nolan and Furman*: Letter from Nolan to Newcomb; Knebel and Bailey, *No High Ground*, p. 46; Newcomb, *Abandon Ship!*, pp. 32–33.
         Now, as the Indy *began steaming*: Stanley Weintraub, *The Last Great Victory: The End of WWII, July/August 1945*, p. 83.
         by 8:30 a.m.: Narrative by: Captain Charles B. McVay.

CHAPTER TWO: GOOD-BYE, GOLDEN GATE

Interviews: Ed Brown, Robert Gause, Dr. Lewis Haynes, Mike Kuryla, Jack Cassidy, Giles McCoy, Richard Stephens, Bob McGuiggan, Gus Kay, Harlan Twible, Jack Miner, Bill Drayton, John Spinelli, Dennis Covert, Charlie Sullivan, Gordon Linke, Jocelyn Linke, Winthrop Smith Jr.

p. 42.   *A CARELESS WORD*: Fussell, *Wartime Understanding and Behavior in the Second World War*, p. 37.
         McVay's orders for this mission: Phillip A. St. John, *USS* Indianapolis *(CA-35)*, p. 31.

p. 47.   *Every ounce of freshwater*: Plan of the Day, USS *Indianapolis*, July 16, 1945.

p. 48.   *McVay's grandfather*: Gene Sultan, "Captain Charles Butler McVay, III," 7/30/74; *Evening Star*, August 15, 1945, "838 Lost, 315 Saved in Sinking of *Indianapolis* by Jap[anese] Sub: Cruiser Had Just Carried Atom Bomb from U.S. to Guam"; Service Record: McVay, Charles Butler.

p. 50.   *Today's practice*: Letter from Nolan to Newcomb.

p. 51.   *Japan, which began*: St. John, *USS* Indianapolis *(CA-35)*, p. 12; Stephen Ambrose, *American Heritage New History of World War II*, p. 122.
         The Indy *was delivering supplies and troops*: Patrick J. Finneran, "A Short History of the USS *Indianapolis*," USS *Indianapolis* (CA-35) Survivors Organization; Testimony of Daniel E. Brady.

p. 52.   *By 1942, however, as the Japanese attempted to fight*: John Keegan, *The Price of Admiralty*, p. 198; Ambrose, *American Heritage New History of World War II*, p. 317.
         Later that year, Admiral Spruance: Thomas B. Buell, *The Quiet Warrior: A Biography of Admiral Raymond A. Spruance*, pp. 185–86.

p. 53.   *During the battle of the Philippine Sea*: James F. Dunnigan and Albert A. Noli, *Victory at Sea*, p. 50.

p. 55.   *In less than three months*: Dunnigan and Noli, *Victory at Sea*, pp. 260–62; Allen and Polmar, *Code-Name Downfall*, pp. 86–88.
          Even now, as the Japanese: John Keegan, *The Battle for History: Refighting WWII*, pp. 27–28.
          The term kamikaze: John Ray Skates, *The Invasion of Japan: Alternative to the Bomb*, p. 148.

p. 56.   *The* New York Times *would call*: *New York Times*, January 9, 1946.
          The pilots, often dressed: Philip Nobile, ed., *Judgment at the Smithsonian: The Bombing of Hiroshima and Nagasaki*.

p. 58.   *McVay received a message*: Moore, *Goodbye Indy Maru*, p. 115.
          Generally speaking, however, the navy suffered: Boyne, *Clash of Titans*, p. 326.

p. 61.   *And, perhaps, for the green hands' sake*: Wren, *Those in Peril on the Sea*, pp. 33–35.
          Nearly six days after leaving: Donald W. Olson, Brandon R. Johns, and Russell L. Doescher, " 'Ill Met by Moonlight': The Sinking of the USS *Indianapolis*," *Sky and Telescope*, 2002.

CHAPTER THREE: THE FIRST DOMINO

Interviews: Dr. Lewis Haynes, Giles McCoy, Ed Brown, Mike Kuryla, Bob McGuiggan, Robert Gause, Harlan Twible, Richard Stephens, Charlie Sullivan, Douw Mac Hallie, David Dorflinger.

p. 65.   *Tinian Island, a mere ten miles*: Gordon Thomas and Max Morgan Witts, *Enola Gay*, pp. 81, 87, 151, 161; Sweeney with Antonucci and Antonucci, *War's End: An Eyewitness Account of America's Last Atomic Mission*, p. 137.

p. 66.   *Capable of carrying a ten-ton load of bombs*: "American Aircraft of World War II," www.ixpress.com/ag1caf/usplanes/american.
          The two officers were seeking: Newcomb, *Abandon Ship!*, p. 43.

p. 67.   *Tinian lay in what was now*: Court Martial.
          As the unloading of the bomb: Dispatch 260152.
          In fact, Nolan was spending: Letter from Nolan to Newcomb.

p. 69.   *a member of McCormick's radio staff*: A principle action source for Guam and Leyte is the 131-page Court of Inquiry document. Like the Court Martial, its concern lies with the order to abandon ship as well as with weather conditions on the night of the sinking. Unlike the Court Martial, however, it gives equal time to the administrative failure to recognize the absence of the *Indianapolis*. The other major source for land-based information is the series of reports carried out after the inquiry and finished in January 1946 by the Navy Inspector General (NIG).

Record of the Proceedings of a Court of Inquiry Convened at the Headquarters of the Commander, Marianas, by order of the Commander in Chief, United States Pacific Fleet and Pacific Ocean Areas for the purpose of inquiring into all the circumstances connected with the sinking of the USS *Indianapolis* (CA 35), on or about July 29, 1945, the rescue operations, and the delay in connection with reporting the loss of that ship. Signed: Vice Admiral Charles A. Lockwood, Vice Admiral George D. Murray, Rear Admiral Francis E. M. Whiting, and Captain William E. Hilbert, Judge Advocate, dated August 13, 1945; Progress Report (NIG); Discussion of Facts in the Further Investigation of the Sinking of the USS *Indianapolis* and the Delay in Reporting the Loss of this Ship, unsigned, undated, (NIG); Investigation of the Sinking of the USS *Indianapolis* and the Delay in Reporting the Loss of that Ship. From: The Naval Inspector General. To: The Chief of Naval Operations. Signed: C. P. Snyder. Dated: Received 7 January 1946; Facts and Discussion of Facts (NIG).

En route to Guam: Narrative by Captain Charles B. McVay.

p. 71.   *At HQ, McVay met Nimitz's*: Discussion of Facts (NIG).

McVay was frustrated: Court Martial; Raymond Lech, *All the Drowned Sailors*, p. 10.

Spruance had left the wounded ship: USS *Indianapolis* Deck Log, April 1945.

Spruance was relaxed: Court Martial.

Two days before this conversation: Skates, *The Invasion of Japan*, p. 242.

p. 72.   *Essentially, there were two battle plans*: Skates, *The Invasion of Japan*, p. 5; Knebel and Bailey, *No High Ground*, p. 70.

Sworn into office: Knebel and Bailey, *No High Ground*, pp. 46, 55.

As they ate, the admiral noticed: Court Martial.

p. 73.   *McVay exchanged pleasantries*: Court of Inquiry; Court Martial; Discussion of Facts (NIG).

p. 74.   *McVay and the* Indianapolis: Court of Inquiry.

Clear as this delineation was: Allen and Polmar, *Code-Name Downfall*, pp. 135–40; Skates, *The Invasion of Japan*, pp. 158–59.

The Indy *had no sonar gear*: Boyne, *Clash of Titans*, pp. 110–12.

When, in the course of the talk: Facts and Discussion of Facts (NIG); Court Martial; Progress Report (NIG); Court of Inquiry; Newcomb, *Abandon Ship!*, pp. 49–50.

p. 75.   *After McVay's navigator*: Court of Inquiry; Court Martial; Discussion of Facts (NIG).

"Here we go again": Discussion of Facts (NIG).

p. 76.   *When McVay next met*: Court of Inquiry; Progress Report (NIG); Court Martial; Discussion of Facts (NIG).

The intelligence report seemed: Court of Inquiry; Court Martial; Facts and

Discussion of Facts (NIG); Office of the Port Director. Subject: Routing Instructions. To: Commanding Officer, USS *Indianapolis* (CA35). From: Port Director, Guam. Dated 28 July 1945. Signed: J. J. Waldron; Operational Intelligence Section, NOB, Guam, M.I. Subject: Intelligence Brief for Guam to Philippines. Dated 27 July 1945. Signed: R. N. Orr, Intelligence Officer.

Three days earlier, on July 24: Samuel Eliot Morison, *Victory in the Pacific*, pp. 317–18; Progress Report (NIG).

p. 77.   *McVay's intelligence report*: von Doenhoff, "ULTRA and the Sinking of USS *Indianapolis*."

Captain McVay, however, was not apprised: von Doenhoff, "ULTRA and the Sinking of USS *Indianapolis*"; Hearing Before the Committee on Armed Services, United States Senate, One Hundred Sixth Congress, First Session, September 14, 1999, "The Sinking of the USS *Indianapolis* and the Subsequent Court Martial of Rear Admiral Charles B. McVay Ill; John Savard, "A Cryptographic Compendium"; Keegan, *Battle for History*, pp. 87–92; Edwin Layton with Roger Pineau and John Costello, *And I Was There: Pearl Harbor and Midway: Breaking the Secrets*, pp. 139, 367, 449–56.

p. 79.   *Sixty feet below the swirling ink*: Mochitsura Hashimoto, *Sunk!: The Story of the Japanese Submarine Fleet, 1942–1945*, pp. 140–48; Weintraub, *The Last Great Victory*, p. 73; "Submarines of the Imperial Japanese Navy," http://www.combinedfleet.com/ss.htm; Court Martial; Investigation of the Sinking, 7 January 1946; "Sinking the *Indianapolis*: A Japanese Perspective," *The Quan*, 1996.

"very low order": Court Martial.

p. 81.   *One well-known disaster*: Boyne, *Clash of Titans*, p. 292.

The carriers Yorktown *and* Wasp: Dunnigan and Nofi, *Victory at Sea*, pp. 113–14.

p. 82.   *Shortly before the Indy's departure*: Dispatch 280032; Lech, *All the Drowned Sailors*, p. 19; Court of Inquiry; Progress Report (NIG); Discussion of Facts (NIG); Facts and Discussion of Facts (NIG).

p. 84.   *At some point during the early evening*: Thomas Helm, *Ordeal by Sea*, p. 38; "Sea Tales: Missing! The *Indianapolis*," A&E Home Video.

p. 85.   *Indeed, while Loran A*: Correspondence with Air Commander "Pinky" Grocott and Walter Blanchard.

And subs were on everyone's minds: Progress Report (NIG); Blue Summary; Discussion of Facts (NIG); Court Martial.

Sometime between 7:30 and 8 p.m.: Court Martial; Progress Report (NIG).

NOTES

CHAPTER FOUR: THE BURNING SEA

Interviews: Giles McCoy, Dr. Lewis Haynes, Mike Kuryla, Jack Miner, Harlan Twible, Robert Gause, Jack Cassidy, Richard Stephens, Ed Brown, Charlie Sullivan, Curt Newport, Dennis Covert, Robert Kraft.

p. 93.　*About twelve miles from where*: Hashimoto, *Sunk!*, pp. 140–48; Court Martial.

As later explained by Goro Yamada: "Sinking the *Indianapolis*: A Japanese Perspective," *The Quan*, 1996.

p. 94.　*The target was some six miles away*: Olson, Johns, and Doescher, "'Ill Met by Moonlight': The Sinking of the USS *Indianapolis*," *Sky and Telescope*, 2002.

p. 95.　*On board the* Indy: Survivor Statements, 7 August 1945.

p. 98.　*Back in his native Tennessee*: Moore, *Goodbye Indy Maru*, pp. 130–31.

p. 100.　*Since July 27, a typhoon*: Court of Inquiry.

About twenty men were stationed: Progress Report (NIG).

The officer of the deck: Court Martial.

Three miles away and closing: Hashimoto, *Sunk!*, pp. 140–48; Court Martial.

p. 101.　*The* Indy *was actually traveling*: Court Martial.

p. 102.　*The first torpedo hit*: Court Martial; Court of Inquiry; Personal Narrative of Captain Charles B. McVay, III, USN. Undated. Correspondence/interview with Robert Kraft about damage caused by torpedo, November 2020.

p. 103.　*Down in engine room 1*: Survivor Statements; Court of Inquiry; Court Martial.

p. 104.　*Chief engineer Richard Redmayne*: Court of Inquiry; Court Martial.

p. 105.　*Up in his battle cabin, Captain McVay*: The following details about the torpedoing, McVay's actions, and the crew's response are drawn from Court of Inquiry; Court Martial; Narrative by: Captain Charles B. McVay; Survivor Statements; *The Bluejackets' Manual*; Personal Narrative of Captain Charles B. McVay; Kenneth E. Etheridge, "The Agony of the *Indianapolis*," *American Heritage* 33, no. 5 (August/September 1982).

p. 110.　*Boys standing or lying*: Bill Van Daalen, videotaped interview with Bob Brundige, 1990.

CHAPTER FIVE: ABANDON SHIP

Interviews: Giles McCoy, Dr. Lewis Haynes, Jack Cassidy, Jack Miner, Richard Stephens, Mike Kuryla, Harlan Twible, Ed Brown, Felton Outland,

John Spinelli, William Drayton, Russell Hetz, Donald Allen, Curt Newport, Dr. Julie Johnson, Dr. Terry Taylor, Gordon Linke.

p. 130. *As the* Indy *sank*: Court of Inquiry; Court Martial; Survivor Statements.

p. 132. *In fact, in a radio shack*: Hearing before the Committee on Armed Services, September 14, 1999.

p. 134. *The prevailing protocol*: Facts and Discussion of Facts (NIG).
Shortly after the distress calls were sent: Narrative by: Captain Charles B. McVay; Court Martial.
Clair Young's account: Hearing before the Committee on Armed Services, September 14, 1999.

p. 135. *It would later be estimated*: Hearing before the Committee on Armed Services, September 14, 1999.

p. 136. *There were no stars*: Olson, Johns, and Doescher, "'Ill Met by Moonlight': The Sinking of the USS *Indianapolis*," *Sky and Telescope*, 2002.

CHAPTER SIX: HOPE AFLOAT

Interviews: Dr. Lewis Haynes, Robert Gause, Ed Brown, Harlan Twible, Giles McCoy, Felton Outland, Mike Kuryla, John Spinelli, Jack Miner, Curt Newport, Bob McGuiggan, Richard Stephens, Bill Drayton, Gus Kay, Charlie Sullivan, Dr. Julie Johnson, Dr. Terry Taylor.

p. 142. *About half of the 900 survivors*: Court Martial. Many details about the Haynes group's initial time in the water also come from Haynes's interviews, his article in the *Saturday Evening Post*, August 6, 1955, and his memoir "Survivor of the *Indianapolis*," in *Navy Medicine* 86, no. 4 (July/August 1995).

p. 143. *Captain McVay found himself*: Narrative by: Captain Charles B. McVay; Personal Narrative of Captain Charles B. McVay.

p. 148. *He was fully dressed*: Bill Van Daalen, videotaped interview with Bob Brundige.

p. 150. *In fact, what they were seeing*: Hashimoto, *Sunk!*, p. 147.

p. 153. *Floating to the northeast*: Narrative by: Captain Charles B. McVay; Personal Narrative of Captain Charles B. McVay; Court Martial; *Bay City Times*, August 15, 1945, "833 Dead and Missing in U.S. Cruiser Loss"; Al Havins, personal interview, 1996; Bill Van Daalen, videotaped interview with Al Havins, 1990.

p. 154. *Kurlick was naked*: Newcomb, *Abandon Ship!*, p. 117.

p. 155. *The tractor planes*: Progress Report (NIG).

p. 157. *A complex web of sea life*: Paul Auerbach and Edward Geehr, *Management of Wilderness and Environmental Emergencies*, chapter 34.

p. 159. *Captain McVay and his ragged*: Narrative by: Captain Charles B. McVay; Personal Narrative of Captain Charles B. McVay; Al Havins, personal interview.

McVay recorded all these sightings: Wylie, "The Last Secret Voyage of the USS *Indianapolis*."

CHAPTER SEVEN: SHARK ATTACK

Interviews: Giles McCoy, Richard Stephens, Dr. Lewis Haynes, Robert Gause, Jack Cassidy, Jack Miner, Mike Kuryla, Bob McGuiggan, Felton Outland, Ed Brown, Harlan Twible, John Spinelli, Curt Newport, Dr. Julie Johnson, Dr. Terry Taylor.

p. 165. *Those sailors who were naked*: Reader's Digest Association, *Sharks: Silent Hunters of the Deep*, pp. 76, 100, 140.

p. 166. *Present-day wisdom*: Capt. H. David Baldridge Jr., "Shark Repellent: Not Yet, Maybe Never," *Military Medicine* 155 (August 1990): 358.

In 1943, the navy had set out: Baldridge, "Shark Repellent," p. 358.

No evidence has ever: David H. Baldridge, "Shark Attack: A Program of Data Reduction and Analysis," *Contributions from the Mote Marine Laboratory* 1, no. 2 (1974): 186–87; Victor G. Springer and Joy P. Gold, *Sharks in Question: The Smithsonian Answer Book*, pp. 82, 127–28, 135.

p. 168. *As the water flashed*: Chip Brown, "Terror of Shark and Sea, 35 Years After," *Washington Post*, August 6, 1980.

Capable of bursts of speed: Springer and Gold, *Sharks in Question*, pp. 59, 82; Samuel H. Gruber, ed., *Discovering Sharks*, p. 36.

p. 169. *Around Captain McVay's raft*: Narrative by: Captain Charles B. McVay.

p. 170. *On Tuesday, McVay*: Narrative by: McVay; Court Martial.

p. 171. *At this latitude*: Matthew C. Barron, NAVOCEANO: Oceanographer and Ocean Services Division Officer, Naval Pacific Meteorology and Oceanography Center/Joint Typhoon Warning Center; USS *Register* (APD 92), Deck Log Additional Remarks, August 3–7, 1945.

p. 173. *Its beaches had been stormed*: Dunnigan and Nofi, *Victory at Sea*, p. 577.

On Leyte there were two: Philippine Sea Frontier. From: Captain Alfred M. Granum, U.S. Navy. To: Commander in Chief, U.S. Pacific Fleet and Pacific Ocean Areas. Signed: Alfred M. Granum. Dated: 1 September 1945; U.S. Naval Operating Base, Navy 3964. From: Lieutenant Commander Jules C. Sancho. To: Commander in Chief, U.S. Pacific Fleet and Pacific Ocean Areas. Signed: Jules C. Sancho. Dated: 31 August 1945; Court of Inquiry; Progress Report (NIG); Facts and Discussion of Facts (NIG); Discussion of Facts (NIG); Expected Arrivals and Departures, 31 July–2 August 1945.

p. 175. *Initiated by chief of naval operations*: Buell, *Master of the Sea*, p. 328.

p. 176. *Of the 1,195 crew*: Court Martial.

p. 179. *Captain McVay was no quitter*: Narrative by: Captain Charles B. McVay; Al Havins, personal interview; Dan Kurzman, *Fatal Voyage: The Sinking of the USS* Indianapolis, p. 115.

p. 182. *One boy chewed*: Wylie, "The Last Secret Voyage of the USS *Indianapolis*."

CHAPTER EIGHT: GENOCIDE

Interviews: Dr. Lewis Haynes, Giles McCoy, Mike Kuryla, Felton Outland, Harlan Twible, John Spinelli, Ed Brown, Robert Gause, Jack Cassidy, Gus Kay, Gordon Linke, Winthrop Smith Jr., Billie Havins, Dr. Julie Johnson.

p. 191. *McVay's four rafts*: Narrative by: Captain Charles B. McVay; Personal Narrative of Captain Charles B. McVay; Al Havins, personal interview; Bill Van Daalen, videotaped interview with Al Havins.

p. 195. *One boy got in his car*: Newcomb, *Abandon Ship!*, p. 131.

p. 205. *Back on Leyte*: Leyte Gulf Expected Arrivals and Departures, 31 July–2 August 1945.
In an air-conditioned bunker: Sweeney with Antonucci and Antonucci, *War's End*, p. 1; Knebel and Bailey, *No High Ground*, p. 164; Richard B. Frank, *Downfall: The End of the Imperial Japanese Empire*, p. 261.

CHAPTER NINE: DEAD DRIFT

Interviews: Giles McCoy, Dr. Lewis Haynes, Robert Gause, Jack Cassidy, Ed Brown, Jack Miner, John Spinelli, Bob McGuiggan, Felton Outland, Gus Kay, Harlan Twible, Hilton D. Logan, Irving Lefkovitz, Curt Newport, Martin Williams.

p. 211. *Something had gone wrong*: Information about Gwinn's patrol and rescue effort is drawn from Lech, *All the Drowned Sailors*, pp. 90–95; Wilbur Gwinn speech transcript, Survivors' Reunion, Indianapolis, Indiana, 1960; Correspondence with Norma Gwinn; Sighting of Survivors of U.S.S. *Indianapolis*: Participation in Air-Sea Rescue and Subsequent Search for Bodies and Debris, 2–7 August 1945. Signed M. S. Langford; Court of Inquiry; United States Pacific Fleet, Air Force, Patrol Bombing Squadron 152. Statement Concerning Sighting of Survivors of CA-35 U.S.S. *Indianapolis* on 2 August 1945. Signed Wilbur C. Gwinn. 3 August 1945.
The plane, like the Miss Deal: "American Aircraft of World War II," www

.ixpress.com/ag1caf/usplanes/american.htm; http://www.usplanes /aircraft/ventura.htm.

p. 213. *At about the same time*: Court of Inquiry.

Gwinn leveled the PV-1: Statement Concerning Sighting of Survivors of CA-35 U.S.S. *Indianapolis* on 2 August 1945; Herbert Hickman, "Six Most Important Words of Your Life," courtesy of John Wassell, "Mission Accomplished . . . But at a Price"; Sighting of Survivors of U.S.S. *Indianapolis*: Participation in Air-Sea Rescue and Subsequent Search for Bodies and Debris, 2–7 August 1945; Questions asked by Correspondents of Lt. (jg) W. G. Gwinn, USNR, Lt. R. A. Marks, USNR, and Lt. Commander G. C. Atteberry, 6 August 1945; Court of Inquiry; Dispatch 020125; Wilbur Gwinn speech transcript, Survivors' Reunion, 1960.

p. 218. *Meanwhile, Gwinn was trying*: Statement Concerning Sighting of Survivors of CA-35 USS *Indianapolis* on 2 August 1945; Gwinn speech transcript, Survivors' Reunion, 1960; Dispatch 020245; Questions asked by Correspondents; Sighting of Survivors of USS *Indianapolis*; Participation in Air-Sea Rescue and Subsequent Search for Bodies and Debris, 2–7 August 1945; Court of Inquiry.

p. 220. *First to receive the message*: Court of Inquiry; Dispatch 020409; Lech, *All the Drowned Sailors*, pp. 99–100.

p. 221. *As the rescue effort heated up*: Sighting of Survivors of U.S.S. *Indianapolis*: Participation in Air-Sea Rescue and Subsequent Search for Bodies and Debris, 2–7 August 1945; Wassell, "Mission Accomplished . . . But at a Price."

p. 222. *Lieutenant Commander George Atteberry*: Sighting of Survivors of U.S.S. *Indianapolis*: Participation in Air-Sea Rescue and Subsequent Search for Bodies and Debris, 2–7 August 1945; Court of Inquiry; Questions asked by Correspondents, 6 August 1945.

The plane belonged: *New York Times*, "Adrian Marks, 81, World War II Navy Pilot"; Adrian Marks speech transcript, Survivors' Reunion, 1960; Wassell, "Mission Accomplished . . . But at a Price"; U.S.S. *Cecil J. Doyle* (DE 368). Memorandum Report on Rescue of Survivors of USS *Indianapolis* (CA-35) August 2–4, 1945. Signed by W. G. Claytor Jr. Undated; *Washington Post*, "No-Nonsense Lawyer Claytor Knows When to Bend the Rules"; "Selected Speeches of R. Adrian Marks"; Bill Van Daalen, videotaped interview with Adrian Marks, 1990; Questions asked by Correspondents, 6 August 1945.

p. 224. *Meanwhile, CINCPAC*: Dispatch 020617.

Then, in the midafternoon: Leyte Gulf Expected Arrivals and Departures, July 31–August 2, 1945; Dispatch 020848; Dispatch 030041; Court of Inquiry; Lech, *All the Drowned Sailors*, p. 100.

p. 225. *Lieutenant Adrian Marks*: Sighting of Survivors of U.S.S. *Indianapolis*: Participation in Air-Sea Rescue and Subsequent Search for Bodies and Debris, 2–7 August 1945; Questions asked by Correspondents, 6 August 1945.
At about the same time, the destroyers: Dispatch 020601.
Marks knew the situation: Dispatch 020625; Bill Van Daalen, videotaped interview with Adrian Marks; Adrian Marks speech transcript, Survivors' Reunion, 1960; Questions asked by Correspondents, 6 August 1945.

p. 227. *Earlier in the day*: Dispatch 020516; Dispatch 020747; Dispatch 020400; Dispatch 020756.

p. 228. *Shortly before Marks landed*: Sighting of Survivors of U.S.S. *Indianapolis*: Participation in Air-Sea Rescue and Subsequent Search for Bodies and Debris, 2–7 August 1945; Record of Flight Operations in Search for Survivors from USS *Indianapolis* (CA-35), 2 August 1945; Joseph M. Lalley, *Search and Rescue*; Bill MacDermott, *A Walk Through the Valley: The History of the 3rd Emergency Rescue Squadron*.
Around 7:15 p.m.: 4th Emergency Rescue Squadron, Flight Detachment, APO 265. Subject: Rescue Operations 2 August through 5 August. Signed: Lt. Richard C. Alcorn. Dated: 6 August 1945; 4th Emergency Rescue Squadron, Flight Detachment, APO 265. Subject: Search Operations of 7 August 1945. To: Sub Area Operations. Signed Lt. Richard Alcorn. Dated: 8 August 1945; Kurzman, *Fatal Voyage*, p. 174.

p. 230. *Circling overhead, Lieutenant Commander Atteberry*: Sighting of Survivors of U.S.S. *Indianapolis*: Participation of Air-Sea Rescue and Subsequent Search for Bodies and Debris, 2–7 August 1945; Questions asked by Correspondents, 6 August 1945; Bill Van Daalen, videotaped interview with Adrian Marks; "Selected Speeches of R. Adrian Marks"; Dan Kurzman, *Fatal Voyage*, p. 167; U.S.S. *Cecil J. Doyle* (DE 368). Memorandum Report on Rescue of Survivors of USS *Indianapolis* (CA-35) August 2–4, 1945; Adrian Marks speech transcript, Survivors' Reunion, 1960.

p. 233. *Captain Graham Claytor*: USS *Cecil J. Doyle* (DE 368), Memorandum Report on Rescue of Survivors of USS *Indianapolis* (CA35), August 2–4, 1945; Wren, *Those in Peril on the Sea*, p. 59; Correspondence with Ruby and Albert Harp; USS *Madison* (DD 425), Narrative of Search Operations, 2 to 5 August 1945. Signed: Donald W. Todd. Dated: 6 August 1945; USS *Dufilho* (DE 423), Rescue-Survivors Search, August 3–6, 1945. Signed: A. H. Nienau. Dated: 9 August 1945.
During the predawn hours: Wren, *Those in Peril on the Sea*, pp. 81–85, 161.

p. 235. *At 4 a.m., the searchlight*: Lewis L. Haynes, "We Prayed While 833 Died," *Saturday Evening Post*, August 6, 1955.

NOTES

CHAPTER TEN: FINAL HOURS

Interviews: Dr. Lewis Haynes, John Spinelli, Giles McCoy, Felton Outland, Bob McGuiggan, Gus Kay, Bill Drayton, Curt Newport, Peter Wren.

p. 239. *Captain Claytor*: Kurzman, *Fatal Voyage*, p. 176; Dispatches 021342, 021500.

The news was a stunning blow: Thomas B. Buell, *Master of the Sea*, p. 327.

On the same day: Weintraub, *The Last Great Victory*, p. 392.

p. 240. *By this time, the last*: Knebel and Bailey, *No High Ground*, p. 100; Rhodes, *The Making of the Atomic Bomb*, p. 696; Weintraub, *The Last Great Victory*, p. 387.

Back in the waters: U.S.S. *Cecil J. Doyle* (DE 368), Memorandum Report on Rescue of Survivors of USS *Indianapolis* (CA-35) August 2–4, 1945; Wren, *Those in Peril on the Sea*, pp. 58–91; U.S.S. *Madison* (DD425), Narrative of Search Operations 2 to 5 August 1945. Signed: Donald W. Todd. Dated: 6 August 1945; 4th Emergency Rescue Squadron, Flight Detachment, APO 265. Rescue operations 2 Aug through 5 Aug Signed: Lt. Richard C. Alcorn. Dated: 6 August 1945; Questions asked by Correspondents, 6 August 1945; Correspondence with Ruby and Albert Harp; Record of Flight Operations in Search for Survivors from the USS *Indianapolis* (CA-35), 2 August 1945.

Some of the boys pulled aboard: Wren, *Those in Peril on the Sea*, p. 157.

p. 241. *The rescue ships were a mess*: Wren, *Those in Peril on the Sea*, pp. 70, 162–66; Lech, *All the Drowned Sailors*, p. 108.

The crew of the Doyle: "Selected Speeches of R. Adrian Marks"; Bill Van Daalen, videotaped interview with Adrian Marks.

p. 242. *The following order was relayed*: Lech, *All the Drowned Sailors*, p. 111; Progress Report (NIG); Dispatch 031406.

By the early morning: Personal Narrative of Captain Charles B. McVay; Narrative by: Captain Charles B. McVay; "Survivors in the Water: Saving the *Indy* Crew," interview with Captain William C. Myer, USN (ret), *Military Heritage*, June 2000; Al Havins personal interview; Bill Van Daalen, videotaped interview with Al Havins.

p. 243. *McVay looked up in surprise*: Roy McLendon Jr., "The Rescue: The Rest of the Story," *Cryptolog*, Spring 1984; Jim Anderson, NCVA, "Tragic *Indianapolis* Story Told"; "Survivors in the Water," interview with Captain William C. Meyer; Dispatch 030855.

p. 245. *Shortly thereafter, the* Madison: USS *Madison* (DD 425), Narrative of Search Operations, 2 to 5 August 1945; USS *Register* (APD 92), Search Operations of USS *Register* (APD 92) for Survivors of USS *Indianapolis*.

315

Signed: J. R. Furman. Dated: 8 August 1945; USS *Ringness* (APD 100) Deck Log-Remarks Sheet,1–5 August 1945; Dispatch 030150.

p. 249. *It has previously been reported*: "Survivors in the Water," interview with Captain William C. Meyer.

By the following day: USS *Madison* (DD 425), Narrative of Search Operations, 2 to 5 August 1945; Record of Flight Operations in Search for Survivors from USS *Indianapolis* (CA-35), 2–8 August 1945.

In all, the Cecil J. Doyle: Commander Western Carolines Sub Area, Rescue and Search for Survivors of the U.S.S. *Indianapolis* (CA-35) and Recovery, Identification, and Burial of Bodies, 15 August 1945; Wren, *Those in Peril on the Sea*, p. 161.

The casualties were astounding: U.S. Naval Base Hospital No. 18, Report of Casualties. From: Charles B. McVay, Ill. To: The Secretary of the Navy. Dated: 9 August 1945.

p. 250. *Adrian Marks would be haunted*: "Selected Speeches of R. Adrian Marks."

CHAPTER ELEVEN: AFTERMATH

Interviews: Giles McCoy, Dr. Lewis Haynes, Harlan Twible, Mike Kuryla, Bob McGuiggan, Jack Cassidy, Ed Brown, Donald Allen, Bill Drayton, Jack Miner, Richard Stephens, Gus Kay, Lee Albright, Gordon Linke, Jocelyn Linke, Scott Linke, Winthrop Smith Jr., Ed Stevens.

p. 253. *"All bodies were in extremely bad condition"*: USS *Helm* (DD 388), Search for Survivors, Period 4–5 August 1945—Report of. Signed: A. F. Hollingsworth. Dated: 6 August 1945.

p. 254. *As the USS* Ringness *had made its way*: "Survivors in the Water," interview with Captain William C. Meyer.

p. 255. *"What would be the normal time"*: As quoted in Newcomb, *Abandon Ship!*, pp. 168–69.

A member of its assembly team: Knebel and Bailey, *No High Ground*, p. 114.

p. 256. *Those rescued by the* Bassett: Wren, *Those in Peril on the Sea*, p. 119.

p. 257. *On August 9*: United States Pacific Fleet and Pacific Ocean Areas, Headquarters of the Commander in Chief. Subject: Court of Inquiry to inquire into all the circumstances connected with the sinking of the USS *Indianapolis* (CA 35), and the delay in reporting the loss of that ship. Signed: C. W. Nimitz. Dated: 9 August 1945.

p. 258. *Minutes before Truman's announcement*: *New York Times*, August 15, 1945; Weintraub, *The Last Great Victory*, p. 616; Lech, *All the Drowned Sailors*, p. 120.

p. 259. *The* New York Times *called*: "The Indianapolis," *New York Times*, August 17, 1945.

p. 262. *Captain McVay had flown*: Moore, *Goodbye Indy Maru*, p. 162; Service Record: McVay, Charles Butler; Newcomb, *Abandon Ship!*, p. 186.

On November 29: Charges and Specifications in Case of Captain Charles B. McVay III, U.S. Navy. To: Captain Thomas J. Ryan Jr., U.S. Navy Judge Advocate, General Court Martial, Navy Yard, Washington, D.C. Signed by James Forrestal.

Admiral Nimitz and Admiral Spruance: Fleet Admiral, U.S. Navy, Memorandum regarding Court of Inquiry to inquire into all the circumstances connected with the sinking of the USS *Indianapolis* (CA 35), and the delay in reporting the loss of that ship. Signed: C. W. Nimitz. Dated: 6 September 1945; Buell, *Master of the Sea*, pp. 328–29.

Unbelievably, the navy: The Naval Inspector General, Investigation of the Sinking of the USS *Indianapolis* and the Delay in Reporting the Loss of that Ship. Signed: C. P. Snyder. Dated: Received 7 January 1946; Facts and Discussion of Facts (NIG); Navy Department, Office of the Judge Advocate General, Memorandum to the Secretary of the Navy. Subject: Charles B. McVay, 3rd, captain, U.S. Navy, trial by general court martial. Signed: O. S. Colclough. Undated.

p. 263. *McVay had less than a week*: Progress of *Indianapolis* case. The Naval Inspector General. Signed: C. P. Snyder. Dated: 10 November, 1945. Includes penciled notation by E. J. King; Hearing before the Committee on Armed Services, September 14, 1999.

Before the trial: as quoted in Newcomb, *Abandon Ship!*, p. 186.

p. 264. Time *magazine suggested*: December 10, 1945, "The Captain Stands Accused."

McVay sat stiffly: Bill Van Daalen, "*Indianapolis*: Ship of Doom," video documentary, 1992.

What McVay didn't know: von Doenhoff, "ULTRA and the Sinking of USS *Indianapolis*"; Progress Report of the USS *Indianapolis* Case (NIG); Investigation of the Sinking of the USS *Indianapolis* and the Delay in Reporting the Loss of that Ship, 7 January 1946.

p. 265. *It's unlikely that*: von Doenhoff, "ULTRA and the Sinking of USS *Indianapolis*"; Progress Report of the USS *Indianapolis* Case (NIG).

Newsweek *carried an editorial*: "A Jap[anese] Bears Witness," *Newsweek*, December 24, 1945.

On the floor of the House: Lech, *All the Drowned Sailors*, pp. 141–42; Department of the Navy, Office of the Judge Advocate General. Con. Res. 116: "To expunge the testimony of an alien enemy officer from the naval records." Signed James Snyder. Undated.

Nevertheless, the prosecution: Court Martial; "'Such Grotesque Proceedings,'" *Time*, December 24, 1945; "A Jap[anese] Bears Witness," *Newsweek*.

p. 266. *In view of his outstanding*: General Court Martial in the Case of Captain Charles B. McVay, 3rd, U.S. Navy, convened 3 December 1945 at the Navy Yard, Washington, D.C., by order of the Secretary of the Navy. From: The Chief of Naval Personnel. To: the Secretary of the Navy. Dated: 22 January 1946; Department of the Navy, Office of the Judge Advocate General. Signed: O. S. Colclough. Dated: 23 January 1946; Department of the Navy. Record of the Proceedings in the General Court Martial in the Case of Commanding Officer, USS *Indianapolis*—Captain Charles B. McVay III, U.S.N. Signed: E. J. King. Dated: 25 January 1946; Secretary of the Navy, "The record of the proceedings in the foregoing general court-martial case . . ." Signed: James Forrestal. Date: Illegible.

p. 267. *McVay had received the announcement*: *Washington Post*, December 20, 1945, "Captain Takes It Calmly."
    Three months after the court-martial: Service Record: McVay, Charles Butler.

CHAPTER TWELVE: BACK IN THE WORLD

Interviews: John Spinelli, Jack Miner, Mike Kuryla, Ed Brown, Jack Cassidy, Harlan Twible, Robert Gause, Gus Kay, Dr. Lewis Haynes, Giles McCoy, Felton Outland, Gordon Linke, Jocelyn Linke, Scott Linke, Winthrop Smith Jr., Ed Stevens, Florence Regosia.

p. 273. *After the court-martial*: Service Record: McVay, Charles Butler; *Times Picayune*, November 9, 1968.
    On the plane ride to Indianapolis: *Indianapolis Times*, July 30, 1960.

EPILOGUE

Interviews: Giles McCoy, Harlan Twible, Dr. Lewis Haynes, Michael Monroney.

p. 279. *Twenty-eight years after*: Summary of Report on the Court-Martial of Captain Charles B. McVay III, USN, Commanding Officer, USS *Indianapolis*. Dated: 18 June 1996; Report on the Court-Martial of Captain Charles B. McVay III, USN, Commanding Officer, USS *Indianapolis*. Prepared by Cdr. R. D. Scott, NJAG. Includes letters to the Honorable Andrew Jacobs Jr., United States House of Representatives. Signed: Steven S. Honigman. Dated: 14 November 1996.
    The answer, explains Captain Bill Toti: Commander William J. Toti, U.S. Navy, "The Sinking of the *Indy* & Responsibility of Command," *Proceedings*, October 1999.

NOTES

p. 280. *"We would've rode to hell"*: Bill Van Daalen, videotaped interview with Bob Brundige, 1990.

The survivors' efforts to clear: Hunter Scott, "Timeline to Justice," *Naval History*, July/August 1998.

On October 12, 2000: Conference Report to H. R. 4205, The National Defense Authorization Act of 2001.

p. 281. *In response, the navy*: Navy spokesperson, October 12, 2000.

Bibliography

BOOKS

Allen, Thomas B., and Norman Polmar. *Code-Name Downfall: The Secret Plan to Invade Japan—and Why Truman Dropped the Bomb*. New York: Simon and Schuster, 1995.

Ambrose, Stephen E., original text by C. L. Sulzberger. *American Heritage New History of World War II*. New York: Viking, 1997.

Auerbach, Paul, and Edward Geehr. *Management of Wilderness and Environmental Emergencies*. St. Louis, MO: Mosby, 2nd edition 1989.

Baldwin, Hanson W. *Battles Lost and Won: Great Campaigns of World War II*. New York: Harper & Row, 1966.

Boyne, Walter J. *The Clash of the Titans*. New York: Touchstone Books, 1997.

Buell, Thomas B. *Master of the Sea*. New York: Little, Brown & Company, 1980.

——. *The Quiet Warrior: A Biography of Admiral Raymond A. Spruance*. Boston: Little, Brown, 1974.

Clemans, Charles. *Harpo: War Survivor, Basketball Wizard*. Tucson: Wheatmark, 2009.

Costello, John. *The Pacific War 1941–1945*. New York: Rawson Wade, 1981.

Dunnigan, James F., and Albert A. Nofi. *Victory at Sea: WWII in the Pacific*. New York: William Morrow, 1995.

Ewing, Steve. *American Cruisers of World War II: A Pictorial Encyclopedia*. Missoula, MT: Pictorial Histories Publishing, 1984.

Frank, Richard B. *Downfall: The End of the Imperial Japanese Empire*. New York: Random House, 1999.

Fussell, Paul. *Wartime Understanding and Behavior in the Second World War*. New York: Oxford University Press, 1989.

Gruber, Samuel H., ed. *Discovering Sharks*. Highland, NJ: American Littoral Society, 1991.

Hashimoto, Mochitsura. *Sunk!: The Story of the Japanese Submarine Fleet, 1942–1945*. New York: Henry Holt, 1954.

Helm, Thomas. *Ordeal by Sea: The Tragedy of the U.S.S.* Indianapolis. New York: Dodd, Mead and Co., 1963.

Herman, Jan K. *Battle Station Sickbay*. Annapolis, MD: Naval Institute Press, 1997.

Hulver, Richard, and Peter Luebke, assoc. ed. *A Grave Misfortune: The USS*

Indianapolis *Tragedy*. Washington, DC: Naval History and Heritage Command, Department of the Navy, 2018.

Keegan, John. *The Battle for History: Refighting World War II*. New York: Vintage, 1995.

——. *The Price of Admiralty*. New York: Penguin, 1990.

——. *The Rand McNally Encyclopedia of World War II*. Chicago: Rand McNally, 1984.

Knebel, Fletcher, and Charles W. Bailey. *No High Ground*. New York: Harper Brothers, 1960.

Kurzman, Dan. *Fatal Voyage: The Sinking of the USS* Indianapolis. New York: Atheneum, 1990.

Lalley, Joseph M. *Search and Rescue*. Asheville, NC: Instiprints, 1997.

Layton, Edwin, with Roger Pineau and John Costello. *And I Was There: Pearl Harbor and Midway: Breaking the Secrets*. New York: William Morrow, 1985.

Lech, Raymond B. *All the Drowned Sailors*. New York: Stein and Day, 1982.

MacDermott, Bill. *A Walk Through the Valley: The History of the 3rd Emergency Rescue Squadron*. Manchester, TN: Beaver Press, 1995.

Moore, Katherine D. *Goodbye Indy Maru*. Knoxville, TN: Lori Publications, 1991.

Morison, Samuel Eliot. *The Two Ocean War: A Short History of the United States Navy in the Second World War*. Boston: Little, Brown, 1963.

——. *Victory in the Pacific 1945*. Boston: Little, Brown, 1964.

Newcomb, Richard F. *Abandon Ship!: Death of the USS* Indianapolis. New York: Henry Holt, 1958.

Nobile, Philip, ed. *Judgment at the Smithsonian: The Bombing of Hiroshima and Nagasaki*. New York: Marlow & Company, 1995.

Reader's Digest Association. *Sharks: Silent Hunters of the Deep*. Australia: Reader's Digest, 1994.

Rhodes, Richard. *The Making of the Atomic Bomb*. New York: Simon & Schuster, 1986.

Sherman, Frederick C. *Combat Command*. New York: Bantam Books, 1982.

Silverstone, Paul. *U.S. Warships of World War II*. Garden City: Doubleday, 1964.

Skates, John Ray. *The Invasion of Japan: Alternative to the Bomb*. Columbia: University of South Carolina Press, 2000.

Springer, Victor G., and Joy P. Gold. *Sharks in Question: The Smithsonian Answer Book*. Washington, DC: The Smithsonian Institution Press, 1989.

St. John, Philip A. *USS* Indianapolis *(CA-35)*. Paducah, KY: Turner Publishing Company, 1997.

Sweeney, Maj. Gen. Charles W., with James Antonucci and Marion K. Antonucci. *War's End: An Eyewitness Account of America's Last Atomic Mission*. New York: Avon, 1997.

Thomas, Gordon, and Max Morgan Witts. *Enola Gay*. New York: Stein and Day, 1977.

Vincent, Lynn, and Sara Vladic. Indianapolis: *The True Story of the Worst Sea Disaster in US Naval History and the Fifty-Year Fight to Exonerate an Innocent Man*. New York: Simon and Schuster, 2018.

Weintraub, Stanley. *The Last Great Victory: The End of WWII, July/August 1945*. New York: Dutton, 1995.

Winterbotham, F. W. *The Ultra Secret*. New York: Harper & Row, 1974.

Wiper, Steve, ed., and T. A. Flowers, illus. *Warship Pictorial: USS* Indianapolis, *CA-35*. Tucson, AZ: Classic Warship Publications, 1996.

Wren, L. Peter. *Those in Peril on the Sea*. Richmond, VA: L. Peter Wren, 1999.

PERIODICALS/MAGAZINES/INTERNET SOURCES

Anderson, Jim, NCVA. "Tragic Indianapolis Story Told," *Cryptolog*, Spring 1984.

Baldridge, H. David, Jr. "Comment on Means for Avoidance or Deterrence of White Shark Attacks on Humans," *Academic Press*, 1996.

——. "Shark Aggression Against Man: Beginnings of an Understanding," *California Fish and Game* 74, no. 4 (1988).

——. "Shark Attack: A Program of Data Reduction and Analysis," *Contributions from the Mote Marine Laboratory* 1, no. 2 (1974).

——. "Shark Repellent: Not Yet, Maybe Never," *Military Medicine* 155 (August 1990).

Benchley, Peter. "Inside the Great White," *National Geographic* 197, no. 4 (April 2000).

Boyd, Carl. "Attacking the Indianapolis: A Reexamination," *Warship International*, no. 1 (1976).

Brockman, Paul. "The Tragedy of the USS *Indianapolis*," The Indiana Historical Society, www.indianahistory.com.

——. "USS *Indianapolis* Records, 1898–1991," The Indiana Historical Society, www.indianahistory.com.

Burlage, Joe John D., USN. "Terror on the *Indianapolis*," *Grit*, December 14, 1975.

Cuadros, Paul. "In Shallow Waters Danger Runs Deep," *Time*, September 4, 2000.

Etheridge, Kenneth E. "The Agony of the *Indianapolis*," *American Heritage* 33, no. 5 (August/September 1982).

Finneran, Patrick J. "A Short History of the USS *Indianapolis*," The USS *Indianapolis* (CA-35) Survivors Organization, www.ussindianapolis.org.

Groves, R. R., Major General. Memorandum for the Secretary of War. Subject: The Test. War Department. 18 July 1945. Trinity Atomic Web Site, www.enviroweb.org/issues/nuketesting/hiroshim.

Guttman, Jon. "Once a Well-Kept Secret, Radar's Role in the Allied Victory Is

BIBLIOGRAPHY

Now Being Told by the Scientists Who Developed It." *The History Net*, www .thehistorynet.com.

Handy, Thos. T., General, G.S.C., Acting Chief of Staff. Letter to General Carl Spaatz, Commanding General, United States Army Strategic Air Force. 25 July 1945. *Children of the Manhattan Project*, http://home.att.net/~cotmp/.

Haskew, Michael E. "The U.S. Navy Bore the Brunt of Kamikaze Fury Off Okinawa During the Desperate Battle to Secure the Island," *The History Net*, www .thehistorynet.com.

Haynes, Lewis L., Capt. "Oral History—The Sinking of the USS *Indianapolis*: Recollections of the Sinking of USS Indianapolis (CA 35)," Naval History and Heritage Command, www.history.navy.mil.

———. "Survivor of the Indianapolis," *Navy Medicine* 86, no. 4 (July/August 1995).

———. "We Prayed While 883 Died," as told to George W. Campbell, Capt., USN. *Saturday Evening Post*, August 6, 1955.

Hays, Paul B. "Introduction to the Atmospheric and Oceanic Environment," http://blitzen.sprl.umich.edu/PHAYS/Chap_6/.

Hulver, Richard, and Sara Vladic. "Setting the Record Straight: Loss of the USS *Indianapolis* and the Question of Clarence Donnor," *Proceedings*, March 2018.

James, Woody Eugene. "In Woody's Words," The USS *Indianapolis* (CA-35) Survivors Organization, www.ussindianapolis.org.

Maier, Timothy W. "For the Good of the Navy," *Insight* 16, no. 21 (June 5, 2000).

Meyer, William C., Capt., USN (ret.), interview. "Survivors in the Water: Saving the *Indy*'s Crew," *Military Heritage*, June 2000.

Miner, Herbert J. "Of Submarines, Sharks, and Survival," *Yale*, October 1996.

Newcomb, Richard. "Four Nights of Terror," *The American Legion*, August 1981.

Nolan, James F., M.D. Letter to William A. Kulick, 12 July 1976. US Department of Energy Open Net Data Base, www.osti.gov/openet/.

———. Letter to Richard F. Newcomb, 12 August 1957. US Department of Energy Open Net Data Base, www.osti.gov/openet/.

Olivi, Fred. "My Mission over Nagasaki," *World War II Times*, September 1988.

Orr, Rodney. "The Great White's Ways," *Discover*, June 1999.

Pierce, Richard C., Jr. Letter to the editor, *The Tin Can Sailor*, January 1996.

Savard, John. "A Cryptographic Compendium," http://home.ecn.ab.ca/~jsavard /crypto/entry.htm.

Scott, Hunter. "Timeline to Justice," *Naval History*, July/August 1998.

Stewart, William H. "The Northern Mariana Islands and World War II with a Review of the Role of Tinian, the Atomic Bomb and the Loss of the U.S.S. *Indianapolis*," *CNMI Guide*, www.cnmi-guide.com.

Toti, William J., CDR, USN. "The Sinking of the *Indy* & Responsibility of Command," *Proceedings*, October 1999.

Wylie, Evan McLeod. "The Last Secret Voyage of the USS *Indianapolis*," *Yankee*, July 1978.

324

BIBLIOGRAPHY

Admiral Jesse B. Oldendorf, Namesake of USS Oldendorf, www.surfpac.navy
.mil.

American Aircraft of World War II, www.ixpress.com/ag1caf/usplanes/american
.htm; www.usplanes/aircraft/ventura.htm.

Dave James's Home Page, www.odyssey.dircon.co.uk.

——. "Rear Admiral Jesse B. Oldendorf."

——. "Admiral William F. Halsey, Commander Third Fleet."

Encyclopedia Britannica, www.britannica.com.

——. "Nuclear Weapon: The First Atomic Bomb."

Haze, Gray and Underway: Naval History and Photography, http://www.hazegray
.org/.

Life, "U.S. Makes Little Island into Mighty Base," July 2, 1945.

——. "F.D.R. on the USS *Indianapolis*," November 30, 1936.

Los Alamos National Laboratory, www.lanl.gov.

——. "Trinity-Completion of the Wartime Mission."

Lynde McCormick, http://members.tripod.com/~LMcCormick/DDG8/DDG
-8-1.htm.

National Archives and Records Administration, www.nara.gov.

Naval History and Heritage Command, www.history.navy.mil.

——. "Burial at Sea"

——. "Casualties: U.S. Navy, Coast Guard Vessels, Sunk or Damaged in War."

——. "Casualties U.S. Navy and Marine Corps Personnel, World War II."

——. "Code Words, World War II."

——. "*Indianapolis*, USS, Loss of."

——. Naval Abbreviations.

Newsweek, "Nobody Looked," August 27, 1945.

——. "The *Indianapolis*: Why?," December 10, 1945.

——. "A Jap[anese] Bears Witness," December 24, 1945.

——. "McVay: The Court Decides," December 31, 1945.

——. "The Navy Relents," March 4, 1946.

The Quan, "Sinking the *Indianapolis*: A Japanese Perspective," 1996.

Royal Institute of Navigation, www.rin.org.uk.

San Francisco History, www.sf50.com/qaboard/quboard.htm. Ron Filion, mod-
erator.

Submarines of the Imperial Japanese Navy, http://www.combinedfleet.com/ss
.html.

Time, "Men Against the Sea," August 27, 1945.

——. "The Captain Stands Accused," December 10, 1945.

——. "Such Grotesque Proceedings," December 24, 1945.

——. "The Good of the Service," December 31, 1945.

——. "End of the *Indianapolis* Case," March 4, 1946.

Trinity Atomic Web Site, www.enviroweb.org/issues/nuketesting/hiroshima.

BIBLIOGRAPHY

——. Eyewitness Account, Atomic Bomb Mission over Nagasaki, War Department, Bureau of Public Relations, Press Branch. Dated: 9 September 1945.

The USS *Indianapolis* (CA-35) Survivors Organization, www.ussindianapolis.org.

——. "The Crew."

——. "Guestbook."

——. "The Legislation."

——. "The Story."

USS Underhill *DE 682*, www.nji.com/~roger/index.htm.

NEWSPAPERS

"833 Dead and Missing in U.S. Cruiser Loss," *Bay City Times,* August 15, 1945, pp.1–2.

"Gentle Giant Stirs Memories of *Indianapolis*," *Dana Point News*, June 3, 1999 (editorial: Dennis Kaiser).

"838 Lost, 315 Saved in Sinking of *Indianapolis* by Jap[anese] Sub: Cruiser Had Just Carried Atom Bomb from U.S. to Guam," *Evening Star,* August 15, 1945, p. A1.

"'You're Out . . . in the Middle of Nowhere,'" *Herald Palladium*, October 22, 1999 (byline: Todd Dvorak), p. 1.

"The 'Hanging' of Captain McVay," *Honolulu Advertiser*, December 10, 1974 (editorial: Cobey Black).

"Pacific Hero Adm. McVay Dies at 70," *Honolulu Observer*, November 8, 1968.

"Tragedy Still Hurts After 15 Years," *Indianapolis Times*, July 30, 1960.

"500 Died in the Shark Horror That Dwarfs 'Jaws,'" *National Star*, September 30, 1975, p. 26.

"*Indianapolis* Is Lost, Suffers Very Heavy Casualties Off Leyte," *Navy News*, August 16, 1945.

"The Search for the Truth About the *Indianapolis*," *Plain Dealer Sunday Magazine,* December 6, 1998 (byline: Bob Sudyk), p. 8.

"Twist of Fate Made Gwinn a Hero," *San José Mercury News*, July 10, 1993 (byline: Dick Egner).

"Survivor Hopes to Clear His Captain," *Sun Post News*, May 29, 1998 (byline: Fred Swegles).

"Ex-Navy Crewman Describes His Surviving Shark-Infested Waters," *Sun Post News*, May 29, 1998 (byline: Fred Swegles).

"Admiral McVay Killed in Conn.," *Times-Picayune*, November 9, 1968.

"Author Wouldn't Write the Same 'Jaws' Today," *Traverse City Record Eagle*, April 5, 2000, p. B4.

BIBLIOGRAPHY

All of the following are from the New York Times:

"Cruiser Sunk, 1,195 Casualties; Took Atom Bomb Cargo to Guam," August 15, 1945, p. 1.

"The *Indianapolis*," August 17, 1945.

"Cruiser's Sinking Laid to Submarine," August 18, 1945, p. 4.

"Captain of Cruiser Pleads Not Guilty," December 5, 1945.

"McVay Guilty in *Indianapolis* Loss: Sentence Is Remitted on His Record," February 24, 1946, p. 1.

"C. B. McVay 3D, 70, Retired Admiral," November 8, 1968, p. 4.

"40 Years After the Birth of the Atomic Age," July 14, 1985 (byline: Lansing Lamont), section 4, p. 27.

"Adrian Marks, 81, World War II Navy Pilot," March 15, 1998 (byline: Richard Goldstein).

Other articles from January 1, 1946; January 2, 1946; January 6, 1946; January 9, 1946.

All of the following are from the Washington Post:

"Navy Secrecy" (editorial), December 4, 1945.

"McVay Court Martial: 850 Men Should Have Survived *Indianapolis* Blast, Says Officer," December 5, 1945 (byline: Marshall Andrews), p. 1.

"Captain Takes It Calmly: McVay Held Guilty of Neglect but Acquitted of Inefficiency," December 20, 1945 (byline: Marshall Andrews), p. 1.

"Court-Martialed in Warship Tragedy: Adm. Charles McVay Dies at 70," November 14, 1968, p. B6.

"Remembering the Hunger and Thirst, the Sharks, and the Screams," August 5 1975 (byline: Steven Norwitz), p. B1.

"No-Nonsense Lawyer Claytor Knows When to Bend the Rules," July 21, 1977 (byline: William H. Jones), p. D8.

"Terror of Shark and Sea, 35 Years After," August 6, 1980 (byline: Chip Brown), p. E1.

"Debates, Doubts Among the Creators," July 21, 1985 (byline: Walter Pincus), p. A1.

"What It Meant for America," July 26, 1995 (byline: Haynes Johnson), p. H6.

UNPUBLISHED DOCUMENTS

Hashimoto, Mochitsura, former captain of *I-58*. Letter to the Honorable John W. Warner, Chairman, Senate Armed Services Committee. Dated: November 24, 1999 (courtesy of Mike Monroney).

BIBLIOGRAPHY

Marks, Adrian. *Selected Speeches of R. Adrian Marks* (courtesy of Robert W. Marks).

Paroubek, Richard A. Letter to Commander Bill Toti, February 24, 1999.

Smith, Bob, U.S. Senator. Letter and summary concerning introduction of Senate Joint Resolution 26, October 13, 1999.

Smith, Keith. "An Archivist's Overview of the Controversy Surrounding the Sinking of the USS *Indianapolis* and the Court Martial of Capt. Charles B. McVay III." Distribution limited to those attempting to get relief for Captain McVay.

Sultan, Gene. "Captain Charles Butler McVay, III, 7/30/74" (Collection, Indiana Historical Society).

Twible, Harlan. *The Life and Times of an Immigrant Son* (by permission of Harlan Twible).

——. *Public Speeches, 1995–1999* (by permission of Harlan Twible).

Wassell, John H. "Mission Accomplished . . . But at a Price."

MISCELLANEOUS

Barron, Matthew C. Correspondence with the author.

Blanchard, Walter. Correspondence with the author.

The Bluejackets' Manual, Annapolis, MD: United States Naval Institute Press, 1943.

Celaya, Adolfo, video interview by Mike Brian, Florence, AZ: July 26, 2013. Southern Arizona Veterans Administration, Veterans History Project, Library of Congress.

Grocott, "Pinky." Correspondence with the author.

Gwinn, Norma. Correspondence with the author.

Harp, Albert, and Ruby Harp. Correspondence with the author.

Havins, Al. Personal interview videotaped by Ruby Tilzel and Linda Day, 1996 (by permission of Billie Havins).

Kraft, Robert. Correspondence/interview with author, November 2020.

Martinson, Alwyn. Correspondence/interview with author about USS *Indianapolis*'s receipt of SOS message, November 19, 2020.

NARA Stock Footage #000960. CR#: 428 NPC 12522.

"Press, Radio and Television Activities During First USS *Indianapolis* Survivors' Memorial Reunion, July 30–31, 1960, Indianapolis, Indiana." Naval Reserve Public Relations Company 9-1, U.S. Naval Reserve Training Center, Indianapolis, Indiana.

"Sea Tales: Missing! The *Indianapolis*." A & E Home Video documentary, Cat. No. AAE-17068. Copyright 1997.

"The Sinking of the USS *Indianapolis* and the Subsequent Court Martial of Rear Adm. Charles B. McVay III, USN." Hearing before the Committee on Armed

Services, United States Senate, One Hundred Sixth Congress, First Session, September 14, 1999.

Solly, Meilan. "See 12 Stunning Portraits of World War II Veterans," www .smithsonianmag. com, August 2019. (Featuring photos by Zach Coco, "Pictures for Heroes," www.picturesforheroes.com.)

"Statement of Paul J. Murphy Chairman, USS *Indianapolis* Survivors Organization, before the Senate Armed Services Committee in support of Senate Joint Resolution 26," September 14, 1999.

"USS *Indianapolis* (CA 35): Second Watch, Information Package." 1999 Reunion, July 10–August 1.

"USS *Indianapolis* (CA 35): Still at Sea." Third edition, prepared for the Indianapolis Reunion, July 1999.

"USS *Indianapolis* Survivors Reunion, Indianapolis, Indiana." Audiotape transcript, 1960.

"USS *Indianapolis:* Tragedy at Sea." Video documentary. Pangolin Pictures.

Van Daalen, Bill. "*Indianapolis.* The Ship of Doom." Video documentary, 1992.

——. Videotaped interviews with Adrian Marks, Bob Brundige, Charles McKissick, Al Havins, and Harlan Twible, 1990 (by permission of Bill Van Daalen).

von Doenhoff, Richard A. "ULTRA and the Sinking of USS *Indianapolis*." *Eleventh Naval History Symposium*, United States Naval Academy, Annapolis, MD, October 1993.

PRIMARY SOURCES

The Court of Inquiry and Court Martial documents were obtained from the Department of the Navy, Office of the Judge Advocate General, Washington Navy Yard. Although the Court of Inquiry itself numbered 131 pages, attached to it were 723 additional pages of exhibit documents. These included the rescue reports for the USS Doyle, Helm, Register, Ringness, *and* Ralph Talbot; *ship reports submitted from the rescue effort; air support logs; casualty lists and reports; press memorandums; over 120 dispatches; and Court of Inquiry memorandums. Navy Inspector General investigation reports were also included among the Inquiry documents, as well as memorandums pertaining to the court-martial of Captain Charles B. McVay, III.*

Additional documents were obtained from various sources, including Naval Academy Archives and personal collections:

Conference Report to H. R. 4205, the National Defense Authorization Act of 2001.

General Plans, CA 35. Bu. C&R #166008–166012. Dated December 1, 1944. (Courtesy of Mike Kuryla.)

BIBLIOGRAPHY

Log Books, USS *Indianapolis*, CA 35, February 1 to June 30, 1945.

Navy and Marine Corps Awards Manual. Department of the Navy. Navpers 15, 790 (Rev. 1953).

Plan of the Day for Sunday, July 15, 1945, and Monday, July 16, 1945. Signed: J. A. Flynn, Commander, U.S.N., Executive Officer (USS *Indianapolis*, CA 35).

USS *Bassett* (APD 73) Deck Log—Remarks Sheet. August 4, 1945.

USS *Cecil J. Doyle* (DE 368) Deck Log—Remarks. August 5–7, 1945.

USS *Helm* (DD 388) Deck Log—Remarks. August 5, 1945.

USS *Ralph Talbot* (DD 390) Deck Log. August 3, 1945.

USS *Register* (APD 92) Deck Log—Additional Remarks. August 3–7, 1945.

USS *Ringness* (APD 100) Deck Log—Remarks Sheet. August 1–5, 1945.

War Diary of Battleship Division Three, from July 1, 1945, to July 31, 1945. From Commander Battleship Three, L. D. McCormick to Commander-in-Chief, United States Fleet. Dated August 4, 1945.

War Diary of Commander Cruiser Division Four, from July 1, 1945, to July 31, 1945. Original to CominCh. Copy to CINCPAC Pearl.

War Diary of the USS *Indianapolis*, May–August 1945. From Commanding Officer, Chas. B. McVay III to Commander-in-Chief, United States Fleet. Dated June 1, 1945.

War Diary of the USS *Pensacola*, July 1945. From Commanding Officer, W. J. Suits to Commander-in-Chief, United States Fleet. Dated August 25, 1945.

War Diary of the USS *Tennessee*, July 1945. From Commanding Officer, John B. Hefferman to Commander-in-Chief, United States Fleet. Dated August 3, 1945.

Weekly Reports of the Joint Army-Navy Personnel Shipping Committee, April 1945–August 1945.

Author's Note

I FIRST became interested in this story in the summer of 1999, when a small local newspaper item caught my eye. It described a reunion being held for a group of survivors from a ship called the USS *Indianapolis*. I had heard of the *Indy* before; immortalized by Captain Quint in *Jaws*, the ship occupied a mythical status in American popular history, a kind of larger-than-life existence. But, I realized, I knew little about the real-life incident.

Something clicked. A few weeks later, I was on a plane to Indianapolis, on my way to the survivors' reunion. My plan was to write a short, 5,000-word article. When it was over, I'd be on to the next assignment.

It's no secret that we celebrate youth in the United States; the average kid has probably never spent any meaningful time around someone older than fifty. For the most part, I had spent my time working for magazines that celebrate this exile of the aged.

But then I met the survivors, about eighty-five of them, as we gathered for three days at the Indianapolis Westin. And I was amazed by their generosity, their courage, their dignity. The reunion marked the beginning of a series of correspondences, interviews, and visits that continue today. It also marked the beginning of my absolute commitment to these men and to telling their story.

Over time, I would become embarrassed by what I had thought of as the hard times in my life. I had spent a portion of it searching out challenges and risk, working aboard a commercial fishing boat and later traveling to far-flung places, once almost drowning on a trip during which I rounded Cape Horn. In retrospect, those adventures were my way of looking for what William James called the moral equivalent of war. But these survivors were the real thing. In writing their story, I knew I would be writing a profile in courage and sacrifice.

The story of the USS *Indianapolis* took over my life. I wrote a 35,000-word magazine piece, which was shortened to 12,000 words and published in the March 2000 issue of *Men's Journal*. It generated more reader mail than any other article the magazine had previously published.

The heart of the story, as I saw it, was the human, elemental drama of men who survived the worst disaster at sea in U.S. naval history. For almost five days, they struggled against unbelievably harsh conditions, fighting off sharks, hypothermia, physical and mental exhaustion, and finally hallucinatory dementia. And yet more than 300 of them managed to survive.

The question I wanted to answer was, *How?*

IN creating this book, I decided to cast the tragedy of the USS *Indianapolis* not as a history of war but as a portrait of men battling the sea. "Don't make me a hero," Giles McCoy told me as I sat in his living room in Florida. Even though his wife was stricken with lung cancer, and Gil (as he's known) was battling life-threatening health problems, he and Betty insisted that I stay with them in a spare bedroom for nearly a week. The interview sessions were lengthy as we sat on his porch poring over photos and memories. Gil was never far from a glass of ice water; fifty-five years after the sinking, he still worried about going thirsty.

Time was of the essence. While I was visiting Gil, we learned that three more survivors had just died, all in the same month. Gil, a husband of fifty-three years and father of three, wanted to tell his full story before it was too late.

Other survivors echoed this sentiment. Which is one of the reasons why in my book readers will find information at odds with that of previous accountings. The book also draws on new information, including U.S. government documents, that only in recent years were made available to the public.

Throughout, I have remained faithful to the bones of the story: that in the dog days of World War II, in a backwater of the Pacific, the cruiser USS *Indianapolis* was sunk.

What ensued was a nightmare.

FOR the survivors, the disaster of the *Indy* is a touchstone moment of historic disappointment: the navy put them in harm's way, hundreds of men died violently, and then the government refused to acknowledge its culpability.

What's amazing, however, is that these men, unlike contemporary generations who've been disappointed by bad government, are not bitter. Somehow, a majority brushed aside their feelings of rancor and went on to help build the booming postwar American economy of the fifties.

Some might say that the America of the World War II era, a country in which people felt a sense of belonging, of being part of a community larger than themselves, is lost to us today. But I don't think so. It lives on in these men, these survivors. They are not our past; they are the future.

IN the course of writing this book, I've read thousands of published pages about the USS *Indianapolis*, conducted hours of personal interviews, and studied miscellaneous materials provided by survivors and people intensely interested in the history of the ship. More than a few of these individuals warrant special mention.

I must first thank Heather Shaw Cauchy, without whose aid completing this book would have been a far more arduous task and to whom is owed much of its texture and breadth. For her perseverance, brilliance, and tireless contributions, I am forever grateful. She has been the perfect colleague in this enterprise. Thank you, H.

Of the survivors of the USS *Indianapolis* disaster, I especially want to thank Gil and Betty McCoy for making me feel like a member of their family. Likewise, I am grateful to Dr. Lewis Haynes and Margaret Haynes, who welcomed me into their home. I'd also like to thank Harlan and Alice Twible, Mike and Lorrain Kuryla, Jack and Muffy Miner, Bob and Gloria McGuiggan, Victor and Dottie Buckett, and Robert and Norma Neal Gause for their support. The men and their families opened their hearts and their homes to me, and I hope I've given back something in return.

Other survivors who generously gave of their time include Felton Outland, Jack Cassidy, Richard Stephens, Bill Drayton, Gus Kay, Ed Brown, John Spinelli, Richard Paroubek, and Grover Carver. Lou Bitonti and Woody James also offered much-appreciated encouragement. Nina Bartasavich generously shared the ordeal of her father, survivor Joseph Naspini.

Besides offering recollections of the sinking and their survival, these former crew members also provided special insight into Captain McVay, as well as into the ship's operation and regimens.

Mike Kuryla, Giles McCoy, Robert Gause, Harlan Twible, Erwin Hensch, and Dr. Lewis Haynes were especially helpful in understanding the captain and his duties, as well as providing insight into his personality. John Spinelli provided a firsthand account of his days afloat with McVay, and Mrs. Billie Havins, Al Havins's widow, answered questions and provided materials concerning her late husband's experience with the captain aboard ship and on a life raft. Documentary filmmaker Bill Van Daalen was generous in supplying interview materials and photographs concerning McVay and the survivors.

David Nelson, director of Second Watch, and his assistant Robin Field were helpful in answering questions about issues facing survivors today, and Michael Monroney took time to explain the effort to exonerate Captain McVay. Keith Smith, an archivist of the USS *Indianapolis* Survivors Organization, also provided valuable assistance. I'm grateful as well for the welcome I received at the 1999 reunion of the *Indianapolis* survivors, led by their organization's chairman, Mr. Paul Murphy. For excellent information about Second Watch and the organization, visit www. ussindianapolis.org.

I also owe a debt of gratitude to McVay's stepsons, Winthrop Smith Jr. and Gordon Linke, as well as Jocelyn, Scott, and Corrine Linke. Winthrop and Gordon arranged for me to tour Winvian Farm in August 1999, and offered particularly keen insight into the captain's character. Likewise, Florence Regosia, McVay's housekeeper, was helpful in understanding McVay's last years, as was Ed Stevens, McVay's fishing, hunting, and bridge-playing companion. Former U.S. senator Spencer Abraham provided assistance in obtaining McVay's military service record.

For accounts of the rescue of the *Indianapolis* crew, I want to thank former navy personnel Albert Harp, John Wilschke, Peter Wren, Roy McLendon, Irving Lefkovitz, Douw Mac Haffie, Max Seisser, Robert France, Hilton Logan, Joseph Lalley Jr., and William C. Meyer. Norma Gwinn answered questions about her husband, pilot Chuck Gwinn, and Robert Marks aided in recounting the role his father, Adrian Marks, played in the rescue effort.

My research was also aided by military historians and researchers Paul Brockman and Eric Mundell at the Indiana Historical Society, and Martin Williams in Washington, D.C. The following historians were also greatly helpful: Air Commander "Pinky" Grocott (naval radar), Bill Roland and Walter Blanchard (loran navigation), William Stewart (*Indianapolis* history and Mariana Islands), Ron Filion (San Francisco in 1945), and John Wassell and Bill MacDermott (rescue planes).

Lee Albright provided information about the USS *Howze*, and Fred Kimball and Rich Tretault described the unescorted voyage of tugboats along the *Indy*'s route. James B. Johnson and Dr. Robert Browning provided historical perspective of the U.S. Navy and the U.S. Coast Guard, respectively.

Russell Hetz and Donald Allen offered detailed information about the *Indianapolis*'s SOS message, and Richard von Donhoeff answered questions about the code-breaking program ULTRA. John Savard was helpful in understanding cryptography.

Former *Indianapolis* crew members Charlie Sullivan and William Collins provided welcome descriptions of the ship. Sullivan, a former altar boy aboard the ship, also aided in understanding the *Indy*'s affable priest, Father Conway. Dennis Covert offered perspective on Captain McVay's situation within the chain of naval command. Deep sea explorer Curt Newport's help was essential in understanding the mechanics of the *Indianapolis*'s sinking and the drift-course of the survivors. David Dorflinger described Guam in July 1945, and detailed his jeep ride on the island with Captain McVay.

Dr. Terry Taylor and Dr. Julie Johnson were instrumental in explaining sea trauma and the effects of saltwater immersion. David Baldridge was helpful in understanding shark attacks, and oceanographer Matthew C. Barron provided climatological information about the South Pacific. Scott Sanford, Andrew Lundberg, Marly Wyckoff, Kathy Erlewein, Gayle Gallagher, and Cindy Lyskawa also offered appreciated encouragement and assistance.

Close to home, I've benefited from the friendship and support of the Stanton, Bott, Edwards, Dennis/Dunn, and Earnest families, and my sister Deb Demin, along with Tony, Genessa, and Wylie Demin; Bob Butz and Nancy Flowers, Dave Scroppo, Glenn Wolff and Carole Simon, Jerry and Gail Dennis, Nick Bozanic and Brit Washburn, Mike and Claudia Delp, Jack and Lois Driscoll, Joe Mielke and Jodee Taylor, Terry and Marlene Caszatt, Jim Fergus, Mike Paterniti, Veronica Pasfield, Larry Grow, Danielle Freund, and Kathy and Bill Thompson. Thanks also to Woody Harrelson, Ron Bernstein, and especially to Betsy Beers.

I want to thank author Richard Newcomb, who patiently walked me through the ins and outs of naval command during the height of the war in 1945. From his vantage point, I think, he saw an effort to tell this story from a new perspective, forty-two years after he had left off. For this, I'm grateful. I was also aided by the published work of Katherine Moore, Raymond Lech, Dan Kurzman, and Peter Wren. And I'd like to thank Kimo and Charles McVay IV, and James Bargsley for their early encouragement.

Sid Evans agreed to let me write the story of the USS *Indianapolis* as an article for *Men's Journal* magazine. I'm thankful for

Sid's friendship and demanding editing, and for then editor in chief Terry McDonell's unwavering support. I am also grateful to Jann Wenner for publishing my work.

Throughout, Jim Harrison and Guy de la Valdéne have given important support, and to them I offer heartfelt thank-yous. My agent, Sloan Harris, has provided sharp advice that's never failed to lift my spirits, and his friendship has been fun, essential, and deeply appreciated. Thank you, Sloan.

Two people who were instrumental in bringing this book to life are Jennifer Barth, Henry Holt's brilliant editor in chief, and Holt's ever-supportive president, John Sterling. Throughout a demanding work period, Jennifer saw both the ocean and the waves, and nursed this tale from its primordial soup into something larger than even I had imagined. She selflessly worked to make it a better book, and I cannot state emphatically enough the importance of her jeweler's precision in all matters editorial. Likewise, John Sterling offered prescient comments and made this writer feel welcome.

George Hodgman provided help at an important juncture. Thanks as well to Maggie Richards, Elizabeth Shreve, Heather Fain, Sarah Hutson, Kenn Russell, Fritz Metsch, and Rebecca Milos at Henry Holt. Photo editor Carin Pearce, Robert Krauss, Tom Flowers, Tim Barrons of Byte Productions, and James Sinclair worked diligently to handsomely illustrate the book.

My mother and father have provided boundless encouragement. I wrote *In Harm's Way* in part because of a story my father first told me when I was kid. "Don't ever forget," he would say (and still says), "the sacrifice somebody has made for you." My parents' example of doing the right thing, even if it's the hard thing, has been an important lesson. And whenever I've suc-

ceeded in doing just that, it's because of three people: Anne, my
wife, who assisted at key moments as this book was nearing com-
pletion, and my children, John and Kate. Whatever I've learned
about sacrifice, love, and endurance through the people I write
about in this book, I want to bring home to them.

Finally, I want to recognize the sailors who were lost at sea
when the *Indianapolis* was sunk. We rely on the living to tell the
story, but not without remembering the men who didn't survive.

Index

Entries in *italics* refer to captions.

About the Author

Doug Stanton is a #1 *New York Times* bestselling author whose books include *In Harm's Way*, *Horse Soldiers*, and *The Odyssey of Echo Company*. *Horse Soldiers* is the basis for a Jerry Bruckheimer–produced movie titled *12 Strong*, starring Chris Hemsworth. *Horse Soldiers* spent nearly three consecutive months at #1 on the *New York Times* bestseller list and was named a "Notable Book." U.S. Army Special Forces at the John F. Kennedy Special Warfare Center and School selected the book as required reading.

In Harm's Way spent more than six months on the *New York Times* bestseller list and became required reading on the U.S. Navy's reading list for officers. The unabridged audiobook edition of *In Harm's Way* is the winner of the **2017 Audie Award in the History category.**

The Odyssey of Echo Company is a **Military Times Best Book of the Year** and recipient of the **Society of Midlands Authors Best Nonfiction Book Award.** Stanton is also the recipient of the **2021 Stephen E. Ambrose Oral History Award,** presented by the Rutgers Living History Society. He has lectured at libraries, civic and corporate groups, book clubs, universities, the U.S. Air Force Academy, the U.S. Department of State, and the Center for Strategic International Studies.

Stanton has appeared on national TV and radio outlets, including the *Today Show*, CNN, Discovery, A&E, History channel, Fox News, MSNBC's *Morning Joe*, C-SPAN's *Book TV*, PBS, and *NBC Nightly News*, and has been covered in prominent publications, including the *Wall Street Journal*, the *Washington Post*, the *Miami Herald*, and the *New York Times*.

He has also written on travel, sport, and entertainment, during which time he camped on Cape Horn, played basketball with George Clooney, and took an acting lesson from a gracious Harrison Ford. His writing has appeared in the *New York Times,* the *New York Times Book Review, Time,* the *Washington Post, Men's Journal, Smart, Sports Afield,* the *Daily Beast,* and *Newsweek,* and at *Esquire* and *Outside,* where he also has been a contributing editor.

Stanton attended Interlochen Arts Academy, Hampshire College, and received an MFA from the Writers' Workshop at the University of Iowa, where he graduated with coursework in both fiction and poetry workshops. Stanton has worked as a commercial sports fisherman in Provincetown, Massachusetts, and caretaker of Robert Frost's house in Vermont.

Doug and Anne Stanton, his wife and a reporter and editor, are devoted to volunteer public service around issues of arts, education, and literacy. In 2017, they were recipients of Michigan Legacy Art Park's **Legacy Award,** and in 2018 Doug was named a **Michiganian of the Year** by the *Detroit News.* He is a recipient of the Interlochen Center of the Arts' **Ovation** and **Path of Inspiration** awards. Doug and Anne live in Michigan and have three children, John, Katherine, and Will. They cofounded with aspiring author Grant Parsons the **National Writers Series**, a year-round book festival featuring great conversations with America's best storytellers; and **Front Street Writers**, a writing workshop and scholarship program for high school students. For more, see www.dougstanton.com and follow him at @DougStantonBook.